Tolstoy :

The Comprehensive Vision

Tolstoy,
The Comprehensive
Vision

E. B. Greenwood

LONDON

J. M. DENT & SONS LTD

Made in Great Britain
at the
Aldine Press · Letchworth · Herts
for
J. M. DENT & SONS LTD
Aldine House · Albemarle Street · London
First published 1975

This book is set in 10 on 11pt Baskerville 169

Hardback ISBN: 0 460 12013 1

Contents

Acknowledgements

I am indebted to the Oxford University Press for permission to quote from the works of Tolstoy in Aylmer Maude's World's Classics translations (in particular *War and Peace* and *Anna Karenina*), from Maude's *The Life of Tolstoy* (in the same edition), from R. F. Christian's *Tolstoy's 'War and Peace': A Study*, Oxford, 1962, and from R. Scholes and R. Kellogg, *The Nature of Narrative*, New York, 1966; and to William Heinemann Ltd and Doubleday and Co. Ltd for permission to quote from Maude's translation of *The Private Diary of Leo Tolstoy*, 1853–1857 (London), 1927.

To Frank Cioffi
without whom this book would not have been written

Introduction

When Rosa Luxemburg was asked by a friend to write a book on Tolstoy she replied:

> Your idea that I should write a book about Tolstoy doesn't appeal to me at all. For whom? Why? Everyone can read Tolstoy's books and if they don't get a strong breath of life from them, then they won't get it from any commentary. . . . Far too many books have already been written: people forget to look into the beautiful world with so much literature all around them.[1]

Yes, there is beauty in the world, though 'beauty' is not a word for which Tolstoy had much use when it came to describing the effects of art. And there is ugliness too. It was, no doubt, the wish to change that ugliness to beauty which impelled Rosa Luxemburg to write books of a very different kind from those she deprecated, books which would teach us something about the evils economic systems cause and give us the knowledge to remove those evils. Here, perhaps, she felt she could say something new and not just draw attention to things others had already said. But this worthwhile undertaking must not distract us from the fact that as old systems alter and new systems arise, whether by revolution or evolution, new woes as well as new benefits arise with them. As Tolstoy himself put it in his story *Lucerne*: 'Centuries pass, and whenever an impartial mind places good and evil on the scales, the balance remains even, and the proportion of good and evil remains unaltered.'[2] The fact that we can still find beauty in this world of mixed good and evil arises far more from literature and art than Rosa Luxemburg's remarks suggest. Far from getting in the way of the beauty of the world, literature and art are very often a means of access to it, and certainly the only means of fully sharing it with others. It is, moreover, not true that works of literature and art are like material objects whose values, so to speak, can just be read off their faces. Tolstoy wrote that there is always a need of disinterested criticism which understands and loves art and is independent of any party, 'criticism which, as Matthew Arnold says, sets itself the task of bringing to the front and pointing out to people all that is best, both in former and in contemporary writers'. [3] That is the task I have tried to carry out with respect to Tolstoy in the following pages.

I have had to concern myself with areas and topics which may be wider than some think the literary critic should try to cover. But it has been well said by Jean-François Revel in his study of Proust that the 'one fundamental condition which must be fulfilled' in talking about an author is that 'what is important to him must be important to you' and that 'Talking about an author means using him as a support for what we ourselves think about the things of which he has spoken'. [4] Consequently I have tried in what follows not just to report on Tolstoy's thoughts and feelings about certain topics, but also to reflect on those thoughts and feelings and to test them against my own experience and reading. I am not only concerned with Tolstoy as a creator of superb characters such as Pierre Bezukhov and Anna Karenina, but also with his engagement from youth to old age with such questions as 'what is the nature of happiness?', 'why is it so difficult to be truthful about human relations?', 'does history have a meaning?', and 'can men find the truth in matters of religion?' Tolstoy embodies the unique combination of a Dickensian power of presenting vivid pictures of character and action with the intellectual penetration of a Schopenhauer. This enables him to appeal to those who enjoy a good story of family life and, at the same time, to a profound philosopher like Wittgenstein, whose view on ethics and religion he strongly influenced.

I have tried, then, to think through for myself the problems raised by Tolstoy's view of the nature of history and of the role of the 'great' man of history, the question whether Tolstoy's views on social problems are relevant today and, finally, the question whether the later Tolstoy's views about Jesus, Christianity and religion in general can be sustained in the light of present-day research and reflection in these matters. But as my title indicates, my basic aim is to outline the striving on the part of Tolstoy and of many of his characters for a comprehensive vision which holds the many-sided confusion of life in a single luminous intuition. I have tried to do justice both to the imaginative drama inherent in this striving and to the intellectual interest of the thoughts and considerations thrown out in the course of it, so that my book will have something to say both to those interested in the novel and to those interested in philosophy and religion.

I am not one of these 'purists', much rarer now than they used to be, who lay it down as a principle that we should not allow our knowledge of an author's life and circumstances to affect our reading of his work. After all, getting to know a work of literature is much more like getting to know a person than a mathematical theorem or a scientific explanation, and it is a fact that the more we know of a person's past and present circumstances the better we can assess his nature. However, the chapters which follow do not constitute a biography. They incorporate biographical and historical information only in so far as it is necessary for my critical purposes. Readers who want a primarily biographical account of Tolstoy should go to the excellent works of Aylmer Maude, Derrick Leon and Henri Troyat. It may, however, be useful to begin with a brief account of the main events in Tolstoy's life and to point out some of the connections between that life and his work which the rest of this book will investigate in detail.

Lev Nikolaevich Tolstoy was born on 28 August 1828 (9 September, New Style) on the Tolstoy family estate at Yasnaya Polyana, the son of a *pomeshchik* (or member of the landed gentry) Nikolai Tolstoy and Princess Mary Volkonsky. Tolstoy's mother died when he was only two, but he drew on certain details of her life and character which he learned from diaries, letters, etc., for his portrayal of Princess Mary Bolkonsky in *War and Peace*. He tells us in his *Recollections* that his father served in the army in the 1813 campaign against Napoleon and then in the Civil Service. But he adds significantly that his father 'simply from a feeling of self-respect did not consider it possible to serve either during Alexander's later reactionary period or under Nicholas I'.[5] There is always a tension in the Ancien Régime between the privileged nobility with their liberty and country estates and the central monarchy. One sees this, for example, during the minority of Louis XIV in France in the hostility of the *Frondeurs* or regionally powerful nobles to the centralized state. The local power of the nobles in Russia during the reign of Catherine the Great is notorious. I shall show in detail, particularly in the latter part of this book, that Tolstoy's later doctrine on non-resistance, which on the face of things seems both Christian and radical, also contains in its hostility to state functionaries a large element of that aristocratic pride, independence and intransigence which Tolstoy's relatives and friends observed in him. When Levin, in *Anna Karenina*, angry at Oblonsky's reference to his rival Vronsky as a 'perfect aristocrat', bursts out:

You consider Vronsky an aristocrat. I don't. A man whose father crawled up from nothing by intrigues and whose mother has had relations with heaven knows whom. . . . No, pardon me, I consider myself and people like me aristocrats; people who can point back to three or four honourable genera-

3

tions of their family, all with a high standard of education (talent and intelligence are a different matter), who have never cringed before anyone, never depended on anyone, but have lived as my father and grandfather did. (II, xvii, 195)

he expresses sentiments which Tolstoy certainly held about his own family. It was because he came from a powerful class that Tolstoy could conveniently overlook the fact that it is not only states which can oppress the weak. We shall see, too, that Tolstoy was consistently hostile to the Westernizing ideas of the *raznochintsy* or urban radical non-gentry intelligentsia. He was rooted in the quasi-patriarchal life of his beloved Yasnaya Polyana without which he once said he could not conceive of existence.

In May 1844 Tolstoy entered the University of Kazan. The grip of French culture on the Russian nobility had long been very powerful. Many of them knew French much better than Russian during the Napoleonic period evoked in *War and Peace*. The influence of the French Enlightenment was very strong, and, in particular, that of Voltaire's scepticism. The portrayal of old Prince Bolkonsky in *War and Peace* with his dry ridicule of his daughter Princess Mary's religion brings out this fact. But the young Tolstoy added to an admiration for Voltaire an interest in Montesquieu with his account of law, history and society, and, more important still, an ardent devotion to Rousseau. He read all twenty volumes of Rousseau's works. At the age of fifteen he even wore a medallion of Rousseau round his neck for a time instead of the Russian Orthodox cross. Rousseau's sense that Voltaire and the *philosophes* of the Enlightenment could not satisfy man's spiritual and religious needs, and that those very needs were legitimate and not merely the result of intellectual aberrations, influenced Tolstoy profoundly.

Tolstoy's sense of the inadequacies of historians was already strong in him while he was a student at Kazan. It emerges with the fruits of much more reading, reflection and experience, in *War and Peace*. An individualism pressed to the point of eccentricity and an impatience with academic discipline prevented him from fulfilling the University's requirements and he left without a degree for the family estate of Yasnaya, which was his own portion of the inheritance, in 1847.

Tolstoy alternated for a time between plans for running his estate, which included a closer relationship with the peasants, and city dissipation. Then in April 1851 he left with his brother Nicholas for the Caucasus where he eventually entered the regular army. He continued to wrestle with the Rousseauistic problems of the contrast between civilized corruption and the Cossack's life of nature and with the conflict in himself between egoism and altruism. He even had a Rousseauistic dream of founding a new religion, a Christianity purged of dogmas and mysticism and giving happiness here and now on earth, not in some merely hypothetical future life. With the outbreak of the Crimean war which, as I shall show, Tolstoy was to interpret as yet another stage in Russia's struggle against the West, Tolstoy applied for a transfer to Sevastopol where he saw some of the bitterest fighting during the siege. His story *The Raid* and his Sevastopol stories anticipate much that is developed in more detail in *War and Peace*. They recognize that war has a 'poetic' or Homeric side even in its fearful cruelty, but ultimately reject it on the grounds of Christian ethics.

The end of the Crimean war in 1855, along with the death of the repressive Nicholas I, brought new hope to Russia. Tolstoy returned to St Petersburg as a promising young author, but he was restive, unsettled and intransigent among 'men of letters' like Turgenev and the intelligentsia. The stories he wrote at this time show him uncertain of his bearings and, with the possible exception of *Lucerne* which I shall discuss in detail as showing Tolstoy's reaction to Western Utilitarianism, are inferior to *Childhood* and the Sevastopol sketches. Tolstoy made visits to Western Europe from January to July 1857 (he based *Lucerne* on an incident during this visit) and from July 1860 to April 1861, the latter visit being particularly concerned with studying methods of education. He threw himself into educational experiments on his estate with his characteristic energy, founding a school for peasant children. He meditated and wrote on the problem of history. In the midst of a struggle with the flesh and the passions that had continued intermittently from his student days on with, at times, an intensity which recalls St Augustine, he continued his long-standing and abiding dream of family life on the old patriarchal lines of Yasnaya Polyana. He even paid court to a young lady called Valeria in the hope that she would prove the right one with whom to turn that dream into a reality. As I shall show, his most conspicuous artistic failure, *Family Happiness*, arose out of the episode.

At last, with his mental and physical powers at their height, Tolstoy married the eighteen-year-old Sonya Behrs in September 1862 when he was thirty-four. From an early period there were tensions in the marriage of a kind which Tolstoy portrays in Levin's marriage in *Anna Karenina*. Diary entries alternate between Tolstoy's intense love for his wife and coldness and fear of what he saw as her egoism. The uncompleted fragment *The Porcelain Doll*, which seems to express the fear that his wife might turn into a doll rather than remain a flesh-and-blood human companion, relates to this period.[6]

Tolstoy certainly need not have feared on this score as far as Sonya was concerned. She, like himself, was 'human all too human'. However, if there were alternations of blissful harmony and stormy estrangement, there was also stability, as with Levin and Kitty. The very month after his marriage Tolstoy wrote to his brother-in-law that he felt drawn towards a work on a large scale, a novel, or something like it. In 1863 he began *War and Peace*. It grew under his hands over the next five years (with Sonya acting as a loving amanuensis) into a unique combination of epic historical material, family chronicle and philosophical reflections which he was always reluctant to call a novel.

As its publication neared completion Tolstoy was exhausted, and in September 1869 he even underwent some kind of mental crisis at the town of Arzamas while he was on a journey from Moscow to Nizhni-Novgorod. The 'Arzamas experience' consisted of an intense Nihilistic conviction of the utter pointlessness of life which overcame him while he was alone in his room. In some ways this experience prefigured the longer-lasting crisis of a decade later on the completion of *Anna Karenina*. During the next few years after finishing *War and Peace* Tolstoy occupied himself with various activities. Apart from estate management, he studied Greek so that he could read his admired Homer in the original; and he became deeply disturbed by the contrast between the heroic ideals of Homer and the renunciation advocated by Jesus. He was to discuss the unbridgeable gulf between the ideals of Greece and the ideals of Christianity in *What is Art?* many years later. He also became interested in Russian folk tales and wrote some religious parables. He began a historical novel about the times of Peter the Great, but abandoned it because the times were too remote for the achievement of that memoir-like psychological intimacy of detail he so much prized and which was to reach its apotheosis in *Anna Karenina* which he began in March 1873 and finished in June 1877.

While he was completing *Anna Karenina*, Tolstoy's thoughts turned more and more intensely (like those of his hero Levin) to the question of ethics and God. He read Pascal's *Pensées* with deep interest and began that period of intense meditation which gave rise to *A Confession* (1879). This work is not designed to stress the meaninglessness of life (as is sometimes the impression) so much as to bring out the fact that those who think life is meaningless (as he himself seemed for a time to have come to do) are making a terrible mistake. What, then, does give meaning to a life always apparently open to the mercilessness of chance and inevitably destined to end in annihilation by an often painful death which most of us try not to think about? Tolstoy came to think that the answer lay in 'that universal and eternal teaching so perfectly expressed, for myself no less than for others, in the Gospels'.[7] The last part of this book will be concerned to explore Tolstoy's account of that teaching which was 'universal' in that it was present in the words of Buddha as well as in the words of Jesus. This account, though disturbed by the turbid currents of Tolstoy's conflicts with his wife, which intensified from 1882 onwards, still remains as one of the most moving examples of that search for God which seems destined to remain with man as long as he is a heart, a mind, and an imagination as well as a physical organism. It was a search which the eighty-two-year-old Tolstoy was still pursuing when he left his beloved Yasnaya Polyana on 28 October 1910 to die at the obscure railway station of Astapovo.

Chapter 1

The Green Stick and the Secret of Happiness

'I lie bound and wish to stretch out my arms, but cannot'.[1] That is how Tolstoy reports the first conscious impression of his life. Struggling in his swaddling clothes, the child had become primitively aware of that contrast between constraint and liberty whose more abstract ramifications were to puzzle the grown man. In *War and Peace* he is obsessed with the problem of freedom and necessity and is driven back on the distinction between the physical and spiritual worlds (in Kantian terms the phenomenal and the noumenal) as the only rational means of solving it.

But, in other moods, Tolstoy was well aware that it is not by reason alone, but by imagination, that we are most deeply united with, and reconciled to, life. His *Recollections* show us that man learns to think through participation in the make-believe and story-telling of childhood's dream world. He recalls being absorbed at this stage as much by the circumstances of the story-telling—his old grandmother all in white, the flickering lamp, the blind Lev Stepanich's monotonous voice—as by the content of the story. Later on, at the beginning of his boyhood, Tolstoy was fascinated by the narrative powers of his brother Nicholas:

His imagination was such that for hours together he could tell fairy-tales or ghost stories or amusing tales in the style of Mrs Radcliffe, without a pause and with such vivid realization of what he was narrating that one forgot it was all invention . . . [2]

When Tolstoy was five, Nicholas announced 'that he possessed a secret by means of which . . . all men would become happy: there would be no more disease, no trouble, no one would be angry with anybody, all would love one another, and all would become "Ant-brothers"'. The name 'Ant-brothers' was probably a childish corruption of Moravian brothers (the name of a religious sect which had strongly influenced John Wesley), as the Russian word for ant, *muravei*, is close to the word for Moravian. Leo, Dmitri, Sergey and Nicholas organized a game of 'Ant-Brothers' which consisted of sitting under chairs, sheltering themselves with boxes and shawls, and cuddling up together in the dark. But though the 'Ant-Brotherhood' itself was revealed, the secret of happiness remained hidden. Nicholas claimed that he had written it 'on a green stick buried by the road at the edge of a certain ravine'.

When he was over seventy Tolstoy looked back on the story of the green stick and wrote:

As I then believed that there existed a little green stick whereon was written the message which would destroy all evil in men and give them universal welfare, so I now believe that such truth exists and will be revealed to men and will give them all it promises.

He was still searching for that secret of happiness when, in his eighty-third year, he left the burdens and conflicts of family life, only to die on a railway station. He was buried, as he had long ago requested, at the very spot where his brother Nicholas claimed to have hidden the green stick.

It is worth reflecting on this story of the green stick, for it is as elusive as what it purports to reveal, namely the secret of happiness. In being so, it suggests both that the elusiveness itself is part of the secret, in that happiness is a road rather than a goal, and that the truth in these matters has to be conveyed in parables rather than in propositions or commandments. And, after all, did not some of the greatest teachers of mankind, the Buddha, Plato and Jesus, have to resort to parables to convey the essence of their doctrines? Certainly part of Tolstoy's greatness as a novelist consists in his ability to make references to philosophic themes arise naturally from the dramatic context he has created. For example Levin in *Anna Karenina* (I, xi, 47) refers to one of Plato's parable-like myths when he reminds the *bon-viveur* Oblonsky of the two kinds of love Plato defines in his *Symposium*: 'Some men understand only the one, some only the other. Those who understand only the non-platonic love need not speak of tragedy. . . . As for the platonic love there can be no tragedy either, because there everything is clear and pure . . .' As the rest of the book shows, Anna's love, which certainly ends tragically, is a mixture of both kinds.

Tolstoy also tells in *Anna Karenina* the story of how Levin himself comes to learn the answer to the question 'Why is it good to be here?', the secret of happiness. Levin learns it, in the end, not from his clever half-brother Koznyshev, an intellectual, but from the peasant Theodore, whose words reveal to him that man is a soul in the sense that he is more than 'a mere bundle of desires and wishes'.[3]

Theodore says that Kirilov, the innkeeper, lives for his belly. That is intelligible and reasonable. We all as reasoning creatures cannot live otherwise. And then that same Theodore says that it is wrong to live for one's belly, and that we must live for Truth, for God, and at the first hint I understand him. (VIII, xii, 413)

Levin, then, learns something from Theodore, but what he learns is knowledge of a peculiar kind. As Levin himself thinks: 'I have discovered nothing. I have only perceived what it is that I know' (VIII, xii, 414). Just as it is worth reflecting on the parable of the green stick, so it is worth reflecting on the nature of this kind of knowledge, for it is knowledge of the kind which literature in general seems to give. Readers of Plato will recall the dialogue called the *Meno* in which Socrates, by skilful questioning, elicits Pythagoras' theorem from a slave boy who had not heard of it before, and on the strength of this argues that the boy somehow knew the theorem already and that all knowledge is recollection. But this notion of knowledge as consisting of our being reminded of what we already know, but with such force that it seems to us as if we were grasping it for the first time, is one which, curiously enough, seems to apply much more appositely to the kind of knowledge we feel that literature gives, than to what we now know are the *a priori* deductions involved in geometry. Tolstoy, in particular, excelled at conveying what one might call insight into insight by giving us supreme descriptions of those moments in his characters' lives when they become aware of truths about personal relationships. Such insight is not easily cast into the form of propositions. It comes to us as experience which we match, so to speak, with experience direct, rather than as propositions which we test scientifically.

One aspect of experience which Tolstoy makes us aware of is the element of irreducible irrationality present in both life and art. The chapter of *Childhood* entitled 'Games' brings this home. The children are outdoors. They have just been absorbed in hunting, itself a curious combination of real activity and play. A carpet is spread under the trees and they sit on the ground and start to pretend to row, imagining they are on a fishing expedition. Volodya annoys the narrator by his cool detachment, his refusal to become absorbed. The narrator cannot help seeing that Volodya is rational, but at the same time reflects that such rationality would rule out the intense enjoyment they all got on long winter evenings indoors by pretending that the armchair was a carriage in which they could ride off to all kinds of adventures. 'If one goes by reality there can be no games. And if there are no games—what will be left?' Art depends on irrationality for its existence, but the pleasure it gives is not, in itself, irrational.

Even in his unduly moralistic *What is Art?* written many years later, Tolstoy, unlike Plato, does not attack art simply because it involves make-believe, and consequently a kind of deceit, as in the case of the boy who fears wolves and invents a story of an encounter with a wolf in order to make his hearers experience this fear. Again, unlike Plato, Tolstoy does not attack art because it works through arousing the passions. Tolstoy simply accepts our susceptibility to make-believe, and consequently to deceit (a susceptibility which is itself bound up with the passions), as a *donnée*, a feature of the species which enables the artist to hold us in his spell. Plato objects to the spell itself, whereas with Tolstoy it is not the spell itself, but what the artist does to us when we are in it, that is subject to moral judgment. Moreover, for Tolstoy, there is a sense in which the artist must be sincere if his work is to succeed, for if he has no acquaintance with the passions (though not necessarily with the situations he sets them in which may be invented) he will not succeed in evoking them. From *Childhood* through *Lucerne* and his great works *War and Peace* and *Anna Karenina* to *What is Art?* and such late works as *Hadji Murad* Tolstoy consistently sees poetic enjoyment as 'a friend to man' and, indeed, the greatest of gifts, because it is the only one which can reveal, like the message on the green stick, the secret of happiness.

It can of course be argued, but in Tolstoy's case inappropriately, that to search for happiness at all is to succumb to vulgar *eudaemonism*, or the pursuit of pleasure, the philosophy of Epicurus in the ancient world and Bentham in the modern, a philosophy which has been called that of 'a pig satisfied'. At worst, it is claimed, the search for happiness leads to egoistic hedonism, the putting of one's own satisfaction before that of others. At best it leads to a kind of universalist hedonism, or Utilitarianism, which sets the happiness of humanity before every other consideration.

Among Tolstoy's contemporaries two in particular reviled the search for happiness as embodied in English Utilitarianism. 'Man does not strive for happiness,' wrote Nietzsche; 'only the Englishman does that.' [4] In *Notes from Underground*, Dostoevsky made a bitter attack on the notion that if men knew that their real interest lay in acting virtuously they would do so:

Oh, the innocence of it! Since when, in these past thousands of years, has man acted exclusively out of self-interest? What about the millions of facts that show that men, deliberately and in full knowledge of what their real interests were, spurned them and rushed in a different direction.[5]

Dostoevsky's eloquence testifies, of course, to the power of men's passions; but those passions only draw their power from the fact that they promise in some cases a more intense, in others an easier, happiness than 'real interests'. If some men seek suffering, as the underground man claims, that is because they find satisfaction in suffering. The underground man himself finds his happiness in whim. Later on Dostoevsky tries to show that he does so because, like Milton's Satan, he lacks love. As for Nietzsche, he, of course, glossed over the fact that the Utilitarians, in claiming that men strive for happiness, were quite prepared to concede that different individuals have the most varied objects as their primary aims. Their contention was that these objects only have their power because men believe that in pursuing them they will achieve happiness. Tolstoy and, for that matter, Jesus and Nietzsche's own revered Buddha, would have agreed with them. Indeed Nietzsche's scorn is put in its place if we remember that St Augustine, who was one of the most passionate strivers for happiness ever known, was not an Englishman. Jesus and Buddha certainly promised happiness, of however exalted a kind, to their followers.

Tolstoy was fascinated in both the first and the seventh decades of his life with the idea of attaining a truth that would give men eternal happiness. In an unfinished article written in 1846 or 1847 in his late teens entitled 'On the Aim of Philosophy' he defined that aim as 'the science of life'. At this time he believed that progress could only come in so far as each individual progresses, and embarked on the period of self-improvement recorded in his diaries from 1847 to 1857. What will be the result, he asked himself, of changing from the life of a student to the life of a landowner:

Some change in my mode of life must result: yet that change must not come of an external circumstance—rather, of a movement of spirit: wherefore I keep finding myself confronted with the question, 'What is the aim of man's life?' and, no matter what result my reflections reach, no matter what I take to be life's source, I invariably arrive at the conclusion that the purpose of our human existence is to afford a maximum of help towards the universal of everything that exists.[6]

The conflict between the pull of altruism and egotism—the cardinal problem of the ethical life—runs right through the diaries and is sometimes spelled out in them explicitly.

The Prince Nekhlyudov of *A Landlord's Morning* tries to find happiness altruistically by helping his serfs, but is weighed down by a world that will not bend to his ideas. Nekhlyudov discovers a kind of egotism at the heart of his altruism. The Olenin of *The Cossacks* tries to put the egotism of his St Petersburg life behind him by going to the Caucasus. Though he admires the vigour of old Daddy Eroshka (whose thieving, lechery and murder Tolstoy alludes to with admirable equanimity), the young Lukashka and the beautiful Cossack girl Maryanka (over whom he plays a youthfully self-regarding drama of renunciation), he realizes that he can never fully enter into Cossack life.

Tolstoy's experience of war in the Caucasus and in the Crimea brought him to his first real crisis of faith in God and Providence. It also laid the foundation for that interest in the physiognomy of war which is evident in *War and Peace*. It awakened that concern with the problem of a theodicy, or justification of God and Providence in the face of the existence of evil and suffering, which is shown in both *War and Peace* and *Anna Karenina*, and which derives so much of its intensity and urgency from the fact that Tolstoy was centrally concerned with happiness as the aim of man. At the end of *Sevastopol in May 1855* Tolstoy stands above the morally blind participants over whose every thought he is a despot, and speaks in the role of a gloomy observer and prophet about the suffering that men who are 'Christians professing the one great law of love and self-sacrifice', inflict on each other. In March 1855 Tolstoy wrote in his diary:

Yesterday a conversation about Divinity and Faith suggested to me a great, a stupendous, idea to the realization of which I feel capable of devoting my life. That idea is the founding of a new religion corresponding to the present development of mankind; the religion of Christ but purged of dogmas and mysticism—a practical religion, not promising future bliss but giving bliss on earth.[7]

It is highly characteristic of Tolstoy that the first thing that his new religion should promise is happiness. It is equally characteristic of him that this happiness should be aimed at here and now and not in some afterlife. He retained this view during his religious crisis in the 1880s when he wrote: 'We only know life in this world and this is because if there is a meaning in our life, then it is here in this world'.[8]

From 1855 to 1861 Tolstoy was looking into Western Utilitarian ideas of Progress to see if they provided the solution to the riddle of the meaning of life that would, once it was found, also bring happiness. He rejected the Utilitarianism of the West in the important story *Lucerne* in which he affirms against it the inner life of a single, despised, itinerant musician. It is no good being concerned with 'the betterment of the whole human race' if one does not have in one's soul 'the simple elemental feeling of human sympathy'[9] for the individual of flesh and blood met face to face.

From 1861 to 1879 Tolstoy was rooted deep in the patriarchal life of Yasnaya Polyana, happy in his marriage and in his writing. In *War and Peace* he identifies God with life itself, but his exploration of the inner uncertainties of Prince Andrew and of Pierre shows that there is no complacency in his affirmation. The insistent realities of suffering and of the death of dear ones are not to be expunged by any false idealism. In *Anna Karenina* God is identified with the Good, with the moral law.

Then from 1879 to 1882 we get the personal crisis reflected in Tolstoy's *A Confession*. But it should be evident from what has already been said that Tolstoy exaggerates in *A Confession* his past forgetfulness of the search for the meaning of life and his past 'unbelief'. He emphasizes, for dramatic purposes, a discontinuity in his life which is not really there. It is enough to recall the diary entry from 1855 about founding a new religion which has just been quoted. Founding such a new religion is the very task he sets himself in all his religious writings from *A Confession* onwards.

At the same time two things should be stressed, the first personal, the second extra-personal. In 1879, after having completed *Anna Karenina*, Tolstoy suffered an 'arrest of life' which was reflected as an inner experience of the futility of things. This experience was similar to that which he had suffered ten years earlier at Arzamas after completing *War and Peace*. Sheer exhaustion after immense labours may well have contributed something in both cases. But, whether because of his age (fifty-one) or some other reason, the second experience was certainly more intense, long-lasting and difficult to overcome. On top of this, the intensification of social problems in Russia with the growth of capitalism, industry and railways and the breakdown of the hegemony of the old patriarchal life on the country estates troubled Tolstoy deeply. The assassination of Tsar Alexander II by a revolutionary group in March 1881 marks dramatically the beginning of a process which was to culminate with Lenin's accession to power in October 1917. The assassination occasioned Tolstoy's noble letter to Alexander III begging him to forgive his father's murderers.

After witnessing the misery of the Moscow poor at the time of the Census in January 1882, Tolstoy could no longer reconcile his individual happiness with such suffering. The task of the minimization of that misery drove away all his peace of mind. He made it his prime task as a writer to awaken the consciences of those who had a superfluity of leisure and wealth. But, unlike both the revolutionaries and the Marxists, Tolstoy, rightly I think, could subscribe to no collectivist solution of the problem of happiness. He could only conceive of happiness in terms of that natural unit of consciousness, the individual life, and not in terms of the collective or swarm life of which he had painted such a terrible picture in *War and Peace*. He saw every human being as an end in himself who should not be sacrificed for a larger whole unless he himself made such a sacrifice spontaneously. If the tormented last days of Tolstoy's life, with all their blunders, occasional self-deception and yet nobility, show anything, they show that true individualism goes with altruism, for it was the misery of the poor, not as a class, but as individual human beings, which would not let Tolstoy rest until he had done something to alleviate it.[10]

Chapter 2

Tolstoy's Early Diaries and his Mastery of 'Literary Psychology'

Many critics have seen that Tolstoy laid the foundation for his great works in the early diaries. In them he was already developing an interest in what Russian critics have called '*dialektika dushy*', 'the dialectic of the soul', that is, the interior monologue which we all carry on with ourselves. Here is a typical entry made in March 1851 :

> I received Poiret over familiarly, and allowed myself to yield to his being a stranger, to the presence of Koloshin and to a misplaced grand-seigneurish sort of feeling: so that I did my gymnastics hurriedly. Out of *fausse honte*, I failed to make anyone hear at the Gorchakov's: while, at the Koloshins I made an awkward exit from the drawing-room—showed too much haste, and in trying to say something very amiable, bungled it.[1]

In such passages as this Tolstoy was developing a technique of self-observation and self-analysis which was later to bear fruit in such passages of psychological truth as that in *Anna Karenina* (I, xiv, 56–58) recording Levin's embarrassment when he finds that he is using a retort for the second time on the same evening to Countess Nordston, a society lady who despises him.

Here is another example of a diary notation which has a counterpart in *Anna Karenina*: 'It sometimes happens that one suddenly feels that an expression of surprise remains on one's face when there is nothing more to be surprised at.' [2] The counterpart is the incident at the beginning of *Anna Karenina* when Oblonsky returns home from the theatre 'merry and satisfied, with an enormous pear in his hand for his wife' and she receives him angrily because she has just found out that he has been unfaithful to her with the governess. As he looks back on the confrontation, Oblonsky is chiefly tormented, not by his wife's suffering, but because he had retained on his face an expression inappropriate to the situation and had smiled 'his usual kindly and therefore silly smile' (I, i, 1–3).

Tolstoy was keenly interested in the awareness of awareness. One entry runs:

There are thoughts which pass through one's mind unnoticed: there are others which seem to leave profounder traces, so that one involuntarily tries to seize them (such are these that I am writing down). Sometimes I forget the thought itself but the trace it has made remains, and I feel that a remarkable thought has passed here.[3]

A little later he writes: 'There was a time when consciousness developed in me to such a degree that it stifled reason, so that I could not think of anything except: "What am I thinking about?"' [4] This preoccupation with thinking about thinking also emerges in the passage on solipsism in chapter XIX of *Boyhood* (1853–54).

An entry for 1 April 1852 shows that Tolstoy was well aware from his own experience that things can easily present themselves in a false light to those who observe them only in order to describe them. The foremost Russian Tolstoy scholar Boris Eikhenbaum sums up in the following interesting passage, which I translate, this whole question of being the spectator of consciousness as it affects Tolstoy:

The matter does not lie in dualism, as is customarily said, but in a dual process, or in two processes of consciousness, one of which works over the material provided by the other; one (the 'daytime' one) is a process of observation which demands from the observer the participation in actuality . . . the other (the 'night' one) is a process of memory freely working on the material provided. . . . Art for Tolstoy consists in the method of calling up memory. . . . Purely historical occurrences, such as those he had thought over for his novel about Peter the Great, were nothing to the purpose. *War and Peace* existed because its war background was the Crimean campaign and its family background the life at Yasnaya Polyana.[5]

Eikhenbaum argues that because memory and analysis turned each thought from a conviction into material for art, they led Tolstoy into a kind of 'cynicism' or 'nihilism'. I am reminded of the so-called 'unmasking psychology' which is the one thing Tolstoy shared with Nietzsche. But Tolstoy's moral resilience comes out in the fact that, like Levin in *Anna Karenina*, he could not bear the lack of positive convictions, the abyss of nihilism which Eikhenbaum rightly saw that his psychological penetration had opened for him. He saw that the moral life was a matter for decisions, but he did not melodramatize these as a series of irrational leaps in the manner of the Existentialists. As I shall show in connection with *Lucerne*, Tolstoy was not as much of a nihilist as Eikhenbaum was led to claim.

The moral resilience of which I have spoken is already present in the early diaries and consists there in the development of a cunning strategy of using the very same psychological penetration which

17

threatens to unbalance his moral equilibrium to find the moves and holds which will enable him to retain it. He achieves, for example, something of the insight of Spinoza or Pascal into the passions in an entry like the following: 'One must apply cunning against oneself and one's passions . . . reason, acting directly, is powerless against the passions, it must try to oppose one to another.' [6] Tolstoy is both calm and pitiless in his analysis of vanity:

Vanity is a sort of immature love of *éclat*, a sort of love of self transferred to the opinion of others. One loves oneself, not for what one is, but for what one appears to be.[7]

His observation has something of the penetration of Pascal's remark: 'We are glad to sacrifice even life, providing our sacrifice is talked about.' [8] These analytic notes on vanity come to their full fruition in Tolstoy's rendering, in *War and Peace*, of Prince Andrew's reflections before the battle of Austerlitz:

I don't know what will happen and don't want to know and can't, but if I want this—want glory, want to be known to men, want to be loved by them, it is not my fault that I want it and want nothing but that and live only for that. . . . And precious and dear as many persons are to me—father, sister, wife—those dearest to me—yet dreadful and unnatural as it seems, I would give them all at once for a moment of glory, of triumph over men, of love from men I don't know and never shall know, for the love of these men here . . . (III, xii, 347)

Tolstoy was also aware that, as he wrote in August 1852, 'Futurity moves us to greater interest than does actuality'.[9] In 1853 he noted that 'Nothing so impedes true happiness . . . as the habit of expecting something from the future'.[10] These remarks recall Pascal's: 'We scarcely ever think of the present; if we do it is only to obtain light wherewith to organize the future. . . . Thus we never live, but only hope to live; and as we are for ever preparing to be happy, we shall assuredly never be so.' [11] And Tolstoy would certainly have assented to Wittgenstein's observation: 'Only a man who lives not in time but in the present is happy.' [12]

The diaries, then, lay the foundation for Tolstoy's great mastery of psychology. But what sort of psychology? Here the philosopher Santayana's distinction between 'literary psychology' and 'scientific psychology' is of crucial importance. Whereas 'scientific psychology' is concerned with the record of how animals act, 'literary psychology is the art of imagining how they feel and think' and as such 'always remains in possession of the moral field'.[13] This is because we can grasp the 'sense' of another's action 'only dramatically, by imitative sympathy'. We make up little stories, or novels, in our minds, not only about others, but also about our own past and future. Our feelings cannot operate except through such mental pictures of the joys and sorrows of both others and ourselves. Our attitudinal life is, so to speak, always mediate rather than immediate, and this is why the skilled novelist can give us just as direct and immediate an access to it as it is ever possible to obtain.

A diary entry for July 1851 shows Tolstoy's intense concern with the problem of how one mind can be enabled to 'run through', so to speak, the feelings of another:

I have been lying outside the camp. It is a marvellous night! The moon is just rising above a low hillock, and shedding its light on two small, thin, ethereal clouds. . . . From the vicinity of the village comes the shouting of Tartars, and, anon, the baying of a dog. Then all is still again—there sounds only the chirrup of a grasshopper as a light, transparent cloud drifts past near and distant stars. To myself I thought; I will go forth and describe whatever I may see: but how shall I describe it? I should need to seat myself at an ink-stained table and to take ink and rough paper, and to cover the paper with letters. Letters make words, and words phrases, but how can one transmit *feeling*? Is there not some way of transmuting one's outlook into the outlook of another while one contemplates nature? Description will not suffice.[14]

He set himself to master the art of conveying the feelings of his characters to the reader by showing the way those characters conveyed those feelings to each other, and, for that matter, to themselves in their own awareness. It was this art which enabled him to evoke the scene in *War and Peace* (VI, ii, 6–8) in which Prince Andrew looks out of the window at Otradnoe on to the moonlit garden and overhears the talk of Natasha and Sonya and feels an unexpected turmoil of hopes within him. It was this art which enabled him to evoke the scene in *Anna Karenina* (III, xii, 314–15) in which Levin spends the night on a haycock and finds his views of life change, after having seen Kitty pass by in a carriage, just as the pearly sky above him has changed.

Tolstoy developed an acute awareness of the phenomenon which the twentieth-century Russian psychologist Lev Vygotsky has called 'inner speech'. This 'inner speech' arises because the mind does not think in separate words but in meaningful wholes, and so operates with a peculiar syntax. The peculiar syntax is caused by the fact that a thinker does not have to name the subjects of his interior monologues to himself and so can confine himself to a stream of predicates. If two people are *en rapport*, as we say, the situation or context leads to a co-incidence of thought, so that such 'external' speech as they use—however telegraphic and opaque it might appear to a third party—is entirely transparent to them. No doubt one of the reasons Tolstoy's works lose so little in translation is that he is often concerned with the dramatic portrayal of those moments when understanding is independent of words, but tied to concrete emotions, actions and situations. In these moments even 'external' speech may become condensed and reduced to predicates. Lev Vygotsky writes: 'Every sentence that we say in real life has some kind of subtext, a thought hidden behind it.'[15] It is when our fellow-speaker cannot guess that subtext that misunderstanding arises. Thus in the magnificent scene in the Vrede gardens in *Anna Karenina* (III, xxii) in which Anna tells Vronsky that her husband Karenin knows their secret, Anna is not 'listening to his words—only trying to read his thoughts from his face'. But some remarks by his commanding officer Serpukhovskoy have alerted Vronsky to the fact that his affair poses a threat to his career, and this is a thought he knows he cannot share with Anna. Vronsky thinks that a duel will settle all. After that Anna will have to leave Karenin. Anna says that she cannot bear to leave her son. Vronsky uses the phrase 'degrading situation' and she is driven back to a tremulous avowal of her pride, an avowal which breaks down as she loses, so to speak, her own subtext, and cannot 'say what she is proud of'.

Much later in the book, shortly before her suicide in fact, Anna, now tragically estranged from everyone, asks herself: 'How is it possible to tell another what one feels?' (VII, xxix, 371). This compares with a famous line from Tolstoy's favourite poet Tiutchev: [16]

Kak serdtsu viskazat' sebia?

which can be literally translated as follows: 'How can you express what is in your heart?' Certainly Anna's thought 'How is it possible to tell another what one feels?' focuses the central problem of Tolstoy's art, the problem we have seen him pose in the early diaries as 'how can we transmit *feeling*?' When Tolstoy came to define art in *What is Art?* (1898)—which cannot entirely be written off as the mere aberration of an old man, but fits in with much that he had thought throughout his life—he does so, significantly enough in view of what we have just seen, in the following terms:

Art is a human activity consisting in this, that one man consciously by means of certain external signs, hands on to others feelings he has lived through, and that others are infected by these feelings and also experience them.[17]

Such a handing over of feelings is the province of what, following Santayana, I have called 'literary psychology'.

The line from Tiutchev's famous poem 'Silentium' which I have just quoted is followed by two more which run: 'How can another person understand you?/Can anyone else understand what you live by?' The three lines bring together for us Tolstoy's two chief concerns, for they point to the fact that if we communicate a human being's inmost feelings, or interior monologue, we at the same time communicate what that human being lives by. All his life Tolstoy was searching for what men must live by if they are to uncover the secret of happiness written on the green stick. The answer to the most basic question of all 'Why is it good to be here?' can only be given in terms of an imaginative projection of a deep conviction that it *is* good to be here. Speculative thought may confirm, but cannot originate, such feeling, and it can carry us no further than the feeling itself.[18] It is for this reason (and not from any sentimental primitivism) that Tolstoy in *Anna Karenina* makes the uneducated peasant Theodore convey to Levin moral knowledge of a kind his intellectual half-brother Koznyshev cannot attain, let alone communicate. It is for this reason that an unintellectual (though intelligent) girl like Kitty is, after her fashion, just as much engaged in a quest for the meaning of life as her husband Levin, that great devourer of books of philosophy. For a time it seems to Kitty that her friend Varenka has discovered the secret: 'What—what is most important? What gives you such peace? You know, tell me!' (II, xxxii, 252). So asks Kitty, not, significantly enough, with her tongue, but with her eyes. But she eventually discovers that Varenka cannot help her. As Kitty says to her: 'I can't live except by my own heart, but you live by principles' (II, xxxv, 266). It is only the heart that can answer, from the depths of one's whole being, the questions 'What is the meaning of life? 'Why is it good to be here?' and it is only art, which, through dramatic psychology, can communicate those reasons which, as Pascal said, reason cannot know.

Chapter 3

Childhood, Boyhood and *Youth*

Tolstoy's first attempt to draw on the self-observation and self-analysis of the diaries for an extended artistic work was the unfinished *A History of Yesterday* written in March 1851.[1] Unfortunately it has not been translated to date. This was a bold attempt to do away with a 'plot' framework and its attendant literary conventions, and simply evoke the 'awareness' of an *homme de société* (including his dream life) during a single day. Boris Eikhenbaum considered that the umbilical cord connecting it to the diaries had not been cut.[2] Tolstoy was greatly influenced at this time by Laurence Sterne; but he was concerned not with Sterne as an elaborator of literary arabesques and as a parodist of literary conventions, but with his rendering of what I have called 'inner speech', the streams of association which sometimes constitute our interior monologues. By August 1851 Tolstoy writes: 'For all his gigantic talent of narration and clever prattle, even my favourite author, Sterne, is tediously discursive.'[3]

In November 1851 Tolstoy began *Childhood* while he was ill at Tiflis. He records finishing it in his diary on 2 July 1852.[4] He wrote to Nekrasov, editor of *The Contemporary*, that it was not intended as an autobiography, but as the first part of a novel.[5] Chapters I–XII describe a day in the country, chapters XIII–XV are transitional, chapters XVI–XXIV describe a day in Moscow and chapters XXVII and XXVIII conclude the piece with the mother's death and the reflection it provokes.[6] In material, themes and *motifs*, *Childhood*, with its evocation of childish first love, its hunting and its society ball, strikingly anticipates the domestic parts of *War and Peace* just as *The Raid* and the Sevastopol stories strikingly anticipate its physiognomy of war. The narrator's intense despair at his shyness and awkwardness gives him a family likeness to Tolstoy's later heroes Pierre and Levin, and his amazement at the would-be 'sophisticate' Volodya's more sensual attitude to the girl he himself idealizes prefigures Tolstoy's subsequent treatments of the same contrast. Tolstoy is objective enough to give the sensualist's case just as much power as the idealist's while at the same time conveying a sense that he is on the idealist's side. This working over of the same territory throughout a whole decade before he began *War and Peace* undoubtedly contributed to the psychological richness and density of that book and of *Anna Karenina*.

The very first chapter of *Childhood* shows Tolstoy trying to make the psychological notation and commentary he had developed in the diaries the focus of attention. In it he explores a phenomenon which will always interest him (and which underlies the whole of art), namely the way in which what starts out as pretence can become so convincing that it takes in, first, the onlooker, and then the pretender himself. The narrator pretends to Karl Ivanych, his tutor, that he has had a fearful dream. So affected is Karl Ivanych by his account of it that the narrator himself starts to believe that his account was true. This is like Sonya's pretence to Natasha, in *War and Peace* (VII, xii, 159), that she has seen a vision of Prince Andrew in the mirror at Hallowe'en. Natasha's reaction makes Sonya begin to believe that she really had seen him.

The narrator's shifts of feeling towards Karl Ivanych are vividly caught and Karl's own peculiarly vulnerable situation as a German tutor to Russian aristocrats is portrayed with great sympathy. When the narrator's father decides to dismiss Karl, the tutor puts before him a claim which includes among its items the amounts he had spent on presents for the children. The commentary which follows brings into focus a theme which always deeply interested Tolstoy— that of the difficulty of judging people's character by their actions alone:

On reading this note, in which Karl Ivanych demanded payment for all he had spent on presents, and even for a present promised to him, every one would conclude that Karl Ivanych was merely an unfeeling and mercenary egotist, and every one would be mistaken. (ch. XI, p. 44)

One is reminded of Nicholas Rostov's discovery, in *War and Peace* (IV, v, 416), that 'Dolokhov the bully' was 'the most affectionate of sons and brothers'.

The passage on vanity and shyness in the diaries bears fruit in the analysis of shyness as the result of uncertainty about the opinions of others. The danger of too much awareness of awareness comes out in the passage towards the end where the narrator feels that his grief at his mother's death is adulterated by the very desire to show it. He contrasts the grief of their nurse Natalya Savishna. Her sorrow is so powerful that she does not find it necessary—as he does

—to disguise the fact that she can attend to other things too. The mention of the 'oppressive smell' of the body shows that willingness to face up to unpleasantness so characteristic of the Russian novelists (it is strongly evident in Dostoevsky too) as opposed to Dickens and Thackeray. At the same time the ethical spiritualism of the Russians saved them from using such detail wholly to shock as the French naturalists and modern realists have done.

An important feature of *Childhood* is the tendency to write in short chapters, each organized round a central action, sentiment, theme or analytic schema. At the end of 1853 Tolstoy wrote in his diary:

> For a composition to be attractive, it is not only necessary for it to be directed by a consistent thought, but it is also necessary for the whole to be penetrated by a consistent feeling. . . . The method I have adopted from the start, of writing only short chapters, is the most convenient. Each chapter should express only one thought and only one feeling.[7]

This almost 'neoclassic' concern with unity and perspicuity was always to be present in Tolstoy. He constantly strives for as much clarity as possible, even in evoking complex feelings. It is this fact which makes the patronizing notion (strongly present, for instance, in Paul Bourget and Henry James) that Tolstoy 'wanted art' so utterly wrong-headed, though ironically akin to Tolstoy's own in part neoclassically conditioned verdict on Shakespeare.

Not surprisingly, however, *Childhood* also has some features which Tolstoy eliminated from his later work. The portrait of the narrator's father in chapter X belongs to a tradition of static 'character' writing revived in the West in the seventeenth century, though ultimately going back to Theophrastus, the pupil of Aristotle. We find a similar somewhat static technique of character portrayal in the story *Two Hussars*. Subsequently Tolstoy always tried to portray character dynamically, in and through action, rather than through purely static retrospective summary. Nevertheless *Childhood* already shows to the full a basic feature of Tolstoy's mature work. This is the objectivity which arises from his bringing his characters forward and letting them think, speak and act for themselves. A passage like the following from chapter two of Thackeray's *Pendennis* would be completely out of place:

> What passed between that lady and the boy is not of import. A veil should be thrown over those sacred emotions of love and grief. The maternal passion is a sacred mystery to me.

Tolstoy's ethical spiritualism has no need for veils of a rhetorical or any other kind because it is strong enough to face the truth. Such rhetoric as there is in *Childhood*, for example, the 'Happy, happy irrecoverable days of childhood!' passage at the opening of the transitional chapter XV, is sparse, brief and contextually appropriate. This passage, and certain solemn passages in the Sevastopol stories, may be too fulsome for modern taste, but they are not evasive.

Though it is not, strictly speaking, autobiographical, *Childhood* has that nostalgia without sentimentality which is peculiarly characteristic of Russian aristocratic memoirs such as those of Aksakov and Herzen. The oppression and rancour which mar so many English middle- and upper-class memoirs are conspicuously absent. The surroundings in which the narrator's emotions first awaken are recorded in loving detail, as, for example, the room where the boys had their first lessons with its view of the lime tree avenue, evoked in the first chapter. These personal 'golden ages' in Russian memoirs are not without moments of stress; but somehow even these elements are seen as part of the sweetness of being alive, neutralized by the fundamental security of the semi-feudal patriarchal life on a large estate. Trotsky, who had a very different sort of childhood, understandably began his autobiography *My Life* by bitterly contrasting it with those of the aristocratic memorialists.

Tolstoy, as we have seen, thought that a composition ought 'to be directed by a consistent thought' and that the whole should 'be penetrated by a consistent feeling'. He noted in his diary that *Boyhood* lacked such a consistent feeling, and that *Youth* lacked unity. His original plan had been that both should be part (along with *Childhood*) of a four-part novel. He started *Boyhood* in 1853 and finished it early in 1854. Work on *Youth* continued intermittently along with other projects until September 1856.[8] *Childhood* had dealt with the closed and basically secure world of the patriarchal estate as seen through a child's eyes. In chapter III of *Boyhood* Katya tells the narrator: 'You are rich, we are poor' and brings home to him for the first time the realization that his is not the only family in the world and that people who have nothing in common with them, do not trouble about them and even have no idea of their existence, share this earth.

Accordingly Tolstoy has to widen the narrative scope in *Boyhood*, but, as he himself felt, he had not yet discovered how to do this and maintain unity of tone, action and theme. The description of the spring storm on the journey to Moscow in the second chapter is an interesting set-piece, but not so well integrated with the developing hopes and fears of the narrator as the famous set-piece on the coming of spring in *Anna Karenina* II, xii–xiii, is with Levin's. In chapters VIII to X ('Karl Ivanych's Story') Tolstoy falls back on the favour-

25

ite eighteenth-century device of the framed narrative. He never resorts to this device again and these chapters have little to do with the boyhood theme. Chapter XVIII ('The Maids' Room') opens as an explicit digression and contains the following untypical 'Thackerayism' (though Gusev does not record the reading of *Henry Esmond* and *Pendennis* till June 1855) : [9]

> Do not disdain, reader, the company into which I am introducing you. If the chords of love and sympathy have not slackened in your soul, sounds will be met with in the maids' room to which they can respond.

The action progresses from improvisation to improvisation and often nothing is added to what Tolstoy had already portrayed in *Childhood*. For example, the account of the sincerity of Agatha Mikhaylovna's grief on the death of the narrator's grandmother seems in many respects a mere re-working of the account of the sincerity of Natalya Savishna's grief at the death of the narrator's mother in *Childhood*. Towards the end of *Boyhood* Tolstoy introduces another protagonist, Dmitri Nekhlyudov, in order to embody a feature of himself the narrator had not embodied, namely the unremitting concern for self-perfection. In the perfunctory conclusion Nekhlyudov, the moral idealist who has not lost his positive convictions, is contrasted with the narrator whose convictions have been eroded by 'constant moral analysis'. Tolstoy here obviously projects two sides of his own nature.

Tolstoy is not yet adept at integrating his psychological and philosophical insights with the drama of individual destinies caught up in an unfolding action, but there are passages in *Boyhood* which show the intrinsic interest of Tolstoy's reflections, notably the one on impulsive and apparently motiveless actions in chapter XIX. The passage on apparently motiveless actions is an example of what might be called the Dostoevsky side of Tolstoy. This side is more important than is often realized. It is not true that the dark depths which Dostoevsky explored were closed to Tolstoy. He sounds them in the early story *A Billiard-Marker's Notes*, in the Arzamas experience of 1869 later fictionalized as *Memoirs of a Madman*, in the treatment of Levin's nihilistic brother Nicholas in *Anna Karenina* (and, for that matter, of Levin himself) and in the later works *The Kreutzer Sonata*, *The Devil* and *Father Sergius*.

Philosophical problems do not just arise because philosophers say bizarre things (as G. E. Moore supposed), or because the natural sciences are puzzling (as Sir Karl Popper claims), but develop spontaneously out of the reflections any sensitive individual is bound to have about his own experience. This is nicely brought out by the passages on happiness and on solipsism in chapter XIX of *Boyhood*. The narrator is struck by the idea that happiness does not depend on external causes. This arouses the hope that has haunted philosophers from Socrates and the Stoics to the early Wittgenstein, namely that if we can inure ourselves to these contingent external causes there is nothing outside us that can make us unhappy. But the philosophical tendency which carries him away the most is solipsism, and the passage on that subject is worth quoting in full as a striking outcome of the concern with the analysis of the awareness of awareness and of vanity which we noted in the diaries:

I imagined that besides myself nobody and nothing existed in the universe, that objects were not objects at all, but images which appeared only when I paid attention to them. . . . In a word, I coincided with Schelling in the conviction that not objects exist but my relation to them. There were moments when, under the influence of this *idée fixe*, I reached such a state of insanity that I sometimes looked rapidly round to one side, hoping to catch emptiness (*néant*) unawares where I was not.

A pitiful, trivial spring of mental action is the mind of man! My feeble mind could not penetrate the impenetrable, and, in that effort lost, one by one, the convictions which, for my life's happiness, I ought never to have dared to disturb.

From all this heavy moral toil I obtained nothing except a flexibility of mind that weakened my will-power, and a habit of constant moral analysis, destructive to freshness of feeling and clarity of reason.

Abstract thoughts form as a result of man's capacity to seize a consciousness of the state of his soul at a given moment, and to transfer that perception to his memory. My fondness for abstract reasoning developed consciousness in me so unnaturally that often when I began thinking about the simplest things, I fell into the vicious circle of analysis of my thoughts, and I no longer thought about what I was thinking about. I asked myself: 'What am I thinking about?' and answered: 'I am thinking about what I am thinking. And now what am I thinking about? I am thinking that I think about what I am thinking about,' and so on. I had thought myself out of my wits.

However the philosophical discoveries I made flattered my vanity extremely; I often imagined myself a great man, discovering new truths for the benefit of mankind, and regarded the rest of humanity with a proud consciousness of my own worth; but strangely enough when I encountered those other mortals I felt shy of each of them, and the higher I set myself in my own estimation, the less was I capable not only of exhibiting the consciousness of my own dignity, but even of accustoming myself to avoid being ashamed of my simplest words and movements.

As phenomenologists like Sartre were later to rediscover, the real undermining of solipsism is to be found in the primitive way in which we sense feelings of embarrassment, shyness and shame which depend on a spontaneous acknowledgement of the existence of others.

Youth (published in 1857) is on a larger scale than *Childhood* and *Boyhood*, indeed it is almost as long as both these works combined. It consists of a series of sketches on the subjects of youthful day-dreams of self-perfection, religious devotion, university examinations, adolescent touchiness and society families. The reflections on adolescent love and on the importance of being *comme il faut* read like interpolated essays. Tolstoy's admiration for Turgenev's *A Sportsman's Sketches* [10] may have encouraged him in a certain looseness of construction, but, as we have seen, Tolstoy himself criticized *Youth* for lacking unity. This lack probably arose partly because he worked on it intermittently over a period of time during which he was also working on other pieces of writing as varied as the Sevastopol stories, *The Cossacks* and *A Landlord's Morning*. *Youth* does not contain passages of quite the same striking intrinsic interest as those to which I have referred from *Boyhood*. However it exercises still further the psychological analysis, the *esprit de finesse* that undermines the individual's self-deception and notes every slight change in the social group. When Tolstoy's friend Druzhinin wrote to assure him (mistakenly perhaps) that there was no falling off from *Childhood* and *Boyhood* he singled out Tolstoy's power of analysis for particular comment:

Do not fear your reflections, they are all clever and original. But you have an inclination to super-refinement of analysis which may become a great defect. You are sometimes on the point of saying that so-and-so's thigh indicated that he wished to travel to India. You must restrain this tendency, but do not extinguish it on any account. [11]

Tolstoy was drawing on memories of his boyhood and youth for these works at the same time as he was serving with the army. We must now turn to those works in which he dealt with his war experiences. For the present he had to deal with these two areas of human experience separately. He was gradually to master them until he became capable of combining aspects of both in a single major work, *War and Peace*.

Chapter 4

The Physiognomy of War: *The Raid, The Wood-Felling* and the Sevastopol Sketches

Childhood, as we have seen, contains much in material, theme and attitude that will be developed in the 'peace' scenes of *War and Peace*. *The Raid* (1852) and the three Sevastopol sketches (1855) foreshadow much of the portrayal of the physiognomy of war in the great novel. The three most striking features of that portrayal are already present: first, a keen interest in the 'internal' aspect of war, second, an equally keen concern with the management (and mismanagement) of war's external paraphernalia (equipment, rations, marching procedures, etc.) and finally, the conflict between Tolstoy's recognition of the truth in the epic view that war *does* have a poetic and heroic side and his acknowledgement of the Christian view that war is evil. This conflict continued throughout Tolstoy's life. During the Russo-Japanese war he wrote one of his most striking condemnations of war, *Bethink Yourselves!* (1904). In it he declared: 'If there is a God, He will not ask me when I die . . . whether I retained . . . Port Arthur. . . . He will ask me . . . Have I fulfilled His law?' [1] Yet his biographer Aylmer Maude tells us that he wept at the fall of Port Arthur and 'indignantly declared that those who had fought at Sevastopol would certainly not have surrendered. . . .' [2] However, where science must provide us with explanations and solutions, art thrives on just such conflict and ambivalence.

The Raid opens with the following declaration which was cut in the original edition by Nicholas I's censor:

WAR has always interested me; not war in the sense of manœuvres devised by great generals—my imagination refused to follow such immense movements, I did not understand them—but the reality of war, the actual killing. I was more interested to know in what way and under the influence of what feeling one soldier kills another than to know how the armies were arranged at Austerlitz and Borodino.

In *War and Peace* Tolstoy's imagination does try to come to terms in a somewhat polemical manner with these larger questions of vast troop dispositions, but for the present his interest is in the question of every combatant's anxiety as to whether he will do as well as his comrades expect, an anxiety partly rooted in the uncertainty as to just what that expectation is. Directly related to this question is Tolstoy's Socratic concern with the nature of courage. Is courage merely a physical endowment like tallness? Are actions prompted by motives like fear of reproach or vanity really worthy of praise? [3]

The narrator tells the experienced Captain Khlopov that the expedition cannot be a long one as only two days' rations have been ordered. The captain replies that they once had only a week's rations, but were away a month and advises him (apparently naively and unironically) to read Mikhailovsky Danilevsky (whom Tolstoy in a diary entry in July 1852 characterized as stupid) if he wants a detailed account of battles with the position of every corps. Tolstoy was later to use Mikhailovsky Danilevsky as a source for his account of the 1805 campaign. The narrator thinks Captain Khlopov's definition of a brave man as 'He who does what he ought to do' is not far from Plato's definition of courage as 'the knowledge of what should and what should not be feared'. The simple captain is obviously puzzled by all this questioning.

Captain Khlopov belongs to the type of soldier Tolstoy admired the most. He foreshadows Captain Tushin at Schön Grabern in *War and Peace*. He has been wounded four times, but has never mentioned this in his letters to his mother who firmly believes that he owes his safety to the intervention of the Virgin Mary whose icon she has sent to him via the narrator. He serves not out of any wish for glory, but because of a simple sense of duty and the fact that the double pay (a sort of danger money) enables him to send money home.

Two other types emerge as the sketch progresses. There is the young ensign Alanin (whose prototype was one of Tolstoy's fellow officers in the Caucasus, Buemsky) [4] who simply forgets fear from youthful inexperience and bravado and is wounded in an unnecessary charge in which he has disobeyed the captain. He looks forward to the young Nicholas Rostov and, later, Petya Rostov in *War and Peace*. Then there is the dare-devil lieutenant Rosencranz who models himself on Lermontov's heroes and sees the Caucasus through Lermontov's eyes. In some respects he anticipates the Dolokhov of *War and Peace*.

'War,' Tolstoy wrote in his diary in January 1853, 'is such an unjust and evil thing that those who wage it try to stifle their consciences.' [5] In a passage in *The Raid* which was cut by the censor he said:

War! What an incomprehensible phenomenon! When one's reason asks: 'Is it just, is it necessary?' an inner voice always replies 'No'. Only the persistence of this unnatural occurrence makes it seem natural, and a feeling of self-preservation makes it seem just.

But the sketch ends with the beautiful and poetic vignette of sunset in the mountains with the moon against deep azure, dark masses of troops moving over the luxuriant meadows, and the voice of the second tenor of the sixth company 'full of feeling and power' floating on the clear evening air.

The Raid is a much more impressive piece of work than *The Wood-Felling* (1855) in which Tolstoy's fondness for classification (effective elsewhere) obscures rather than clarifies. *The Wood-Felling* contains many characters, but none is striking either as an individual, or as a type, and Tolstoy is unable to bring any of his concerns to a thematic focus as he had done with the theme of courage in *The Raid*.

The fact that Tolstoy's first personal experience of war was an experience of irregular skirmishing may well have led him to underestimate what generalship and planning can achieve when he came to write of the Napoleonic campaigns. His service in the Crimean war (notoriously mismanaged on both sides) would confirm such an underestimation rather than correct it.

During the war against the Turks in what is now Rumania in 1854 Tolstoy took part in the siege of Silistria. A letter to his aunt Tatyana shows his keen concern with the accurate observation of the feelings of men under fire. He notes that the Russian commander, Prince Gorchakov, was so intent on the business in hand that the bullets just did not exist for him.[6] In *War and Peace* he portrayed Prince Bagration as acting in the same way and conceded that this aspect, at least, of a general's conduct is important. The letter then goes on to describe the unease before an assault. All pretend not to be thinking of the coming day more than of any other day. As the moment for action approaches fear proportionally diminishes until, when the whole thing is unexpectedly called off at the last moment, the predominant feeling is one of disappointment. This experience stood Tolstoy in good stead when he came to describe the feelings of Prince Andrew, Pierre and others on the eve of Borodino.

By the time Tolstoy reached Sevastopol on 7 November 1854, the battles of the Alma and of Inkerman had already been fought. Tolstoy heard about the latter while on his journey and referred to it in his diary on 2 November as an 'outrageous treacherous business'.[7]

Tolstoy could not help seeing the Crimean war as he was later to see 1812 in retrospect, namely as part of the long struggle of Russia against the West. The defence of Sevastopol impressed him because it was conducted against an enemy greatly superior in numbers and equipment. Many of the Russian soldiers still only had muskets, while their opponents had rifles. Tolstoy himself was an artillery officer and drew attention in a memorandum to the fact that the Russians needed guns with a longer range to match those of the allies.[8] He wrote to his brother Sergey of the fineness 'morally and physically' of the English prisoners.[9] He wished to found a non-official army journal that would truthfully express the spirit of the Russian army.

The first Sevastopol sketch, *Sevastopol in December 1854*, was actually done in its earliest form in the month it describes.[10] It is written in the dramatic present and in the second person (grammatically rare in fiction except in the epistolary form) and invokes the imaginary observer of a set of typical aspects of the besieged town. There are no character types or narrative complications. If we normally thought of journalism as truthful, dignified and restrained, we could certainly call this sketch journalism. It moves from the animated quay (where the narrator acknowledges an initial disappointment at the ordinariness of it all) to the grim operating theatre in the assembly hall which contains 'the clear and personal sense of suffering and death' that military pageants and funerals obliterate. You then see officers in the restaurant talking about girls and about the terrors of the famous fourth bastion, the most dangerous part of Sevastopol. Houses are unoccupied with doors boarded up and windows smashed. As you draw nearer to the fourth bastion itself, passers-by become more infrequent. An occasional cannon ball tempts you to walk in a trench knee-deep in stinking yellow mud. You are struck by the 'simplicity and obstinacy' of the sailors at their gun, but also by 'the feeling of animosity and thirst for vengeance' which animates them. As a sailor whose breast has been torn open by a mortar bomb is carried away the officer remarks, 'That's the way with seven or eight every day', yawns and rolls a cigarette. What power keeps men going under such conditions of life? Tolstoy is haunted by this question because he believed, as we have seen, that what men really (and rightly) desire is happiness.

In April and May 1855 Tolstoy served at the fourth bastion. In June he began to write *Sevastopol in May 1855*.[11] This has much more in the way of characters and their inner lives than the first sketch. The protagonists are: Captain Mikhaylov, a shy and vain man who is frightened of being snubbed by his fellow officers and pretends to be a *roué* to impress them; Prince Galtsin, in whose consciousness the horrors of the operating theatre are mirrored; Kalugin who imagines himself in the role of one of Napoleon's lieutenants, but looks around to see if anyone has noticed his fright when a bomb bursts near him, and, as a newcomer, always needs to test himself; Captain Praskukhin, treated with *hauteur* by his fellow officers, but quietly brave; and cadet Pesth who, like many of the characters in *War and Peace*, gives a sincerely insincere account of a hand-to-hand fight he had witnessed in a state of confusion.

Captain Praskukhin is killed by a bomb and the interior monologue which Tolstoy gives him as he watches it spinning marks an important stage in Tolstoy's mastering the use of this device. The interior monologue will be of a great importance in *War and Peace* and *Anna Karenina*. It stands in the same relation to Tolstoy's art that the soliloquy stands to Shakespeare's. The Russian critic Chernyshevsky singled out this instance of Tolstoy's use of the device for special attention as a new departure in literature and was the first to use the name 'inner monologue' for it.[12]

Inclusive of the minds of Mikhaylov, Galtsin, Kalugin, Praskukhin and Pesth and of what they witness is the mind of Tolstoy himself. It is the mind of an omniscient narrator who hears the very thoughts of men and denounces their moral blindness and vanity with the eloquence and authority of a prophet.[13]

The piece opens with a solemn introduction the second paragraph of which contains a sentence thirteen and a half lines long. The whole sketch concludes with a picture of a ten-year-old child gathering a bunch of flowers in a valley covered with corpses and the amazed reflection that 'Christians professing the one great law of love and self-sacrifice' do not fall down on their knees in repentance and 'embrace like brothers with tears of joy and gladness'. There are no heroes and villains in the story. 'All are good and all are bad.' Tolstoy has earned the right to the somewhat rhetorical concluding sentence in which he claims that the real hero of his tale is truth.

Shortly after the withdrawal from Sevastopol on 27 and 28 August 1855 in which he took part, Tolstoy started to make notes for the third sketch, *Sevastopol in August 1855*. He began the piece on 19 September and finished it in December 1855 after his return to Yasnaya.[14] The story centres on a Lieutenant Koseltsov and his young brother Volodya. At this stage the family tie is, as Eikhenbaum says, a rather 'external' element in the story.[15] Tolstoy later made much more skilful use of it as an 'internal' constructive element motivating much that happens in the great novels. Koseltsov dislikes staff officers and red tape and is eager to return to the front line after being wounded. In this respect he foreshadows Nicholas Rostov in *War and Peace*, and his relation to Volodya (who is keen to see fighting for the first time, but anxious about what he will find) parallels that of Nicholas to his young brother Petya. Both Koseltsovs are killed in the storming of the Malakhov and Redan redoubts by the French on 27 August. Volodya is mourned by a fellow officer, Vlang. The Russian army withdraws to the north side of the road-stead, and as the soldiers cross themselves and look back each feels 'inexpressible bitterness in his heart'.

War and Peace united the portrayal of patriarchal and domestic life found in *Childhood* with the portrayal of the psychology of men under fire and of the physiognomy of war found in *The Raid* and the Sevastopol sketches. Much twentieth-century literature about war has concentrated solely on the pathos of individual flesh caught in the impersonal machinery of death. Tolstoy manages to transcend what he is portraying so that he can see it steadily and see it whole (however limited the vision at times of his *dramatis personae*) without being overcome by its complexity, multiplicity and horror.

At the same time Tolstoy's lifelong desire for God led him to set the phenomenon of war against the Scriptures and, in particular against 'the great law of love and self-sacrifice'. *Sevastopol in May 1855* in its small way foreshadows *War and Peace* not only in its use of 'a reliable, omniscient, omnipresent' objective narrator but also in its ultimate rejection of the epic-poetic view of war for the Christian condemnation of it.

Chapter 5

New Paths: The Portrayal of Peasant Life; 'A Landlord's Morning', 'Polikushka'

After his return from the Crimea, with *Childhood* and the Sevastopol sketches to his credit, Tolstoy was for a time accepted in St Petersburg as a 'man of letters'. He fitted into this category most uneasily. He distrusted Turgenev who had made being a 'man of letters' his only calling and quarrelled with him constantly. He also intensely disliked Turgenev's 'emancipated' attitude to sex and marriage. In 1856 Tolstoy was associated with Nekrasov's 'progressive' journal *Sovremmenik (The Contemporary)*, but as it was more and more taken over by the radical *raznochintsy*, and by Chernishevsky in particular, he abandoned his connection with it, though in some ways he was closer to a radical like Chernishevsky than to Turgenev. Tolstoy wrote to Botkin in October 1857: 'Thank God I did not follow Turgenev when he told me that a man of letters should be a man of letters and nothing else. That doesn't suit my nature at all, You can't make literature a crutch, as Scott said.' [1] It was typical of him that he asked Botkin to show Turgenev the letter.

There are five main characteristics in the works Tolstoy published about this time. First there is a lack of emphasis on 'narrative' as such. It is replaced by a concern with the inner world of the characters and with the general bearing of the moral problems with which they wrestle. As Tolstoy wrote in his diary in 1853: 'the new tendency is for interest in details of feeling to predominate over interest in the events themselves'.[2] Second is the extent to which the germ of many of the stories is an actual experience of the author. Third is the use of parallelism through similarity or contrast for thematic emphasis. This was a device which he was later to use masterfully on a large scale in *War and Peace* and *Anna Karenina*. In these early works he is gaining practice in it. Parallelism is particularly evident in *Two Hussars* and *Three Deaths*. Fourth is Tolstoy's fondness for clarity and classification into types. Fifth is Tolstoy's concern, not with social utility, but with the 'moral' utility of art. Each of his short works has some kind of moral point to make, or moral attitude to convey.

Tolstoy was at this stage very much concerned with the problem of art and its function. The radical *raznochintsy* led by Chernishevsky, Dobroliubov and Pisarev, the so-called 'civic' critics, were convinced that art should have an immediate use in the narrowest Utilitarian sense. It should inculcate the correct 'progressive' viewpoint on the burning social and political questions of the day. In some ways they anticipated the Soviet critics who were to subordinate literature to 'social command' such as the increase of output in cement or steel. Tolstoy wrote to Botkin in January 1858 suggesting that they, Fet and Turgenev, should combat the Utilitarian view of art with a journal not out to 'prove' or 'investigate' anything, but to give artistic pleasure to those with cultivated taste. Seven years later, when deep in *War and Peace*, Tolstoy forcefully averred:

If I were to be told that I could write a novel whereby I might irrefutably establish what seemed to me the correct point of view on all social problems, I would not devote two hours to such a novel: but if I were to be told that what I should write would be read in twenty years' time by those who are now children, and that they would laugh and cry over it and love life, I would devote all my life and all my energies to it.[3]

The works which Tolstoy wrote about this time, such as *Two Hussars* (written in 1856), *Albert* (written in 1857) and *Three Deaths* (written in 1858), are feebler than the earlier *Childhood* and *Sevastopol*.[4] *Lucerne* does, I think, stand apart, as I shall show in a later chapter. But it would be wrong to attribute this weakness to the negative effect of Tolstoy's joining Druzhinin and Botkin in an art for art's sake movement against Chernishevsky.[5] There is a lot in Boris Eikhenbaum's summary of Tolstoy's situation at this period (1856–1860) as being that of a man hailed as an officer hero, but uncertain of what to write about and of what being a writer meant. He is right also to see Tolstoy as needing to reach some kind of 'absolute' moral truth as a basis for a piece of writing.[6]

Tolstoy could never have become an advocate of art for art's sake in the hedonistic sense in which Western writers such as Théophile Gautier (and, later, Oscar Wilde) understood this conception. What Tolstoy wanted was simply to prevent art from being subordinated to the social demands of a particular generation, whether those demands came from a Westernizer like Chernishevsky or a Slavophil like Homyakov. Addressing the Moscow Society of Lovers of Russian Literature on 4 February 1859 in Homyakov's presence he claimed that literature must reflect not just the interests of the society of a given time, but 'eternal human interests'.[7] At the same time for Tol-

stoy these 'eternal human interests' involved a concern with goodness and truth. Such a view is not 'quite different', as Aylmer
Maude claims, from the position taken in *What is Art?* forty years
later.[8]

Tolstoy's portrayal of peasant life affords a fine example of his
ability to penetrate to 'eternal human interests' in the handling of a
subject which was of peculiarly intense topical interest because the
question of the emancipation of the serfs was in the foreground of
attention. This may be because Tolstoy's interest in the peasant
as a type and individual was deep, of long standing and bound up
with his most profound personal concerns. It was linked, for example,
with the quest for the secret of happiness which obsessed him. Could
it not be that the secret was *oproshchatsia* 'to make oneself simple'?
Nekhlyudov in *A Landlord's Morning*, Olenin in *The Cossacks*, Levin
in *Anna Karenina* and, finally, Tolstoy himself in *What is Art?* and
some of his later religious and political writings, actually try to
become peasants to a greater or lesser degree. Pierre in *War and Peace*
learns wisdom from the simple Karataev, who becomes a kind of
moral touchstone for both him and Natasha when, in 1819, at the
end of the book, they consider the merits of Pierre's ideas on organizing a society of like minded men to further political and social reform. Tolstoy is here alluding indirectly to the fact that Pierre was
the type of man who would have joined the Decembrist Conspiracy
of 1825.

Max Weber pointed out that the peasant's becoming 'the dis-
tinctive prototype of the pious man who is pleasing to God'[9] is a
thoroughly modern phenomenon. Jesus himself was an artisan, a
carpenter in the building trade, not a peasant. In early Christian
times the rustic or *paganus* was stubbornly resistant to Christianity,
as our very word 'pagan' shows. Even Tolstoy wrote in a letter to
his cousin Alexandra of a peasant in one of his stories (the slight
Three Deaths published in 1859) dying calmly precisely because he is
not a Christian, 'although he has kept up the Christian rites by force
of habit'. His religion is Nature. Weber finds the belief in the peasants' special worth and piety in Lutheranism as opposed to Calvinism and in 'modern Russian religion' as influenced by the
Slavophils.[10]

This Slavophil influence certainly enters Tolstoy's works and
emerges, for example, in his *The Meaning of the Russian Revolution*
(1906)[11] in which he claims that 'the Christian understanding of
life' has manifested itself among the Russian people (by which he
means the peasants) 'in various traits peculiar to themselves alone'.
He mentions their sense of brotherhood and equality, their complete
religious toleration, their not condemning criminals but regarding

them as unfortunate, their use of the word 'forgive' when taking leave, their respect for beggars, their readiness for self-sacrifice and their distrust of power. He even conjectures whether their agricultural life may not have something to do with this as well as the fact that the Russo-Greek Church was too stupid to hide 'the true meaning of the Christian teaching'. The later Tolstoy certainly owed much to sectarians like the peasant Sutaev whose practice of their moral beliefs impressed and eluded him. He was undoubtedly touched by the general peasant tendency to conservatism and fatalism, the 'Asiatic' fatalism which offended Lenin. Nevertheless there was always a strong rationalist and anti-mystical streak in Tolstoy. He had no more sympathy with the peasants' concern with ritual (the *raskol* or schism in the seventeenth century had been a revolt in favour of ritual conservatism involving such things as continuing to make the sign of the cross with two fingers instead of the new-fangled Orthodox three) than he had with that of Orthodoxy.

The most burning question concerning the peasantry by the late 1850s was that of serfdom itself. In his *Recollections* (1908) Tolstoy wrote of the ownership of serfs:

The idea that such ownership should not exist, and that serfs should be liberated, was quite unknown in our circle in the eighteen forties. The ownership of serfs by inheritance seemed a necessary condition and all that could be done to ensure that such ownership should not be evil, was to attend not only to the material but also to the moral condition of the serfs.[12]

In the spring of 1847 the nineteen-year-old Tolstoy left the University of Kazan without a degree in order to manage his estate at Yasnaya Polyana. He began a book on domestic economy and in 1849 started a school for peasant children. He was to run such a school again ten years later. In October 1852 when he was in the Caucasus he had the idea for a novel on the life of a Russian landowner. He linked this to the theme of the quest for happiness:

Basis of the life of a Russian landowner: The hero seeks in rural life the realization of an ideal of happiness and justice. Not finding it, and disillusioned, he would seek it in the life of the family. But a friend of his suggests that happiness rests not in an ideal at all, but in constant labour of a life whose object is the happiness of others.[13]

He worked on this story, *A Landlord's Morning*, intermittently in 1853 and 1855 and then laid it aside for the Sevastopol sketches. Back at Yasnaya Polyana in May 1856 Tolstoy called together a village assembly and made a speech about a proposal to give the peasants their freedom. Two months earlier the new Tsar Alexander II had announced to the marshals of the Moscow nobility that it would 'be much better' for emancipation 'to come from above than from below'.[14] Tolstoy found the peasants distrustful. It was while engaged with this issue that he completed *A Landlord's Morning*. The work does not deal with the emancipation as such, but with the conflict between the landowner (Nekhlyudov) and the peasants over Nekhlyudov's schemes for estate improvement. It honestly reflects (in E. Lampert's words), 'the unsurmountable estrangement and lack of understanding between the landowners and "the people"'.[15]

The young Tolstoy had been deeply influenced by Rousseau's sense of the evils of civilization and his cult of simplicity. He had written in his diary in 1853: 'The common people are so far above us by the work they accomplish and the privations in their lives, that it seems wrong for one of us to write anything bad about them.' [16] Nevertheless anyone who thinks that Tolstoy always idealizes the *muzhik* and pictures himself living in conditions of idyllic patriarchal simplicity will be quickly disabused if he reads both *A Landlord's Morning* (1856) and *Polikushka* (1861). They contain the sordid side of peasant life quite as much as Chekhov's story 'Peasants'. They certainly do not show any pious inwardness on the part of their protagonists. In some cases there is fatalism, in others superstition. One very important feature of Tolstoy's portrayal of peasant life is that he always shows it in relation to the life of the landowning class. Even in *Polikushka* the 'mistress', Polikushka's owner, has an important role to play.

A Landlord's Morning [17] begins with its nineteen-year-old protagonist, Prince Nekhlyudov, writing in French to his aunt about his determination to improve the peasants' lot. She replies (also in French) that his motives may not be as disinterested as he supposes. He has a wish to be original that is rooted in egoism. He is sincere and yet deceiving himself. Ivan Churis, the first peasant he goes to see, distrusts Nekhlyudov's fine feelings. The poverty in which he and his family live is so wretched that Nekhlyudov, although he has long known it by personal observation, involuntarily keeps forgetting about it. At the same time he cannot make any headway against Churis's passivity and resistance to improvement: 'it is not manure that makes the corn grow, but only God'. The next peasant, Epifan, wants to sell a horse. He treats Nekhlyudov with feigned humility and eventually provokes him into an angry outburst. The third peasant, David, lives in a mere hovel and is even more shiftless than the other two. His mother, whom the peasants call Arina the barge hauler, complains that David killed his first wife from overwork, but this does not stop her from wanting Nekhlyudov to arrange a second marriage. She is so superstitious that she is thinking of having David cured by the spells of the local wizard Dunduk. Finally Nekhlyudov goes to see the Dutlovs, a family of wealthy peasants of the type who were to be called kulaks (the class of prosperous individualistic peasants whom Stalin had to destroy in enforcing collectivization). He wants Dutlov's sons, Karp, Ignat and young Ilya, to farm some land for him, but Dutlov wants them to go off as teamsters and it is obvious that Nekhlyudov is no match for old Dutlov in the conflict.

As Nekhlyudov walks home Tolstoy presents us with his memories of his fantasies of the previous year. He had dreamed then of a beautiful woman. Suddenly 'the thought that love and goodness are truth and happiness' had entered his mind : 'Love, self-denial— that is the only true happiness—a happiness independent of chance !' Then he had pictured a harmonious life with himself happily married to a wife who also wants to help the peasants, and the father of a family. Where are those dreams now? Was not his aunt right when she said he should try to find happiness for himself rather than to give it to others? After all his plans for helping the peasants have come to nothing. Even the new threshing machine does not work, much to their amusement. He thinks of his fellow students now settled down in successful careers.

Nekhlyudov's reflections bear out his aunt's caution in her letter that he is too ambitious and that his plans for social amelioration are, in fact, rooted in his wish to appear original and in his 'excessive self-esteem'. The search for happiness has involved him, as it involved Tolstoy, in the perennial and intractable conflict between egoism and altruism. After talking to his old nurse Malanya, who says that what his aunt wrote was true, Nekhlyudov begins to improvise chords at the piano. Fantasies throng his mind. He sees Karp and Ignat and Ilya galloping over Russia in three troikas as far as Kiev, Odessa and even Constantinople. 'Why am I not Ilya?' he thinks.

Just as Tolstoy reworked the domestic material of *Childhood* and the war material of the Sevastopol sketches in *War and Peace* so he reworked the material on the peasant question in *A Landlord's Morning* into the complex structure of *Anna Karenina*.

Polikushka is an even grimmer portrayal of peasant life.[18] Tolstoy's friend the poet Fet (who was a conservative landowner) admitted it was truthful, but that only made it so much the worse. It smelled of a corrupt environment and lacked the purity of idealism.[19] Turgenev, however, admitted its power and wrote to Fet:

After you left, I read Tolstoy's *Polikushka* and marvelled at the strength of his huge talent. But he has used up too much material, and it is a pity he drowned the son. It makes it too terrible. But there are pages that are truly wonderful! It made a cold shudder run down even my back, though you know my back has grown thick and coarse. He is a master, a master! [20]

Tolstoy was working on *Polikushka* during his second trip to Europe in 1861 and he had it ready for the press two years later.[21] It was thus, along with *The Cossacks*, one of the last pieces of fiction Tolstoy worked on before beginning *War and Peace*. He was at this time much preoccupied with the problems of peasant education in his school at Yasnaya. *Polikushka* has more of a narrative element in it than Tolstoy's other early works. It begins with Egor Mikhaylovich, the steward, discussing with his mistress the question of which three peasants are to go for soldiers. This is a matter for the peasant Commune to ratify, but the steward wants to put forward the good-for-nothing drunkard and thief Polikushka, a house serf, rather than one of the hard-working Dutlovs who will otherwise have to go. The mistress is bent on morally improving Polikushka, however, and will not give him up. At the same time she is too stingy to fork out the three hundred roubles necessary to buy off a recruit. To test Polikushka she sends him to a market gardener in town to bring back a sum of over four hundred silver roubles.

Tolstoy shows us the awful living conditions of the peasants, four families (Polikushka's has seven members) in one room twenty-three feet square with a stove in the middle. He shows, too, the quarrelling and back-biting to which this gives rise. At a stormy meeting of the Commune the peasants insist that one of the Dutlovs must go, and the lot falls to Elijah, Dutlov's nephew. Meanwhile Polikushka goes to town, having sworn to his wife Akulina not to touch a drop while he is away. Well pleased with himself, he accomplishes his mission, but accidentally loses the roubles from inside his cap on his way home. He disappears and is eventually found hanging in the loft. Akulina is washing the baby in the trough when the discovery is made. She faints and in the general consternation the baby is forgotten and drowns. I think Turgenev was wrong to see this as a flaw in the story. It is not like the somewhat gratuitous suicide of Father Time in *Jude the Obscure* which too overtly underwrites Hardy's 'accursed Fawleys' theme, but is, given the circumstances, a perfectly natural, if terrible, happening. The superstitious peasants fear Polikushka's ghost and the mistress is so upset by the whole business that when Dutlov comes to her, having found the money, she tells him to keep it. The avaricious streak in him is so strong that at first he is still disinclined to buy his nephew Elijah off, but at the same time he has a queer feeling that a sort of evil spirit haunts the money. He is so overwrought that he thinks he sees Polikushka's ghost; after this, he tells the steward he wants to buy Elijah off, and when he has done so falls on his knees and asks Elijah and his wife for forgiveness. Another peasant who has volunteered because he was in debt goes off to serve drunk and cursing. Truly 'One man's sorrow is another man's luck!'

One of the reasons why *A Landlord's Morning* and *Polikushka* hold such a great interest for the reader of Tolstoy is that they make a striking contrast with the way he tended to idyllicize the life of landlord and peasant in *War and Peace* and even occasionally in *Anna Karenina*, although there Tolstoy is sometimes critical of the way his hero Levin does this. Completely absent in these stories is a figure like the Karataev, of *War and Peace*, in whom Tolstoy tried to incarnate once and for all the Slavophil idea of the godly peasant. The grim portrayal of peasant life in *A Landlord's Morning* and *Polikushka* only serves to point up the somewhat forced 'exemplary' quality of Karataev. It may be that, for whatever reason, Tolstoy was deeply concerned in *War and Peace* to show the possible unity in spirit of a nobleman like Pierre and a peasant like Karataev. Nevertheless his honest recognition of the conflict of interest between landowner and peasant comes out in his portrayal of the restiveness of Princess Mary's peasants at Bogucharovo (X, ix–xiv, 412–37). Here we meet once again the peasant distrustfulness that permeates *A Landlord's Morning*, as we also meet it in *Anna Karenina* (III, xxiv, 363–7) in the reaction of Levin's peasants to his schemes of improvement and his new English agricultural machines.

Chapter 6

The Cossacks, Strider: The Story of a Horse and Family Happiness

Apart from *Family Happiness*, *The Cossacks* is the longest work Tolstoy wrote before starting *War and Peace*, though it is only a *nouvelle* by modern standards. It is based on Tolstoy's relationship in the years 1851–52 with an old Cossack, a young Chechen tribesman and a Cossack girl. Tolstoy began *The Cossacks* in the autumn of 1852 and worked on it intermittently in 1853 and then laid it aside. He took it up again in 1856 on receiving some notes on the Caucasus from his brother Nicholas, and wrote more of it while in Europe in 1857.[1] He revised it in 1862 and it was published in January 1863. The next month he began writing *War and Peace*.[2]

The Cossacks [3] begins with Olenin, a young man of twenty-four (Tolstoy's own age when he began the story) not yet started on a career, and in love with the goodness in himself, for he is at a stage when it seems to him that there is nothing else. In November 1853 indeed Tolstoy noted in his diary: 'I have not yet met a single man who was morally as good as I.' [4] This looks odd taken out of its context, but when it is put back there it emerges not as moral Pharisaism (no one could be more critical of his own faults) but as part of Tolstoy's youthfully exuberant pursuit of individual perfection.

Olenin turns his back on Moscow society and on a failed love affair (it is not surprising that it failed, for in all his 'experiments' so far, from farming to women, he has always kept himself free) to go to the Caucasus. When he sees the stern majesty of the mountains there he feels freer still. Tolstoy then gives an admiring account of the Grebensk Cossacks, Old Believers who act as a bulwark against the Chechens, Tartar tribesmen in the region of the river Terek. The Cossack women are strong, used to heavy labour and enjoy perfect freedom, when unmarried girls, in their relations with men. One of them, Maryanka, attracts Olenin, who comes to lodge in her house. He meets the experienced old Cossack, Daddy Eroshka, who offers to teach him hunting and fishing and find him a girl, but when Olenin asks him about Maryanka, Eroshka tells him she is betrothed to Lukashka, a Cossack. He offers to get Olenin another girl and when Olenin is shocked and replies 'it's a sin' Eroshka exclaims:

A sin? Where's the sin? . . . A sin to look at a nice girl? A sin to have some fun with her? Or is it a sin to love her? Is that sin in your parts? . . . No, my dear fellow, it's not a sin, it's salvation! God made you and God made the girl too. He made it all: so it is no sin to look at a nice girl. That's what she was made for: to be loved and to give joy. That's how I judge it, my good fellow. (ch. XII, pp. 326–327)

(This attitude to sexuality is, of course, the complete antithesis of that in *The Kreutzer Sonata, The Devil* and *Father Sergius*, but what all four have in common is their sense of its immense power.)

At the same time Eroshka is proud of having been a drinker, a horse-thief, a singer. He has killed in battle, but not wantonly ('It is a serious thing to destroy a human being'). He seems to have no belief in an after-life. He reports an old friend as saying, 'When you die the grass will grow on your grave and that's all!', and though he characterizes this friend as 'a desperate fellow' there is no indication that he disagrees with him. Yet at the same time, he speaks of a wild pig as 'God's creature' and 'wise' because it scents the hunter, whereas man is foolish.

When out hunting one day Olenin meditates on the perennial Tolstoyan theme of man's innate desire for happiness and the consequent conflict between living for oneself and living for others. Feeling that love and self-sacrifice are the only desires not dependent on external circumstances, it is to these he turns. This does not prevent his panicking at being lost in the forest. When he finds a Russian outpost he is naively surprised that a Chechen prisoner whose brother has been killed treats him with contempt. Lukashka is there and Olenin, aware that Lukashka loves Maryanka, conceives the pleasantly grandiose idea of 'sacrificing' her to his comrade. An old Moscow friend Beletski arrives and his presence distastefully reminds Olenin of his former life in the city. At a party at Beletski's Olenin forgets all about his idea of self-sacrifice and starts to make up to Maryanka. Olenin sees his former life as vile and is more and more attracted by the freedom of Cossack life. He even dreams of becoming a Cossack, as Levin in *Anna Karenina* dreams of becoming a peasant. Yet the very thought, which continually haunts him, that happiness lies in self-sacrifice seems to him alien to Cossack morality. One day he is writing in his diary that the one way to be happy is 'to love self-denyingly, . . . to spread a web of love on all sides and to take all who come into it' (Tolstoy made a similar

entry in his own diary on 12 May 1856), [5] when Eroshka enters
drunk. He assumes that Olenin must be engaged in some sort of
useless legal complaint about his wrongs because he associates all
writing with nothing but legal trickery. Even though Maryanka
is to be betrothed to Lukashka, he insists that Olenin will get her
if he gives enough money.

At the grape harvest Olenin is once again attracted to Maryanka.
He writes a long letter to himself, in the manner of Rousseau, contrasting her natural beauty with the falsity of civilization. He still
thinks that she cannot share his deepest interests, but feels that this
is no longer so important. His self-renunciation now strikes him as
false. She is 'Nature' to him and yet a human being as well. He
resolves to tell her all. But when he proposes she says: 'Do gentle-
men marry Cossack girls? Go away!' Later he proposes a second
time, but she is non-committal.

Lukashka is wounded in an expedition against some marauding
Chechens. Maryanka is grief stricken and tells Olenin she is sick of
him. Olenin realizes that she can never love him and leaves, drop-
ping rapidly out of the lives and concerns of the Cossacks.

When Tolstoy took up *The Cossacks* again in 1857, he was dis-
satisfied with it. He noted in his diary on 18 August 1857 that he
could not write without an idea (this is that need for an absolute
moral truth of which Eikhenbaum speaks) and that the idea 'that
a savage condition is good, is not sufficient'.[6] Yet *The Cossacks*
remains an impressive example of Tolstoy's constant tendency to
seek the secret of happiness in Rousseauistic terms of following the
'natural' and turning from the 'artificial'. Olenin, however, is the
least interesting of Tolstoy's major focuses of consciousness, and at
the time of conceiving the tale, Tolstoy himself did not sufficiently
transcend Olenin to be able to compensate for this in either the
commentary or the narrative. The presentation of Olenin's psychology lacks Tolstoy's customary density of detail, and his life outside
the Caucasus (unlike Levin's, say, outside his contact with the peasants) lacks any complexity of circumstance. The presentation of war
is too much in the picturesque mode of Fenimore Cooper through
whose books Olenin himself sees the Caucasus. The contrast with
The Raid, not to speak of the Sevastopol stories, is striking in this
respect. Olenin's love affair with Maryanka is presented with a
certain monotonous repetitiveness of situation. In fact Olenin is
simply a vehicle for Tolstoy's own moral interests, in particular his
conflict-ridden quest for happiness. No doubt, too, as Eikhenbaum
suggests,[7] the work had lost its freshness for him by 1859–62 when
he was more and more occupied with questions of education, ideology and history and rather remote from the twenty-four-year-old

in the Caucasus. He could not work these new preoccupations into it. Nevertheless the egoism/altruism and artificial/natural antitheses still remain central to *War and Peace* and *Anna Karenina* and this is why the reader of Tolstoy should not neglect *The Cossacks* where they are present with, of course, much less complexity of detail and subtlety.

Strider: the Story of a Horse (drafted in 1863),[8] the most extreme example of Tolstoy's presenting things from an unusual viewpoint, led the Russian Formalist critic Victor Shklovsky to speak of the device of *ostranenie* or 'making it strange'.[9] In it many aspects of human life and, in particular, the institution of property, are made to look bizarre by being viewed through the eyes of a horse. But Tolstoy does not make the horses' view of life into the 'ideal' as some have (perhaps mistakenly) thought Swift intended to do with the houyhnhnms in *Gulliver's Travels*. In 'equine ethics' the ruthless cruelty of the young to the old is the rule and it is simply a fact that love depends on physical conditions so that when Strider's mother becomes interested in the stallions again she grows cold to him. The possible dependence of the 'higher' spiritual qualities on physical conditions worried Tolstoy deeply and he returns to the problem at crucial points of *War and Peace* and *Anna Karenina*. To see life consistently from the assumption that everything we do is conditioned by our physical states to the point of being determined by them would be to 'make it strange' indeed, and in a way from which, as we shall see, Tolstoy shrank to the extent of affirming a dualism of the phenomenal and noumenal like that of Kant and Schopenhauer.

As to *ostranenie* or 'making it strange' in general, one of the most striking parallels to *Strider* in *War and Peace* (see VII, v, 116) is Tolstoy's presentation of the wolf hunt seen momentarily from the wolf's point of view. We are also given the thoughts of Levin's dog, Laska, in *Anna Karenina* VI, xii. There are plenty of examples in which characters are made to see other characters or the surroundings as if for the first time: Nicholas and Sonya at the mumming, Andrew wounded at Austerlitz, Petya serving with Denisov's band, the six-year-old Malasha at the Council of War after Borodino in *War and Peace* and Levin waiting to go and make a formal request for Kitty's hand in marriage and many other instances in *Anna Karenina*.

In *The Cossacks*, as we have seen, the 'making it strange' or, to use the American critic Kenneth Burke's term, 'perspective through incongruity', was effected by removing a spoiled *homme de société* from the environment of Moscow to that of the Caucasus and recording the changes this effected in the way he saw things. Tolstoy began work on it at a time when he himself was in a situation identical with that of his own Olenin. But it is typical of him that at the same time that he entertained the project of submergence in the 'simpler' life of the Cossacks, he should also daydream of continuing family life in a traditional way on his estate at Yasnaya Polyana. He outlines this daydream in the following passage from a letter to his aunt Tatyana written in 1852 from the Caucasus. The passage is a marvellous illustration of the way in which we grasp the sense of our own lives and those of others by making up little novels about them. It also shows Tolstoy rehearsing in his mind the domestic material of *War and Peace* eleven years before he actually began work on the novel:

I let myself dream—I am married. My wife is a gentle creature, kind and affectionate: she has the same love for you that I have. We have children who call you Grandmamma: you live upstairs in the big house, in what used to be Grandmamma's room. The whole house is as it was in Papa's time, and we recommence the same life, only changing our roles. You take the role of Grandmamma, but you are still better: I take Papa's place, though I despair of ever deserving it: my wife that of Mamma: the children take ours: Marya, that of the two aunts (except their misfortunes) . . . but some one will be lacking to take the part you played in our family—never will anyone be found with a soul so beautiful, so loving, as yours.[10]

Before Tolstoy could begin *War and Peace* in 1863, however, first-hand experience of married life on his part was essential. The chief interest of *Family Happiness* (1859) is that its failure to portray married life convincingly bears out this contention.

Family Happiness arose out of Tolstoy's return to his project of family life during the years 1856–57 and his unsuccessful courtship of a girl called Valeria Arsenev.[11] The rather grumbling tone Tolstoy uses about Valeria in his diaries is certainly not the tone of a man in love, but fits the situation of a man in search of someone suitable for marriage. On 26 June 1856 he notes: 'Valeria was in a white dress. Very charming. Spent one of the pleasantest days of my life. Do I love her seriously?' But two days later he writes: 'Valeria is extremely badly educated, and ignorant if not stupid'. Two days later he writes that she does not please him, but that if they go on seeing each other so often, he might suddenly marry her and then the whole thing would turn out badly. One day her unshapely arms displease him, but another day she is 'nicer than ever.' Nevertheless he is terrified by her frivolity and 'afraid hers is a nature that cannot even love a child'. (For her part, she, not surprisingly, shows him a letter in which she calls him an egotist.[12]) In September 1856 he writes in his diaries that she is shallow and cold, but the next month he draws near to her again.[13] Between January and July 1857 he is away on his first trip to Europe. Even while comparing and contrasting it with Russia, however, he is also deeply occupied with reflections on 'family life' and with what had already come to be known as 'the woman question'. On 4 September 1857, after his return from Europe he notes: 'At the Arsenevs everything is as of old—one might begin over again. She is kindly but the emptiest of girls.' [14]

Fortunately Tolstoy's letters to Valeria have survived and have been translated.[15] In them we can see him setting out to educate her in the rather fearsome way the 'sheltered' young ladies of the time were thought to require. In the course of the letters, Tolstoy invents a little novel for Valeria in which he becomes a Mr Khrapovitsky and she becomes his wife. Khrapovitsky is a man who has committed many follies and so is 'morally old'. He has now found his vocation in literature. He despises *society* and 'adores a peaceful, family, moral life', whereas 'for her, happiness consists in balls, bare shoulders, a carriage, diamonds, acquaintance with chamberlains, lieutenant-generals, etc.'.[16]

Paul Biryukov, who collected the letters into a volume, contends, in an essay, 'Autobiographical Elements in L. N. Tolstoi's Works', following them, that *Family Happiness* grew out of the 'little novel' Tolstoy had imagined in his letters to Valeria; and in chapter IV of *Family Happiness* itself Sergey Mikhaylych makes up a little novel about his relations to the heroine, with three possible endings, as his way of proposing to her. Biryukov sees *Family Happiness* as Tolstoy's justification for his belief that marriage with Valeria would not have been *the right thing* because it could not have produced what Tolstoy thought marriage existed to produce, namely the family happiness of its title, the family happiness he also alludes to in the famous opening sentence of *Anna Karenina*.

Family Happiness is, then, an 'as it might have been' story told rather unconvincingly (and it is not clear why) from the woman's point of view. The first part deals with Sergey Mikhaylych's courtship of the narrator, and the second part with the unhappiness of their married life. The story ends with an over-explicit and wooden reconciliation in which they agree to be 'friends'. The narrator somewhat implausibly suggests in the last paragraph that 'a new feeling of love for my children and the father of my children' has dawned. Can it be that the title of the story was not ironic, as the reader has all along been led to think, after all?

Boris Eikhenbaum calls the book 'schematic and poor in material'.[17] He sees Tolstoy as reacting against the Turgenev love novel of the 1830s and 1840s which had set aside any concern with family life for loftier and more 'poetic' preoccupations. But, at the same time, he thinks that Tolstoy is uncertain about tone and style and gives us an uneasy mixture of Turgenev type landscape and lyricism (as in the passage on the nightingale in chapter II) and Tolstoyan detail and objectivity. The uneasy mixture can be seen in such a passage as the moonscape in chapter III. The secondary characters in the work are mere ciphers. Katya, the narrator's old governess, and Sonya, her younger sister, are for the most part quite superfluous artistically.

Sergey Mikhaylych tries to educate the narrator and correct her taste (as Tolstoy had done with Valeria), but is used by Tolstoy in chapter III for an attack on the notion of being 'in love' (à la Turgenev?) which makes the narrator's 'I knew from that day he was mine, and that I should never lose him now' jar incongruously; and there is no indication of irony at the narrator's expense, which is always difficult to achieve in a first person novel. The 'I felt I was wholly his' at the end of chapter V is also incongruous and ill prepared for. It follows a frigid description of the wedding that dwindles to nothing when set beside the evocation of the wedding of Levin and Kitty in *Anna Karenina*.

But it is in part two, in his description of his narrator's married life, that Tolstoy ventures furthest into territory which is as yet outside the range of his personal experience. The narrator reports her boredom with life in the country in too dry and abstract a manner. Her mother-in-law Tatyana Semenovna is a wraith when compared to the rich characterization of Levin's old nurse Agatha Mikhaylovna and his relations with her in *Anna Karenina*, and, in fact, the contrast with the full dramatization of Levin's feelings after the first few months of married life is most striking. The couple go to St Petersburg and here there is quite a good dramatic scene over whether the narrator should go to a ball or not which shows a slight touch of Tolstoy's later skill in anatomizing quarrels. But it peters out in too unnatural and forced an allusion to the theme 'We compete in generosity—what an example of family happiness'. Tolstoy avoids this mistake in *Anna Karenina*, where he excels in inventing situations and dialogue in which the themes can be brought to a focus in a perfectly natural and spontaneous way which often involves subsidiary and minor characters as much as the chief protagonists. It is interesting, too, that Tolstoy never again uses the first person narrator who simply recounts what happened in the past from a standpoint of calm, as it were, and is not subject to the scrutiny and irony of the author. The first person narrator of *The Kreutzer Sonata* is something of an exception here, but he is dramatically involved with the imagined listener to his story and is anything but calm.

There are two other important aspects of Tolstoy before he began

War and Peace that we have not yet considered in our exploration of his concerns, and these are the questions of his attitude to the problem of Russia and the West and to the problem of history. The Crimean war had shown Russia and the West in acute conflict and could not fail to remind men like Tolstoy of the great days of 1812 when the Russians had gloriously expelled the Western invader. Naturally such a reminder made the recent performance of the Russians in the Crimea ignominious by contrast. One of the motives for Tolstoy's journey to the West in 1857 was his wish for a first-hand acquaintance with what the West had to offer, particularly in the areas of education and social philosophy. What should Russia take from the West and what should she reject? The spiritual conflict produced in Tolstoy by his investigation of Western ideas of Utilitarianism and Progress is interestingly dramatized in his story *Lucerne*. He was deeply suspicious of the idea of Progress, seeing it as an example of that philosophical view of history which has since become known as historicism—but, as we shall see, he did not find the question of historical truth all that straightforward when he came to write *War and Peace*.

Chapter 7

The Struggle Against the West: *Lucerne*

In spite of the fact that he did criticize deeply certain aspects of the Western doctrines of Utilitarianism and Progress, Tolstoy owed much to the West. As a thinker he was profoundly influenced in his youth by Rousseau and in middle and later life by Kant (who 'wrote horribly, and yet . . . makes an epoch'[1]) and Schopenhauer. As a novelist he read and learned from the Brontës, Dickens (whose satire of parliament had an unfortunate influence on his political views by confirming him in his contempt for 'merely' political freedoms[2]), Thackeray, Trollope and George Eliot. The English novelists were much closer to him in their moral outlook (for example in their fondness for family life) than the French novelists Flaubert, the Goncourts and Zola. It is true that Stendhal's account of Fabrice at Waterloo in *La Chartreuse de Parme* influenced his portrayal of war, but the vanities of *Beylisme* left him untouched. The portrait in *War and Peace* of Captain Ramballe (for whom '*L'amour* . . . consisted principally in the unnaturalness of his relations to the woman and in a combination of incongruities giving the chief charm to the feeling') is a genial attack on that side of the Gallic character.

For all his indebtedness to Western thinkers and writers, however, Tolstoy took part, with Dostoevsky, in what his friend, the critic Nikolai Strakhov, was to call the struggle against the West in Russian literature.[3] This is yet another aspect in which the often-posed question Tolstoy *or* Dostoevsky is misplaced. In this matter it is a case of Tolstoy along with Dostoevsky against the Westernizer Turgenev, with whom Tolstoy's relations between 1856 and 1861 were in a state of great strain. This strain reached its climax in May 1861 when the two practically came to blows over Tolstoy's criticism of the Westernized education which Turgenev was giving his illegitimate daughter.[4]

In *Notes from Underground*, *Crime and Punishment*, *The Devils* and *The Brothers Karamazov* Dostoevsky struggled against what he felt to be the Godlessness of the purely 'naturalistic' interpretation of life with which the scientific-materialist thinkers of the West had infected the *raznochintsy*—the Russian radical intelligentsia, the 'devils' of his novel of that name. Dostoevsky was deeply agitated by this issue, because, like his own Ivan, he himself was infected by scepticism. Dostoevsky had revolted against the radical intelligentsia from within. He had been a protégé of the critic Belinsky and a member of the radical Petrashevsky circle.[5] The ethos of such groups was remote from a *pomeshchik* like Tolstoy. Tolstoy shrewdly remarked to Goldenveizer in 1902: 'Dostoevsky was seeking for a belief, and, when he described profoundly sceptical characters, he described his own unbelief'.[6] Tolstoy himself puzzled Gorky when the latter came across Tolstoy's cryptic note 'God is my desire'.[7] But the four words spoke truly. The basis of Tolstoy's reaction against the West, as of Dostoevsky's, was his disgust with what he conceived to be its self-satisfied assumption that its material civilization constituted 'progress'. It was in the name of the soul that both Tolstoy and Dostoevsky reacted against the West. The soul was not, however, a conception of metaphysics and mysticism for them, but an ethico-religious conception. In fact Tolstoy once remarked to Goldenveizer that he thought that materialism was 'the most mystical of all doctrines'.[8] Tolstoy differed from Dostoevsky, however, in that he saw that it was absurd to identify spiritual universalism with Pan-slavism. This was an area in which, it must be admitted, Dostoevsky sometimes clouded the issues with a mystique of nationalism.

It is clear, too, that one of the reasons for Tolstoy's immense admiration for Rousseau was the fact that Rousseau had anticipated him in his scepticism about whether the great developments in the arts and sciences that marked Western civilization from the seventeenth century onwards had increased human happiness. Did not material progress come into conflict not just with man's unreasoning animal instincts, but with his spiritual needs?

Tolstoy's first journey abroad lasted from January to July 1857. He oscillated between favourable and unfavourable impressions. At first he liked Paris. He wrote to Botkin on 5 April about his awakened sense of his own ignorance and about his admiration for 'all this social liberty of which we have no idea in Russia'.[9] But the very next day he was deeply disturbed when he witnessed a public execution. All his disgust at the power of the State was awakened and he left for Switzerland.

Here at Lucerne in June 1857 he came into contact with the class which best embodied all that the vaunted 'progress' of nineteenth-century civilization was achieving, the English *bourgeoisie*. This is how Herzen, the exiled Russian revolutionary whom Tolstoy was to visit in London on his second journey to the West in 1861, summed up what *bourgeois* 'manners' had done to the life of Western Europe:

Chivalrous honour is replaced by the honesty of the book-keeper, elegant manners by propriety, courtesy by stiff decorum, pride by a readiness to take offence, parks by kitchen gardens, palaces by hotels, open to *all* (that is, all who have money). The old out of date, but consistent conceptions of relations between men have disappeared, while no new recognition of the *true* relations between men has appeared.[10]

Tolstoy reacts against the *bourgeoisie* not with the irony of a Matthew Arnold, or the spleen of a Flaubert, but with the fervent indignation of a prophet. In a long letter to his friend Botkin he describes an incident in which these respected citizens, all Christians and humanitarians, listen with pleasure to a poor Tyrolean singer, but give him no money when he has finished. In the letter he declares:

One could write the history of civilization, basing oneself on these facts. There it is, this famous civilization. Rousseau wasn't talking nonsense in his discourse on the evil civilization has done to manners. . . . Where is the original *spontaneous* sentiment of man? It is not to be found and it disappears just as civilization, that is to say the interested, rational, egoistic association of men, spreads.[11]

This incident, and his passionate reaction to it, form the basis of his story *Lucerne* published in that same year, 1857.

Lucerne is a complex and interesting work, for in it we see Tolstoy reacting not only against Western civilization, but also against his own indignation. This latter reaction is connected with Tolstoy's need to separate himself from the *raznochintsy*, the Russian radical intelligentsia, of whom Chernyshevsky was the contemporary, and Belinsky the earlier, representative. He disliked them, in part, merely because he was a *pomeshchik*, a member of the landed gentry (one may recall Levin's pride in being a *pomeshchik* in *Anna Karenina*). But he also disliked them because they were sympathetic to that very Western civilization of which he was so critical. The writings of such men as Mill, Buckle and Spencer were translated, welcomed and eagerly discussed in Russia among this group in the late fifties and early sixties.

This is how Tolstoy attacked Chernyshevsky in a letter to Nekrasov written on 2 July 1856:

One only hears his fractious disagreeable voice which ceaselessly mouths obtuse spite. It gets excited because it does not know how to speak and its voice sounds false. All this sort of thing comes from Belinsky. However he spoke like that because he had really been hurt whereas this writer thinks that in order to speak well one must speak insolently and in order to speak insolently one must get angry. . . . It has come to be thought among us, and not only in criticism, that it is *the thing* to show oneself indignant, bitter, testy. I find all that in bad taste. People like Gogol better than Pushkin. Belinsky's criticism is the height of perfection. Your poems are preferred to all others. I find all this very regrettable, because a bitter and irritable man is in an abnormal state. A loving man is just the opposite. Only in a normal state can one do good and see things clearly.[12]

In October of the same year Tolstoy wrote to Kovaleski: 'I've discovered that indignation, the wish to draw attention to what makes us indignant is a great vice and particularly the vice of our century'.[13]

Lucerne [14] purports to be from the memoirs of a Prince Nekhlyudov (a 'persona' Tolstoy used in other stories and in his late novel *Resurrection*), who recounts an incident which occurs when he is staying at the best hotel in Lucerne. He tells how he is struck by the faces of the well-to-do English guests. These faces express 'a consciousness of their own well-being and a complete lack of interest in all that surrounded them unless it directly concerned themselves'. A wandering Tyrolean singer appears and Prince Nekhlyudov is struck by his 'immense natural gifts'. His skilful yet spontaneous songs arouse delight among the guests, but when he has finished singing and holds out his cap not one person throws him a single penny. Prince Nekhlyudov grows indignant. He contrasts the 'comfortable, convenient, clean, and easy' life of the English guests with that of the 'tired and perhaps hungry' singer. He tries to anger an Englishman. He follows the musician and insists on taking him back to the hotel and ordering him champagne. He tries to awaken indignation in him against the guests, but finds that he bears no resentment, though he complains that the 'republican laws', unlike 'natural laws', do not allow singing in public. Prince Nekhlyudov gets angry with the waiters in the inferior public bar to which they have been sent, and insists on taking the musician to the other room and sitting with him ('more dead than alive') next to a wealthy Englishman and his lady who get up in anger and complain to the waiter.

Eventually the musician goes and, after a spell in his room, Prince Nekhlyudov walks out into the town and reflects how the guests would say that 'the best thing in the world is money' and yet show by their listening to the musician that they have a need for art, 'this greatest blessing in the world'. But their slighting this need and their ingratitude to those who, like the poor musician, meet it, are overwhelming. It seems to Prince Nekhlyudov that this crowd's rejection of a poor singer on 7 July 1857 'is an occurrence the historians of our time ought to record in indelible letters of fire. This incident is more significant, more serious, and has a profounder meaning, than the facts usually printed in newspapers and histories'. Such facts as the English killing of a thousand Chinese, or the French massacre of a thousand Arabs, or Napoleon III's assurance that 'he reigns only by the will of the whole nation' reveal nothing new about the history of mankind, but this apparently trivial incident 'appears to be something quite new and strange, and relates not to the eternally evil side of human nature, but to a certain epoch in social evolution'.

Boris Eikhenbaum is right to stress the ardently moralistic element in *Lucerne* as showing Tolstoy's transcending the world of journalism and letters, but he makes a bad mistake in suggesting that Prince Nekhlyudov's reflections in the passage immediately following the one I have just quoted, are rooted in 'nihilism'.[15] In this passage Tolstoy/Nekhlyudov begins to think about the difficulties of the notion of 'progress' in the moral sphere, and about the impossibility of one individual judging another:

What an unfortunate, pitiful creature is man, with his desire for positive decisions, thrown into this ever moving, limitless ocean of good and evil, of facts, conceptions, and contradictions! For ages men have struggled and laboured to place good on one side and evil on the other. Centuries pass, and whenever an impartial mind places good and evil on the scales, the balance remains even, and the proportion of good and evil remains unaltered. . . . Whose soul possesses so absolute a standard of good and evil that he can measure all the confused and fleeting facts? . . . And who has seen a condition in which good and evil did not exist together? And how do I know that it is not my point of view which decides more of the one than of the other?

Why is this scrupulous awareness of the complex interweaving of good and evil in life to be called 'nihilist?'

At the very end of *Lucerne* Prince Nekhlyudov, hearing the musician singing in the distance, turns round and condemns himself for his moral pride. Take the rich Englishman and the poor musician:

Who has weighed the inner happiness to be found in the soul of each of them? He is now sitting somewhere on a dirty door-step, gazing at the gleaming moonlit sky and gaily singing in the calm of the fragrant night: in his heart there is no reproach, or malice, or regret. And who knows what is now going on in the souls of the people within these palatial walls? Who can tell whether among them all there is as much carefree benign joy in life and harmony with the world as lives in the soul of that little man?

These things only seem contradictions to those who try to penetrate God's laws and intentions. But there is a nice little reflexive touch at the end of the story. Prince Nekhlyudov should not be too indignant with his own 'mean and petty indignation', for he too is only playing his 'necessary part in the external and infinite harmony'. Such a notion of 'harmony' would be an odd one for a nihilist, and Eikhenbaum would have done better to speak of disillusionment rather than of nihilism in connection with *Lucerne*. Prince Nekhlyudov is disillusioned both with his fellow men and, at the end of the story, with himself. But the disillusionment with himself is, so to speak, a 'positive' disillusionment on which he can build. In thinking that happiness could be reduced to a set of homogeneous units and measured on a single scale, Prince Nekhlyudov had momentarily fallen into the very error of the Western Utilitarians which he and Tolstoy rejected.

Tolstoy also rejects in *Lucerne* the Western doctrine of progress. This is a historicist doctrine in that it assumes a law underlying the unfolding pattern of human history. Tolstoy found the doctrine of progress in contemporary English writers such as Buckle in his *History of Civilization*; but whereas they claimed that the 'epoch in social evolution' which England had reached, with its progress and civilization and 'equality before the law' was a wholly good thing, he pointed to what he saw as losses to counterpoise the gain. He could not, in a story like *Lucerne*, deal with the wider implications of the historical views implicit in, say, the famous third chapter of Macaulay's *History of England*, with its 'progressivist' contrast of nineteenth-century England with the England of the 1680s—for too many theoretical implications were involved. Before he started writing *War and Peace*, however, he thought deeply about the issues raised by Western views of history and education and dealt with them in a series of essays, notably in 'Progress and the Definition of Education', an essay published in 1862, the year after his second trip to Europe. It will be interesting to see now in more detail how Tolstoy both reacted against and was influenced by the historicism he found in Western thinkers, and how, indeed, he might even be claimed to have capitulated to 'historicist' thinking in parts of *War and Peace*.

Chapter 8

Tolstoy and Historicism

In the early 1860s, before starting *War and Peace*, Tolstoy wrote a number of articles in connection with his study of Western ideas about education, culture and history. These ideas were not of purely theoretical concern to him, but intimately linked to his educational work in his peasant school at Yasnaya Polyana. In these articles, particularly 'Progress and the Definition of Education', he attacked with great vigour certain tendencies in the philosophy of history present in different ways in the work of Hegel, Macaulay, Buckle, Herbert Spencer and Mill, tendencies which have since been labelled 'historicism'. Sir Karl Popper sees the basic assumption of historicism as being that there are general laws governing the whole of human history which determine the transition from one period to another.[1] If one knows them, one can prophesy at a given stage what the next stage will be and, at the same time, adopt only such courses of action as will further the 'inevitable' changes. Historicism, in short, discerns in history the plot, rhythm and predetermined pattern that the historian H. A. L. Fisher claimed he was unable to find.[2] It can, in fact, be viewed as a secularization of the Christian idea of Providence, with historical laws taking the place of the will of God. It is a well-known paradox that doctrines of 'inevitabilism' such as are found in Islam, Calvinism and Marxism, have not led to the passive resignation that might have been expected, but, on the contrary, have often stimulated heroic activism, a *jihad* or 'holy war', whether against infidel, papist or capitalist. Perhaps, indeed, this was one of the reasons why Tolstoy, having perceptively attacked historicism in his articles, succumbed to it, as we shall see, in parts of *War and Peace*. He saw a great tide of Russian national sentiment aroused by the Napoleonic invasion of 1812 with such vividness, that he found himself swept along by that vision into a foamy acclamation of national destiny and invested the defeat of Napoleon with historicist overtones.

Alongside historicism as a view of history, there often goes a his-

57

toricist type of moral theory which we might call 'moral inevitabilism'. Sir Karl Popper (who called it 'moral modernism' or 'moral futurism') formulated its cardinal tenet as follows: 'The morally good is the morally progressive, i.e. the morally good is what is ahead of its time in conforming to such standards as will be adopted in the period to come'.[3] This view has a pernicious effect when it leads people to refrain from condemning policies they recognize as evil on the incoherent grounds that those policies will somehow be justified before a kind of 'court of history'. The defect of such moral inevitabilism is that it involves a kind of Sartrean bad faith, an attempt to delegate judgements one should make oneself to an abstraction such as 'the historical process'. The phrase 'history will judge' is unobjectionable if it simply means that man in the future will endorse our present judgements. It is pernicious if it is used to mean that men in the future will, by some mysterious process, make our judgements for us. A kind of bad faith also lurks in the claim that the views of a particular generation must *ipso facto* be the right ones and in the pseudo-objectivity bestowed by certain uses of such idioms as: 'the demands of the time', or 'the needs of the age', or 'out of date'.

In this guise it should be evident that historicism is no mere bogy of the nineteenth century, but a view which is still very much in the air at the present time. It is, therefore, salutary to see the withering scorn with which Tolstoy met arguments using historicist idioms in the 1860s in his essay 'Progress and the Definition of Education':

> We are told . . . one must teach in conformity with the demands of the time, and we are told that that is very simple. I understand teaching according to the demands of the Christian or of the Mohammedan religion, but teaching according to the demands of the time is something of which I fail to comprehend a single word. What are these demands? Who will determine them? Where will they be expressed? [4]

Tolstoy strongly objected to the reductive view that a thinker's work was merely the result of 'historical conditions' which compelled him to express himself in a certain way. He insisted that if, for example, I want to understand Rousseau, 'I can verify and comprehend his thoughts only by thinking and not by reflecting on his place in history'.[5] A man's situation is important, no doubt, but it is a fallacy to see his thoughts as determined by history.

In the early 1860s Tolstoy met historicism in two forms. First there was the practical historicism of the Western liberal doctrine of inevitable social progress which he found in Mill and Buckle. Tolstoy claimed that as long as the law of progress or perfectibility remains personal' it is fruitful (we have seen in his diary how concerned with this kind of progress he was), but 'when it is transferred to history, it becomes an idle, empty prattle, leading to the justification of every insipidity and to fatalism'.[6] Tolstoy thought that Buckle really meant no more by progress than gunpowder, printing, roads, science and industry; and as man, on the contrary, has many other sides to his existence, why should men believe that such progress was *ipso facto* good. Many years later when Tolstoy met the practical historicism of Marx himself (which in its notion of inevitable progress parallels the 'bourgeois' ideology of Mill and Buckle) he protested against its regarding 'that gradual destruction of small private production by large capitalistic production now going on around us, as an inevitable decree of fate'.[7]

The second form of historicism which Tolstoy met was the 'theoretical' historicism stemming from Hegel which influenced both rightist and leftist thought. Tolstoy condemned this Hegelian historicism in an eloquent and forceful passage:

Since the day of Hegel and the famous aphorism, 'What is historical is reasonable', there has reigned in the literary and oral debates, especially in our country, a very singular mental hocus-pocus called the historical view. You say, for example, that a man has a right to be free and to be judged only on the basis of the laws which he himself regards as just, but the historical view replies that history evolves a certain historical moment, which conditions a certain historical legislation and the people's historical relation to it. You say you believe in God, and the historical view replies that history has evolved certain religious conceptions and the relations of humanity to them. You say that the Iliad is the greatest epical production, and the historical view replies that the Iliad is only the expression of a nation's historical consciousness at a certain historical moment. On this foundation the historical view does not contend with you whether liberty is necessary for man, whether there is a God or not, whether the Iliad is good or bad: it does nothing to obtain that liberty for you, after which you have just been striving, to persuade or dissuade you of the existence of God, or of the beauties of the Iliad,—it only points out to you that place which your inner need, the love of truth or beauty, occupies in history: it only recognizes, not through direct consciousness, but through historical ratiocinations. Say that you love something and believe in something and the historical view tells you, 'Love and believe, and your love and faith will find a place for themselves in our historical view'. Ages will pass, and we shall find the place which we shall occupy in history: but you must know in advance that that which you love is not unconditionally beautiful, and that that which you believe in is not unconditionally true: but amuse yourselves, children,— for your love and faith will find a place and a proper application for themselves. Add the word historical to any conception you please and that conception at once loses its vital, actual meaning and receives an artificial and barren meaning in some kind of an artificially framed world conception.[8]

A little later on in 'Progress and the Definition of Education' Tolstoy characterizes what he sees as the inhuman pride of the 'calm historical view' in the following burning passage:

You yourself stand on some imaginary height, and below you act Rousseau, and Schiller, and Luther, and the French Revolution. From your historical height you approve or disapprove their historical acts and classify them according to historical patterns. More than that. Each human personality is crawling about somewhere there, subject to the immutable historical laws, which we know: but there is no final end, and there can be none,— there is only the historical view! [9]

Tolstoy, on the contrary, believes with the natural law theorists that, in some sense or other, there is a 'common eternal law . . . written in the soul of each man'.[10] After a discussion with a friend he had noted: 'Christ did not impose, but revealed, the moral law which for ever remains the standard of good and evil.' [11] He repeats this idea at the end of chapter XVIII of book XIV of *War and Peace* in which he rejects the notion that the 'great' men of history are beyond judgement by this standard: 'For us, with the standard of good and evil given us by Christ, no human actions are incommensurable.'

But when he came to write the account of 1812 and the second epilogue to *War and Peace*, Tolstoy himself could not resist the attraction of historicist explanation. This comes out in three ways.

The first is in Tolstoy's succumbing to the ambition (shared by many eighteenth- and nineteenth-century thinkers, including Hume and Kant) to do for the human world what Newton had done for the material world. In Tolstoy this takes the form of what Eikhenbaum called 'Urusovism' [12] because of the influence on Tolstoy of a friend called Urusov, who was a professor of mathematics interested in history. Tolstoy's 'Urusovism' is to be found in those passages of *War and Peace* in which the movements of men and armies are conceived in purely physical terms as 'forces' so that they can be treated in terms of Newton's laws of motion and viewed as 'determined'. Thus at the opening of book XI Tolstoy speaks of the motion of these forces as continuous, and therefore open to treatment by the infinitesimal calculus, whereas history selects discrete units and therefore falsifies. Tolstoy's 'Urusovism' is at its height in the following passage on the possibility of precise investigations of a phenomenon Tolstoy rightly sees as crucially important, namely 'the spirit of the army'.

Ten men, battalions, or divisions, fighting fifteen men, battalions, or divisions, conquer, that is—kill or make captive—all the others, while themselves losing four, so that on the one side four and on the other fifteen were lost. Consequently the four were equal to the fifteen, and therefore $4x = 15y$.

Consequently $\dfrac{x}{y} = \dfrac{15}{4}$. This equation does not give us the value of the unknown factor but gives us a ratio between two unknowns. And by bringing various selected historical units (battles, campaigns, periods of war) into such equations, a series of numbers could be obtained in which certain laws should exist and might be discovered. (XIV, ii, 290)

Many years later Tolstoy remarked to Goldenveizer apropos Urusov: 'I was always surprised that mathematicians who are so exact in their own science are so vague and inexact when they try to philosophize.'[13] It is a pity Tolstoy did not bear that in mind when he wrote a passage of utter mystification like the one above.

The second way in which Tolstoy succumbs to the attraction of historicist explanation is in his surrender to a kind of Deistic 'Providentialism'. This can also be linked to Newton, for Newton himself had thought that God continually directs the goings-on in the universe he has created. Tolstoy explicitly claims that Voltaire was mistaken in thinking 'that the laws of astronomy destroyed religion'. Tolstoy was attracted by the grandeur of this eighteenth-century Deism (which is also found in Kant) because it contrasted with the materialist hostility to religion of the self-confident 'naturalists' of his own day whom he compared, in *War and Peace* (Second Epilogue, ch. xii, p. 537), to plasterers who cover all the complexities and beauties of a church and are then delighted that 'from their point of view . . . everything is now so smooth and regular'.

It is true that Tolstoy says that it is impossible to return to a belief in the direct intervention of the Deity in human affairs, but in his polemic against Buckle he makes the fatal mistake of asking the 'essentialist' question, 'What is power?' This gets him into such difficulties that he ends by writing of the 'inevitability' of events in such a way as to imply that, though no direct intervention is observable, everything which occurs in time is in some mysterious way 'the expression of the will of the Deity, not dependent on time'.[14] Only in such a way can discrete events and periods be seen as part of a continuous whole. It is not just a matter of causes in a purely physical world. The passions of men are connected with that physical world in some obscure way left unexplained and are just as 'determined' as the movements in that physical world. In yielding to their passions men are 'but blind tools of the most melancholy law of necessity'[15] and that law is, in some mysterious way, identical with God's will.

At the beginning of book IX Tolstoy claims that the whole mass movement of men in 1812 resulted from a host of causes each of which was necessary and none of which was sufficient and that the actions of Napoleon and Alexander were no more voluntary than those of their lowliest soldier. He writes: 'We are forced to fall back on fatalism as an explanation of irrational events.' He identifies 'History' with what he calls the 'swarm-life of mankind' and states that it uses every moment of the life of kings for its own purposes. Their every act 'is related to the whole course of history and pre-destined from eternity'. Again, just before his account of Borodino, Tolstoy argues that it is contrary to reality to suppose that the war with Russia was begun by the will of one man: 'To the question of what causes historic events, another answer presents itself, namely that the course of human events is predetermined from on high—depends on the coincidence of the wills of all who take part in the events, and that a Napoleon's influence on the course of these events is purely external and fictitious.'[16] It seems to Tolstoy that Napoleon merely 'fulfilled the inhuman role predestined for him'.[17] Sidney Hook in *The Hero in History* formulates very clearly the view to which Tolstoy was committed. It is that 'neither Napoleon nor any other figure in history *could* have acted differently in any important respect'. As Hook says, this historical fatalism, like all fatalism, 'cannot be supported by any evidence, but it can be held in the teeth of any evidence marshalled against it'.[18] Hook sees Hegel, Buckle and Spencer as all committed to this kind of historical fatalism. Ironically enough we have seen Tolstoy in his anti-historicist essays in disagreement with all of them. Tolstoy's capitulation to a sort of Deistic Providentialism is a surrender to the assumption that history has a pattern and Tolstoy, in making it, forgets his earlier (and, I think, correct) view that it is impossible to find a historical law or laws.

The third way in which Tolstoy succumbs to historicist explanation is in his surrender to what the German visitor who saw him gripping his peasant pupils with the story of 1812 called the *ganz Russisch* view.[19] This surrender (which, as I shall show, is not constant) involves falling into the neo-Slavophil temptation of seeing Russia as having a special kind of mission and as producing a special kind of hero, the 'humble' Kutúzov to set over against the Western type of hero, the lackey's hero—Napoleon.[20]

Sir Isaiah Berlin has called the passage on the bringing of the news of Napoleon's abandonment of Moscow to the aged Kutúzov 'one of the most moving in literature'. Kutúzov is so full of feeling that he cannot speak to his fellow officers, but turns 'to the corner darkened by the icons' and says 'in a tremulous voice': 'O Lord, my Creator, Thou hast heard our prayer . . . Russia is saved. I thank Thee, O Lord!' [21] But Berlin points out that we are now 'in an imaginary realm' in that the historical evidence for this 'emotional atmosphere' is 'flimsy' despite all Tolstoy's repeated professions of his undeviating devotion to the sacred cause of the truth.[22] This raises in an acute form the problem of poetry and truth which I shall wrestle with in the next chapter. What I want to do at the moment is to suggest that the 'national epic' element in *War and Peace* reinforces the tendency to historicist Providentialism present in the work. In the prayer of Kutúzov's just quoted I feel that it is not just Kutúzov's view (whether imagined or actual) which is being presented, but a view sanctioned by the author.

There are passages in *War and Peace*, however, which, while not exactly contradicting this nationalist 'Providentialism', bring out the fact that there were strong tensions between it and Tolstoy's moral universalism. One of the most moving of these passages evokes Natasha's conflict of feeling on hearing the Orthodox Church's special prayer for victory when she goes to mass. It is one of the most effective of the many links in the book between the personal life and the 'swarm' life, the contrast between which so tormented Tolstoy. Natasha, her head turned by the superficial Anatole Kuragin, has in spirit betrayed Prince Andrew to whom she is betrothed. She has tried to poison herself and has been under medical treatment. Pierre, who has earlier declared his devotion to her, treats her with great delicacy and is the only person she can bear to see. A country neighbour, Belova, who is visiting Moscow, suggests that Natasha should prepare to receive Holy Communion at the end of the fast of St Peter, and Natasha, filled with a sense of her own fault and baffled in her wish to understand the 'why' of things, comes to see the wish itself as a kind of pride and throws herself upon repentance and commitment to God.

During Communion she is more and more drawn by a sense of man's erring and his need for forgiveness and for submission to God, until the usual order of the service is suddenly interrupted and a special prayer for the destruction of the French is offered up in solemn language. Tolstoy writes:

She shared with all her heart in the prayer for the spirit of righteousness, for the strengthening of the heart by faith and hope, and its animation by love. But she could not pray that her enemies might be trampled under foot when but a few minutes before she had been wishing she had more of them that she might pray for them. (IX, xviii, 335)

Yet, at the same time, she cannot doubt 'the righteousness of the prayer'. She is in awe at the punishment that overtakes men for their sins and that comes from God.

63

In this portrayal of Natasha torn between Christian universalism and nationalism, Tolstoy transcends his own nationalism, with its sense that Russia had a special historical destiny, though that sense weaves a strand of historicist thinking into much of the book. Another feature of the work is Tolstoy's tendency to see as peculiarly Russian the characters with whom he sympathizes most deeply, such as Natasha with her almost instinctive response to folk song and dance, and the bear-like expansive Pierre. However, as a degree of instinctive ethnocentrism seems to be a ubiquitous feature of human life, this feature may, paradoxically, contribute to the universalism of the work. It does not have to be the case that benevolent feelings towards our own nation, community or group need involve malevolence towards others, despite many unfortunate examples of this happening. As Tolstoy's friend and biographer Aylmer Maude pointed out in his criticism of some of Tolstoy's later writings on the topic of patriotism, the evil side of patriotism should not obscure 'the rational basis that exists for national feeling of a non-malevolent kind'.[23]

Finally, a potent reason for Tolstoy's succumbing to historicism in *War and Peace* may well lie in the fact that, as we saw in the very beginning of this book, he felt deeply that the discovery of the meaning of life was a necessary condition for happiness. At the time of writing *War and Peace* he may well have thought that if life has a meaning, then so must history. But in order to give history a meaning, or in Fisher's words, 'a plot, a rhythm, a predetermined pattern', he was pulled towards showing it as ultimately illustrative of his deepest moral convictions, in short, making it 'exemplary'. This made for difficulties when it came to the presentation of such characters as Napoleon and Kutúzov, and of such events as the battle of Borodino. Although he claimed truth as his primary concern, historical truth had to give way where it conflicted with his deepest moral convictions.

Chapter 9

The Problem of Truth in *War and Peace*

Tolstoy's interest in the problem of *historical* truth (a problem which is crucial in *War and Peace*) was awakened early. In 1853 he wrote in his diary:

Every historical fact should be explained humanly, and routine historical expressions avoided. I should write an epitaph to history 'I conceal nothing'. It is not enough not to tell direct lies, one should try not to lie negatively by silence.[1]

In chapter one of the second epilogue to *War and Peace* Tolstoy states that 'modern history, like a deaf man, answers questions no one asks'. This seems meant to imply that modern history is silent on questions men *do* ask. Men, of course, expect history to tell them what happened, why it happened and what went on in the minds of those to whom it happened. One has the feeling from both the diaries and *War and Peace* that it is really the third of these questions which is the most important to Tolstoy, and it is, of course, the one which it is often the most difficult for the historian proper to answer, and the one where the novelist gifted with dramatic sympathy is most strongly tempted to compete with him. True, the historian is bound to 'hypothesize' about the thoughts and attitudes of the people he is describing, but he is more professionally concerned to let the extant evidence control his hypotheses than the novelist, even when that novelist, like Tolstoy, proclaims the primacy of truth.

The earliest story we have about Tolstoy's attitude to history is an amusing one. It comes from a fellow student at the University of Kazan called Nazarev. He recounts that in January 1846 he and Tolstoy were punished for lateness at a history lecture by being placed in detention. Tolstoy noticed that Nazarev had a volume of Karamzin's *History of Russia* with him and

attacked history as the dullest and almost the most useless of subjects. A collection of fables and useless details, sprinkled with a mass of unnecessary figures and proper names. . . . Who wants to know that the second marriage of Ivan the Terrible, with Temrúk's daughter, took place on 21st August 1562; and his fourth marriage, with Anna Alexéevna Koltórskaya, in 1572? Yet they expect me to grind all this, and if I don't, the examiner gives me a one.[2]

No doubt much in this can be set down to pique and should not be taken too seriously, but the passage does illustrate Tolstoy's quest for where the 'vital interest' of history lay. He was to try to convey this 'vital interest' in his teaching of history to the pupils at his Yasnaya Polyana school many years later. But what was the result? A visiting German found Tolstoy's account of the events of 1812 'not history, but a fanciful tale arousing the national sentiment'.[3] One is tempted to see this remark as applicable to parts of *War and Peace* itself.

It is, then, perhaps not surprising that some professional historians have spoken dismissively of Tolstoy. The great Dutch historian, Pieter Geyl, for example, who made a famous study of the views of other historians on Napoleon entitled *Napoleon: For and Against*, characterized Tolstoy's own view of Napoleon as 'fundamentally unhistorical'.[4] Yet after all Geyl's book itself brings out in the end how elusive a figure Napoleon is and how the professional historians themselves leave us with a multiplicity of Napoleons. Moreover Geyl himself feels called upon to judge Napoleon quite as much as Tolstoy, and his verdict is remarkably close to Tolstoy's. Geyl writes:

I should like to see the eternal postulates of respect for the human personality, of the feeling for spiritual freedom, of lofty idealism, of truthfulness taken into account when the final reckoning is made.[5]

Even if Geyl's dismissive view of Tolstoy as a historian is the right judgement to reach in the end, he reaches it far too quickly, easily and complacently for three main reasons.

The first arises from the fact that Geyl himself, like many other professional historians, is not concerned with military history. He explicitly disavows dealing with Napoleon as a general. But this is the aspect of Napoleon with which Tolstoy is centrally concerned. Another professional historian, G. R. Elton, has written interestingly on this lack of concern among his fellow professionals with the history of war:

In both general and particular works of history, the agonies of wars and battles rarely appear at any length comparable to the impact they had on the people of the day . . . professional historians who specialize in the history of war are astonishingly few. Since so much of man's history is concerned with his efforts to kill others and avoid being killed by them, this fastidious attitude, though highly civilized, is also highly unrealistic.[6]

Elton finds much written by historians about war 'intellectually undemanding and unsatisfying' perhaps because of the lack of 'direct acquaintance' with warfare among most of them, and moral revulsion on the part of the rest. He sees war as too serious a matter to be left to military historians and to the social scientists of RAND. The latter lack the feeling, intellectual equipment and vision to do it justice.

The second reason is that Geyl says nothing about the immense suggestiveness of Tolstoy both for the historian and for the student of history, particularly where it comes to being critical of explanations of actions and events. It was perhaps this suggestiveness which led a leading practitioner of contemporary history, Walter Laqueur, who is keenly interested in certain defects of professional historians, to write apropos Tolstoy and Stendhal:

War and Peace and *Le Rouge et Le Noir* ought to figure at least as prominently in the education of the student of Borodino and Waterloo as Kolyubakin, Horsburgh, or Nazev.[7]

The sort of suggestiveness I am thinking of comes out in Tolstoy's rejection of deep and over-subtle explanations designed primarily to demonstrate the insight and ingenuity of their inventors, in favour of explanations in terms of what Sir Karl Popper has termed the logic of situation. An example Popper himself cites is Tolstoy's answer to the question why the Russians withdrew from Moscow after Borodino by way of the famous flank march to the Kaluga road due south, instead of eastward to Ryazan as seems to have been the original intention.[8] According to Tolstoy this was because there were good provisions for the army in the area to which it withdrew rather than because of any profound tactical considerations, as some subsequently assumed. It is typical of Tolstoy, however, that he presents his view that the praise of the Russian generals for reaching this decision was undeserved as an out-of-the-way one. He does not mention that it was shared by the most famous nineteenth-century theorist of war, Von Clausewitz.[9] We shall find another example of this sort of thing in the account of Borodino itself.

The third reason is that a reading of Tolstoy brings home to us the fact that to give a proper explanation of what actually happened we must always take into consideration (even if we do not refer to it explicitly) what *might* have happened. Tolstoy is acutely aware that historians 'are not much concerned with also-rans and drop-outs. They have a bias towards success'.[10] At the same time it should be said in criticism of Tolstoy that he is too prone to overlook the fact that gaps may exist in a historical account simply because of lack of evidence, so that incompleteness, far from necessarily reflecting bias or untruth (as he is apt to suppose), may on the contrary reflect scrupulousness. Tolstoy sometimes implies that when a historian does not give us *all* the facts, the ones he does give are therefore false. He demands, in short, a kind of 'total' descrip-tion. But it should be evident that such a demand is *logically* inco-herent. All descriptions of an object or an event must be selective according to the purpose of the describer. As a critic of Tolstoy's view in this matter correctly remarked: 'from the fact that not all has been said it does not follow that what has been said is false'.[11]

But is there a problem of *historical* truth in the first place? R. F. Christian thinks not. He contends that the question of 'the historical accuracy of Tolstoy's alleged facts' in *War and Peace* is unimportant. All that matters for him is that 'the underlying artistic idea should be clearly and convincingly expressed' and that the characters should act 'consistently' with the roles Tolstoy assigns them in the work itself.[12] But why then did Tolstoy make the claim in his after-word 'Some Words About *War and Peace*' that he told the truth while the historians did not, and why were historians of the time like Norov, Vitmer and Glinka worried by his innaccuracies? [13] More-over Christian overlooks an important complication of the problem. Anyone, including a professional historian, can make mistakes in-advertently; but supposing someone points out cases where Tolstoy has omitted (or introduced) details in such a way as to falsify what was actually the case with the tendentious purpose of influencing our view of the historical characters concerned—would we not then be uneasy, whatever our theory about the relations between novels and history? As a small example of what I mean, consider how Tolstoy tells us that on the eve of Borodino 'Another valet . . . was sprinkling eau-de-Cologne on the Emperor's pampered body . . .' (X, xxvi, 490). The Russian critic Victor Shklovsky points out that Tolstoy's only warrant for the eau-de-Cologne was De la Case's description of Napoleon's domestic habits many years later during exile on St Helena.[14] Are we not legitimately disturbed on learning that this historically false detail was introduced in order to make Napoleon look petty?

Tolstoy's account of Borodino is, in fact, inseparable from his portrayal of Napoleon, for much in that account emerges as designed to undermine Napoleon's status as a great commander. Tolstoy begins with three claims about the battle. His first claim is that the 'histories' are wrong in saying that the Russians chose the best position for battle deliberately.[15] Characteristically he implies that he is something of a maverick in taking the opposite view—and this has a certain prima facie implausibility when we recall that one of his recurrent complaints against historians is that they contradict each other. He nowhere mentions that Von Clausewitz was, in fact, in complete agreement with the view that many other positions might have been as good, or even better.[16] Tolstoy's second claim is concerned with the problem of the position of the Shevardino redoubt. This fortified redoubt was well in front of the Russian lines during the actual battle of Borodino and had in fact been captured by the French in a preliminary action on the 24 August (5 September New Style). Why was it so senselessly isolated? Tolstoy conjectures that the redoubt was originally intended to be on the left flank of the Russian positions in a plan which had had to be abandoned. Whatever the truth of the matter, Tolstoy seems to be trying to solve a genuine puzzle here.[17] Tolstoy's third claim is directly concerned with Napoleon and immediately involves us in a tendentious *non sequitur*. He attacks Napoleon's battle plan by saying that it was ill conceived and could not have been executed.[18] In the case of two of the four orders (those given to Campan and Poniatowski), Tolstoy simply assumes that, by mentioning contingent circumstances (Poniatowski's meeting Tuchkóv's troops and Campan's running into grape shot) which led to the two generals failing, he has done sufficient to establish the very strong claim that they could not have succeeded. But can we infer from the simple fact of failure the impossibility of success and the folly of the plan attempted? This fallacy might well be called the schoolboy's comforter.

When Tolstoy reaches the actual fighting he even gets involved in some self-contradictions. For example, he claims that Napoleon was so far away from the battle that 'not one of his orders during the fight could be executed'. Yet he himself shows Napoleon deciding not to send Claparède's division into battle, but Friant's instead, and explicitly states that 'the order was carried out exactly'. Later on he shows Napoleon refusing to allow the Old Guard to be used in the action.[19] This order was certainly carried out; and although there is naturally dispute about the matter, some writers think that Napoleon's decision was crucial in ruling out the possibility of a French victory. Tolstoy was so concerned to establish the *ineffectuality* of Napoleon that he was prepared to overlook Napoleon's errors.

Tolstoy's continual tendentiousness in his account of the battle is apt to provoke the reader to disagreement. He had said at the outset that the battle was senseless given its outcome: 'What the result must be was quite obvious, and yet Napoleon offered and Kutúzov accepted that battle' (X, xix, 458). Tolstoy here forgets that both he and the historians know the outcome, whereas Napoleon and Kutúzov at the time *did not*. In doing so he makes the commanders' actions look more irrational than they were, given the circumstances. Napoleon wanted to achieve a position which would enable him to impose advantageous peace terms and Kutúzov had the perfectly intelligible wish to defend Moscow. They were not 'the blind tools of history' that Tolstoy at this point portrays them as being. He lapses here into that very Hegelian superciliousness—in which from a historical height 'you approve or disapprove . . . historical acts and classify them according to historical patterns' [20]—which he had condemned in his attack on historicism. It is, moreover, self-contradictory of Tolstoy to maintain on the one hand that Napoleon's commands did not cause any of the killing at Borodino and yet, on the other hand, to claim that Napoleon was the figure 'on whom the responsibility for what was happening lay more than on all the others who took part in it' (X, xxxviii, 540). Napoleon could not both be completely ineffectual in bringing about what happened and most to blame for it.

At the end of the nineteenth century a Russian general called Dragomirov wrote an interesting critique of Tolstoy's account of war.[21] He contended that many of Tolstoy's difficulties arise because he blurs the crucial distinctions between the two stages of a battle, the first in which the tactical positions are assumed under the general's eye and influence and the second when the engagement has begun and the subordinate commanders and troops do what they can for themselves. He takes Tolstoy up on a number of issues of the type to which I alluded in my suggestion that Tolstoy's tendentiousness is apt to provoke the reader to disagreement. He finds Tolstoy's contention that it was the soldiers and not Napoleon who killed the enemy at Borodino specious because, by the same process of metonymy, one could argue that it was not the troops who did the killing, but the bullets. As I have already pointed out, it is inconsistent of Tolstoy to say at one point that Napoleon did no killing and then to blame him solemnly at another for the deaths inflicted. Dragomirov points out that Tolstoy's argument that if Napoleon had ordered the troops *not* to fight they would have turned round and killed him ignores the fact that Napoleon's troops did not turn on him at even more opportune moments such as the crossing of the Beresina.

To come to a larger issue, what are Tolstoy's grounds for assuming that Napoleon's cold *could* not have affected the outcome of Borodino by impairing his performance as a general? They rest on the prior claim that the will of one man *could* not have directed an army. And what does that claim rest on? It rests on the judgement that such a notion outrages human dignity because 'each of us is, if not more, at least not less a man than the great Napoleon'. But as Dragomirov points out the last of these judgements may be true as an ethical one without having any relevance whatsoever to the argument as to whether or not a general can control an army by his will. The pathos of Tolstoy's need to vindicate his theory by such slender means may lead us to an ambivalent view of *War and Peace* —in that we find the treatment of historical events and the portrayal of Napoleon unacceptable, and yet are gripped with admiration for the intensity and moral seriousness with which Tolstoy wrestled with the problems they posed for him.

In fact Tolstoy's portrayal of Napoleon is deeply affected by the historicist fatalism we discussed in the last chapter. He is committed, as we saw there, to the general thesis that Napoleon could not have acted differently in any significant respect because any other figure in the same position would have had to act identically and so would have produced the identical effects. The French historian Albert Sorel thought that Tolstoy had adopted the position of Montesquieu. Sorel wrote of Montesquieu:

he has shown us in great men the great instruments of history; he established that if Caesar had not arisen another would have taken his place. He has written this sentence which sums up all his philosophy: 'If the luck of a battle, that is to say a particular cause, ruined a state, there was a general cause which brought it about that that state had to perish through a single battle. In a word the main cause draws with it all the particular contingencies.[22]

Such a view is naturally very tempting to a writer like Tolstoy who is concerned to belittle great men in general and Napoleon in particular partly for ethical reasons, partly, one sometimes suspects, out of an aristocrat's disdain for a bourgeois parvenu. But is the view a true one? Would not the history of France between 1793 and 1815 have been very different in its detail if Desaix, Hoche or Carnot had occupied Napoleon's place? Would the October revolution have taken the course it did without Lenin?

Tolstoy's judgement of Napoleon is open to the same objections as that of his own Prince Andrew who had reflected:

And Bonaparte. . . ! I remember his limited, self-satisfied face on the field of Austerlitz. Not only does a good army commander not need any special qualities, on the contrary he needs the absence of the highest and best human attributes—love, poetry, tenderness, and philosophic inquiring doubt. (IX, xi, 308)

You cannot argue that the absence of certain qualities you may well rightly admire is a sufficient reason for assuming that a man has no merit in his own *métier*. If a man can be a good dentist though he is beastly to his wife and unable to appreciate Shakespeare, might not a man be a good general and lack the moral qualities Tolstoy praises? Reflection on this last example brings out how complex the problem of truth in literature is. Factual discrepancies may not disturb us, at least not when we feel that they are genuine errors, such as the most scrupulous historian might make, and not tendentious distortions. But we might well be disturbed if all the facts are right but there is a discrepancy between the moral judgement a writer makes about the persons and actions he presents and our own. In this respect the issue of 'truth' applies to pure fiction, to history proper and to 'mixed' works like *War and Peace*. I think the problem in Tolstoy's case, at least as far as my own judgement is concerned, is, however, not so much disagreement with his moral judgement of Napoleon, but the sense that he has let this moral judgement distort his presentation of historical events and the part Napoleon actually played in them.

Perhaps one solution for Tolstoy would have been to advance the concept of a hierarchy of greatness. This was the course adopted by a famous American Unitarian writer and preacher of the early nineteenth century whose pacifism had some influence on the later Tolstoy's teaching: William Ellery Channing. Indeed Channing's combination of influence from the eighteenth-century enlightenment with a commitment to Christianity is in many ways similar to Tolstoy's own. When Sir Walter Scott brought out his biography of Napoleon, Channing reviewed it in an essay entitled 'Remarks on the Life and Character of Napoleon Bonaparte'. In this essay Channing sets up three orders of greatness, *moral* greatness or magnanimity, of which 'we see not a trace in Napoleon', *intellectual* greatness in science and art, and last and least, greatness of *action*, the power of conceiving bold plans and bringing such machinery and energy to bear on them that 'great outward effects' are accomplished. Channing says of Napoleon: 'All must concede to him a sublime power of action, an energy equal to great effects'. Channing thus avoids Tolstoy's mistake of denying Napoleon the power to subdue men to his will. He does not, like Tolstoy, imply that Napoleon must have been a bad general because he was a bad man. At the same time he anticipates Tolstoy in his moral condemnation of Napoleon in particular and of militarism in general.

Tolstoy, in fact, is not just attacking Napoleon in *War and Peace*, but the phenomenon of Caesarism or one-man dictatorship in general, and more than that even, the moral theory underlying

Caesarism, namely the theory that there is one morality for the ruler, or exceptional man, and another morality for the rest of us. It may have been the contemporary adulation in some quarters of such figures as Napoleon III and Bismarck which irritated Tolstoy into making this attack. In this matter Tolstoy is in agreement with Dostoevsky, whose *Crime and Punishment* appeared while he was writing *War and Peace*. Dostoevsky portrays Raskolnikov as led into crime, and, worse than crime, sin, by his worship of Napoleon and the idea of the great man. Both Tolstoy and Dostoevsky take an antithetical line to that veneration for men of will that Nietzsche was to adopt very soon afterwards. In 1859 Tolstoy had noted in his diary that 'Christ did not impose, but revealed, the moral law which for ever remains the standard of good and evil.' [23] Whereas Nietzsche was explicitly to reject this moral law Tolstoy evokes it at the end of the eloquent passage on false greatness which follows his account of Borodino :

'*C'est grand!*' say the historians, and there no longer exists either good or evil, but only '*grand*' and 'not *grand*'. *Grand* is good, not *grand* is bad. *Grand* is the characteristic, in their conception, of some special animals called 'heroes'. And Napoleon escaping home in a warm fur coat and leaving to perish those who were not merely his comrades but were (in his opinion) men he had brought there, feels *que c'est grand*, and his soul is tranquil. . . .

And it occurs to no one that to admit a greatness not commensurable with the standard of right and wrong is merely to admit one's own nothingness and immeasurable meanness.

For us, with the standard of good and evil given us by Christ, no human actions are incommensurable. And there is no greatness there where simplicity, goodness, and truth are absent. (XIV, xviii, 337–338)

Back in 1857, however, Tolstoy had noted in his diary : 'The Gospel words "judge not" are profoundly true in art : relate, portray, but do not judge.' [24] Many years later he was to take the text stating that vengeance is God's not man's as the epigraph for *Anna Karenina* and to make the reluctance to condemn others a feature of the most morally sensitive characters in the book. Is there any inconsistency between the condemnation of the worship of false greatness from *War and Peace* on the one hand and the 1857 passage about not judging and many similar passages from *Anna Karenina* on the other? Is Tolstoy himself not falling into the moral pharisaism which tends to accompany all censoriousness? I do not think so, for Tolstoy's judgement is not a first order judgement about the conduct of others, but a second order judgement about the false standard underlying the judgements of others. He judges not others, but the basis of the judgements made by others. Moreover in doing so he appeals to something outside himself, a norm not imposed, but revealed, by Jesus.

Tolstoy's account of Borodino undoubtedly makes a fitting artistic climax to his novel. In retrospect the battle had come to be seen as the high point of a great national struggle against the West; and in the book it marks the union of the 'war' side with the 'peace' or domestic side, because Pierre, a civilian, is used as a focus of awareness for much that goes on and because the battle has such a shattering effect on the civilian population of Moscow and its surroundings, including the Rostov family. It is at Borodino that Prince Andrew receives the fatal wound which ultimately leads to reconciliation with Natasha before his death in circumstances which enable Andrew's sister Princess Mary to draw close to Natasha whom she had previously regarded coldly. Borodino also admirably suited the purposes of Tolstoy the moralist. After battles on the scale of Stalingrad and Kursk and horrors like the concentration camps and Hiroshima it may not seem so shattering to us, but we must remember that for the time it involved a huge number of men in a single engagement (about 250,000) and that the number of those killed and wounded on both sides has been estimated at the huge proportion of almost one-third of the combatants involved (about 70,000).[25] This, for one day's fighting, is carnage on the scale of the 1914–1918 war. The primitiveness of medical resources (no anaesthetics, for example) must also be borne in mind. Commentators agree that both armies were drawn up in unusually deep and crowded formations which made tactical finesse peculiarly difficult, with bloody frontal assaults by the French on prepared Russian positions and much use of artillery by both sides. This made it 'butchery' on an extraordinary scale. All these facts have prepared the ground for a sympathetic response when at the close of his account Tolstoy steps forward with something of the authority of an Old Testament prophet in his call to repent:

Over the whole field, previously so gaily beautiful with the glitter of bayonets and cloudlets of smoke in the morning sun, there now spread a mist of damp and smoke and a strange . . . smell of saltpetre and blood. Clouds gathered, and drops of rain began to fall on the dead and wounded, on the frightened, exhausted, and hesitating men, as if to say: 'Enough, men! Enough! Cease . . . bethink yourselves! What are you doing?' (X, xxxix, 543)

In many ways it is the atypicality of Borodino which stands out if we set it by, say, Marlborough's campaigns, Suvorov's tactics in Italy against the armies of the Directory, Napoleon's own Italian campaigns, Wellington's tactics in the Peninsular War, or even

Austerlitz as it appears in Tolstoy's own account which shows Wey-rother's poor tactics and Kutúzov's slowness as contributing to Napoleon's victory. The atypicality of Borodino lies in the absence of those tactical strokes which are decisive without being unduly bloody.[26] But because Borodino is atypical the truth of the *general* theory as to the unimportance of commanders and tactics that Tolstoy undoubtedly uses it to demonstrate is gravely impaired. He could have thrown all the stress on the anomaly of Borodino and the difficulty of finding a philosophy of war, so to speak, to cope with it. But, unfortunately for his theorizing, he takes the very opposite course. He uses this exceptional battle as evidence for his *general* thesis that the will of one man cannot make decisions which affect the course of events one way or the other, a thesis which, as we have seen, not even his own account of Borodino really bears out. If this thesis is an empirical one (and his arguments and his using examples as evidence for it indicate that it starts out as an empirical thesis even if like many others it turns under pressure into an 'unfalsifiable' and thus 'metaphysical' one) then it is false and shown to be so by the considerations I have already advanced.

Tolstoy gives us, then, like any historian, statements of fact which can be true or false. If we feel they are false because of human inadvertence and errors such as anyone (including a professional historian) might make, we are not disturbed; but if we feel that facts are being distorted (or relevant facts suppressed) in the service of establishing a theory or an ideology, or both, then we are uneasy. Next Tolstoy gives us inferences as to what happened or did not happen, and why, and these inferences, like any inferences, are open to charges of being valid or invalid. I have suggested that Tolstoy gets involved in self-contradictions and *non sequiturs* on this level. Finally, by various means, Tolstoy conveys to us his attitudes to the actions of the characters he presents and to the grounds on which those actions have been assessed by others, and we feel these attitudes appropriate or inappropriate as the case may be.

This question of the attitudes conveyed concerns not only the problem of *historical* truth in *War and Peace* but also the wider problem of truth as it concerns Tolstoy's portrayal of human life in general, a consideration which touches on both the historical and fictional materials in the work. I want to consider, in particular, the nature of Tolstoy's portrayal of suffering in a work largely devoted to showing the impact of war on human life. But it must be borne in mind that it was not just war which brought Tolstoy face to face with the problem of the place of suffering in the moral economy of things, the so-called theodicy problem. War simply afforded some of the most spectacular and dramatic illustrations of that problem.

The most important feature of Tolstoy's portrayal of suffering was noticed by Renato Poggioli when he remarked that cruelty in Tolstoy is always portrayed in such a way as to make us feel the situation of the victim.[27] There is a tremendous contrast here with such twentieth-century 'tough' writers as Babel and Hemingway. We feel the poignant situation of the victim in the portrayal of Pierre's experiences as a prisoner, and, most strikingly, in the account of the lynching of the scapegoat figure Vereshchagin by the Moscow mob.[28] But Tolstoy's ability to make us feel the victim's situation is never accompanied by the masochism we find in Dostoevsky, or by a cheap indignation against the people who inflict the suffering. On the contrary, Tolstoy has a tendency to show that the people who inflict the suffering are, in a sense, victims too, victims of circumstances and temperament. A good example here is Count Rostopchin, the highly nervous Governor of Moscow, who gives Vereshchagin to the crowd as a victim. Tolstoy often shows those who cause suffering as affected by compunction and guilt, either at the time or subsequently. This is perhaps why his portrait of Davout's sparing of Pierre has been found unconvincing.[29] Underlying Tolstoy's portrayal of suffering there seems to be a thesis which I would phrase as follows: 'No normal human being deliberately inflicts suffering on another so long as he (or she) really recognizes that other as a fellow human being.' But it should be evident that the concession renders the thesis unfalsifiable (and in that sense 'metaphysical') because whenever suffering is inflicted we can always claim that those who inflicted it did not recognize their victims as human beings like themselves in all relevant respects. The reasons for such a lack of recognition could of course arise from traditions, education or pressure of circumstances, or a combination of all three. Tolstoy's need to believe his thesis may, however, have contributed to the intensity and merit of *War and Peace*, just as his need to believe in the incompatible combination of Napoleon's ineffectuality and guilt may have done.

Moreover, no reader of such a first-hand account of the fighting in 1812 as that given by General Sir Robert Wilson in his *Journal* can doubt that Tolstoy greatly underplays the cruelties inflicted on the French prisoners during the retreat, despite his suggestive hints about the hardness of Dolokhov, the partisan leader who rescues Pierre. Tolstoy tells us nothing about peasants such as those Wilson saw beating out the brains of prisoners to the time of a song.[30] We do not hear of such characters as the village elder Shklovsky mentions,[31] who asked for advice about new ways of killing a man, as he had tried out so many on the French. Undoubtedly Tolstoy's reticence in portraying cruelty was partly due to the artistic reasons outlined above, but as far as the underplaying of peasant cruelty in particular is concerned, I am convinced that Tolstoy was still strongly under the influence of the attitude he had expressed in his diary in 1853 when he wrote:

The common people are so far above us by the work they accomplish and the privations in their lives, that it seems wrong for one of us to write anything bad about them.[32]

As to the question of the infliction of suffering and of conscious cruelty in general, Tolstoy's implicit thesis that such suffering is always inflicted unwillingly deep down, does not stand up as an empirical one. Nevertheless it may be that his work does not give us as distorted a picture of the part these things play in the general economy of human life as a whole as does the work of those who deliberately emphasize such elements. Tolstoy's artistic sense may have been sure here, for the interest that readers have in stories of torture and suffering, whatever their avowed motives, is rarely a 'pure' one.

Tolstoy's reticence in his portrayal of physical violence (so different from the procedure of twentieth-century writers) also derives from a kind of classicism that was both instinctive to him and reinforced by his admiration for Homer. He was happy to accept the truth that art is a revelation of life and not, as academics, aesthetes and so-called 'realists' suppose, a substitute for it, for brutal realism often arises as a reaction against academicism and aestheticism. Tolstoy has an inborn sense that art is the product of a spirit that has grasped the energetic diversity of life in a single sustained intuition; and, paradoxical as it may seem, it is his very grasp of the autonomy of art which makes for the 'lifelikeness' of his work. He can represent violence, lust and cruelty in such a way that not only does no vicarious indulgence in them arise, but we feel purged of them as we read.

There is a most important and artistically fruitful tension in Tolstoy's work which arises out of the clash in him between two ideals: the ideal of the primacy of right conduct and the ideal of the primacy of beauty, what Matthew Arnold called Hebraism and Hellenism. Tolstoy's moral attitude to war, for example, is already fully present (as we have seen) in *Sevastopol in May 1855*, and it is one of righteous condemnation from a Christian standpoint. At the same time, however, no reader of his works can doubt that Tolstoy felt to the full the 'poetic' beauty of war that occurs at certain moments when a heightening of consciousness takes place in the participants. It was this poetic beauty to which Tolstoy immediately responded in Homer's *Iliad*. On 25 August 1857 he wrote in his diary:

Finished reading the incredibly delightful conclusion of the *Iliad* . . . After the *Iliad* read the Gospels, which I have not done for a long time. How could Homer not know that goodness is love! It was a revelation.[33]

This passage focuses the 'clash of ideals' very clearly. Tolstoy was so impressed by Homer that, after he had finished *War and Peace*, he started to learn Greek in order to appreciate him more fully. I think there is a lot in Aylmer Maude's suggestion [34] that the intense melancholy which overcame him about that time owed some of its force to the powerful opposition between two rival views of life which were both immensely attractive to him: the view of Homer and the view of Jesus. Three decades later, when he wrote *What is Art?*, we find Tolstoy still opposing the Greek discovery of the meaning of life in earthly happiness, beauty and strength to the Christian view that it lies in renunciation, humility and the love of others. This shows how deep and persistent was his sense of the contrast between the two views. There is certainly a strain in Tolstoy which sympathizes with his own Prince Andrew's hatred of the French and glories Homerically in the strength which threw them out, but there is also an equally powerful strain which sympathizes with the efforts of Princess Mary to turn her brother's thoughts away from revenge to Christian forgiveness. As R. F. Christian rightly says: 'To Tolstoy no war—not even a 'just' defensive war—can be anything but a human tragedy.'[35] Homer, no doubt, could appreciate the tragedy of Hector, Andromache, Priam and the defeated Trojans; but even if Homer's work portrays many situations in which men must enact hell, he was basically reconciled to life on earth *as it is*. Nietzsche, indeed, thought that the fact that Homer made his gods so like men in their loves and hates was not only a kind of celebration of earthly life, but the best justification of it, and, in fact, the only true solution of the theodicy problem. The contrast between Tolstoy and Homer in this respect comes out in Tolstoy's protest *against* life on earth as it is, a protest which arises from his Christianity. Tolstoy would have seen the point of Ivan Karamazov's protest that, given the conditions of human life, he wants to 'return God his ticket'; and, indeed, Tolstoy himself furnished the great psychologist William James with an example of what James called 'the sick soul'. Tolstoy saw earthly life as in need of redemption and salvation, whereas Nietzsche condemned the very notion of such a need.

In considering where the truth in this momentous matter lies, it is necessary to begin by defining the theodicy problem more closely. The term 'theodicy' comes from two Greek words, *theos*, meaning god, and *diké*, meaning justice. The traditional theodicy problem was that of reconciling the belief in a divine justice of some kind with the indubitable existence of evil. The problem is presented in dramatic form in the *Prometheus* of Aeschylus and in the *Book of Job*. With the spread of monotheism and the development of the view that the one God's attributes include omnipotence and benevolence (which Homer's rival gods, of course, lack) the problem became even more acute, for it seems logically inconsistent to assume that God can be omnipotent and benevolent if evil exists. Both Milton and Leibniz in the seventeenth century used various traditional arguments and distinctions to try to resolve the difficulties, but by the eighteenth century the traditional arguments seem to have become unacceptable, for a variety of reasons, to men as different as the deist Voltaire, the atheist Hume and the devout Christian Dr Johnson. In the nineteenth century Mill argued in his discussion of Theism that if there is a God and he is benevolent, then the existence of evil shows that he cannot be omnipotent. Nietzsche, as we have seen, held that the problem should not arise for a healthy creature. He thought that the questioning of the meaning of life was an impertinence on the part of a being who was a small part of existence and therefore could not hope to comprehend existence as a whole: 'One must reach out,' he wrote, 'and try to grasp this astonishing *finesse, that the value of life cannot be estimated*. Not by a living man, because he is a party to the dispute, indeed its object, and not the judge of it; not by a dead one, for another reason.' [36] To question the meaning of life was, for Nietzsche, a sign of impotence and decadence, whether such questioning was done by Socrates or by one of Nietzsche's own contemporaries. What, then, is the view of this matter implicit in *War and Peace*?

For this we have to interrogate the experience of those portrayed as the most sensitive characters in the book—Prince Andrew, Princess Mary, Pierre, Natasha, and along with them the commentary of the narrator—and, if we do, it emerges that the narrator holds the view that one of the hall marks of sensitivity is that the sensitive person cannot fail, at some stage, to be aroused to grapple with the problem of the suffering that the economy of things seems calculated to inflict. A battle such as Borodino with its horrible pain and its thousands of dead and maimed brings this home in spectacular form. But Tolstoy is quite clear that so long as *one* sentient being suffers amid the happiness of others, the theodicy problem is raised.

Princess Lise's death, bearing the child of a husband grown

cold to her, in the house of a frightening cantankerous father-in-law, raises the theodicy problem just as much as Borodino. Her death deeply troubles the thoughtful and sensitive Princess Mary (whose consciousness Tolstoy uses as a dramatic focus of this problem) so that she even argues herself at one point into the notion that it was perhaps better for Lise to have died because she would probably have made a bad mother. Tolstoy is well aware that such a view would be grotesque if offered as a justification of Providence, but he treats it with a tender rather than scornful irony because of his dramatic sympathy with the inevitable human need to come to terms with the often cruel nature of things.

We saw in the chapter on historicism that Tolstoy himself occasionally capitulated to a sort of Deistic Providentialism. But this only shows that he, like his own Princess Mary, sometimes resorted to desperate remedies in order to come to terms with an intractable problem. Borodino may have enabled Prince Andrew to forgive his bitterest enemy Anatole Kuragin and that is an important moment in both their lives and gives the event a meaning for them (just as Princess Mary imposes a meaning on the death of Lise), but there is no suggestion that this 'justifies' Borodino in terms of an 'objective' meaning in some quasi-Hegelian world-historical plan. Neither is there a suggestion that the ultimate defeat of the French does so. The notion that God stepped in to hurl Napoleon down at the height of his power may sometimes cross our minds as we read *War and Peace*, but I don't think the work can be read naturally as an unproblematic vindication of Providence. As Sir Isaiah Berlin rightly said, Tolstoy felt that 'all previous attempts at a rational theodicy . . . were grotesque absurdities'.[37]

What Tolstoy shows us, then, is the truth that man as an *active* dramatic being has to come to terms with situations which he cannot encompass as a *thinking* theoretic being. There is a measure of agreement with Nietzsche so far. In the end this is an area where we, as struggling finite beings in an infinite drama, are just as involved in making decisions as in registering truths. Given the nature of things, are we right even in wanting God to exist, quite apart from the question whether or not we believe He does? And it is here, in this area of decision, that Tolstoy parts company with a 'vitalist' like Nietzsche and sees God as the 'natural' assumption of a troubled spirit in a material world. At the same time Tolstoy indulges us neither in the Hegelian complacency that everything we do is ultimately reasonable nor in the Existentialist complacency that everything we do is ultimately absurd. He shows us the infinite complexity of existence on the one hand and the need of finite individuals to make sense of it on the other. When Princess Mary argues herself into thinking that some good possibly came from Lise's death [38] Tolstoy presents her view in a larger, and, in effect, ironic perspective as an example of the difficulties and bad arguments to which even the good are driven in order to come to terms with what strikes them as unjust suffering. Tolstoy himself rarely gives a dramatized sanction to the quasi-Hegelian notion that good comes out of evil by a kind of cunning hidden 'necessity', and in so far as his treatment of Napoleon does this I have already been critical of it as showing a lapse into historicism. He never sanctions even for an instant the still more pernicious notion that the sufferer secretly desires his suffering, that as D. H. Lawrence's Birkin puts it, 'a man who is murderable is a man who in a profound if hidden lust desires to be murdered'.[39] Birkin's view is the most perverted form the theodicy can take, apart perhaps from the ridiculous view pilloried by Dr Johnson, namely that sufferings may be justified by the enjoyment they afford to 'higher' beings. Tolstoy avoids both the grosser and the subtler pitfalls in his dealings with the theodicy problem. The fact that he seems to have achieved a human centrality in this difficult matter, and that most of the judgements implicit in his dramatization strike us as true, is surely one of the reasons why we think he is a great writer.

Chapter 10

What is *War and Peace*?

Before we can criticize something we must know what it is. Tolstoy himself denied that *War and Peace* was a novel. In 'Some Words about War and Peace' [1] (1868) he wrote:

What is *War and Peace*? It is not a novel, even less is it a poem, and still less an historical chronicle. *War and Peace* is what the author wished and was able to express in the form in which it is expressed.

This is an interesting statement, but Tolstoy was only able to make it because the novel, like the epic before it, is not a single form, but, in the words of Scholes and Kellogg's *The Nature of Narrative*, 'an unstable compound' of mimesis, history, romance and fable, just as the epic was a compound of 'primitive legend, folk-tale, and sacred myth'.[2] Thus *War and Peace* includes history in Tolstoy's critical attitude to accounts of 1805 and 1812, myth in the form of Pierre's preoccupation with Freemasonry and the Apocalypse, and romance in the use of such coincidences as Prince Andrew and his enemy Anatole Kuragin ending up in the same operating theatre after Borodino, and Nicholas Rostov being on hand to rescue Princess Mary from the restive peasants at Bogucharovo, as well as much representational mimesis of character and action.

Tolstoy's friend the critic Nikolai Strakhov wrote of *War and Peace*:

We see all that he describes and hear all that he is informed of . . . the author tells nothing from himself; he leads his characters forward straightaway and makes them speak, feel and act.[3]

It is not true, of course, that Tolstoy, 'tells nothing from himself', but when we compare him with Thackeray, Dickens, George Eliot or Trollope, the exaggeration seems pardonable. Certainly in Fielding, Thackeray, Stendhal, George Eliot and Trollope there is often an ironic distance between the narrator and his story, created by the commentary. They cultivate an intimacy with their audience at the expense of their intimacy with the story. This is not true of the 'authoritative and reliable narrator' of the *Iliad*, say, or of the narrators of the stories in the *Old Testament*, and it is not true of Tolstoy either. He gives us a unique combination of the 'naive objectivity' of the oral narrator with the interest in detail characteristic of realism. This is the reason for our trust in his presentation.

But what about the portrayal of historical events and the polemic accompanying it? Doesn't this break that unity which Manzoni, for example, claimed was essential to art, by causing an uneasy shift between fact and fiction? Tolstoy solves this problem by building into the book the thesis that *all* narrative involves fiction because, as Nicholas Rostov comes to realize, 'nothing happens in war at all as we can imagine or relate it' (IX, xii, 312). As Scholes and Kellogg put it:

The convergence of the novel with the history, biography, and autobiography has resulted not so much from impatience with the story-teller's fantasy as from a modern skepticism of knowing anything about human affairs in an entirely objective (non-fictional) way. Science seems to have demonstrated that Aristotle's distinction between history and fiction was one of degree not of kind. All knowing and all telling are subject to the conventions of art.[4]

Tolstoy himself speaks in 'Some Words About *War and Peace*' of the 'necessary lie' involved in every description of a battle in which a few words must stand proxy for 'the actions of thousands of men spread over several miles, and subject to most violent moral excitement under the influence of fear, shame, and death'. Tolstoy seeks to make knowledge by description as vivid as knowledge by acquaintance while remaining conscious of the fact that the two types of knowledge can never be identical.

But, it may be urged, is not this just the point? The historian does not delude himself into thinking that he can give us anything more than knowledge by description. Yes, Tolstoy could reply, but in so far as the historian tries to convey his knowledge in narrative, he is subject to the conventions of narrative art and there he is far from having an advantage over the novelist. This may be so, but it does not affect the question of truth. Victor Shklovsky claims that we must simply regard Napoleon and Kutúzov as invented characters like Natasha.[5] This is not possible because Tolstoy makes truth claims within the book. Scholes and Kellogg write:

The novel's combination of factual and fictional elements is not naive and instinctive but sophisticated and deliberate, made possible by the development of a concept called realism, which provides a rationale for a marriage that rationalism had seemed to forbid.[6]

But in the particular case of *War and Peace* this general defence of the realistic convention will not do because of the peculiar nature of Tolstoy's presentation and use of historical materials. Perhaps we will just have to admit, in the end, that as far as its use of such material is concerned, *War and Peace* is a fascinating 'sport', *sui generis*, but, possibly, flawed as art.

We must, however, also consider Tolstoy's presentation of those materials and characters that are unproblematically fictional. Here we need first to dispose of the question of 'prototypes' of the fictional characters. Was Natasha really based on Tolstoy's attractive young sister-in-law Tatyana Kuzminskaya? Was the whole domestic side of the work based on the literature of family memoirs, as Boris Eikhenbaum suggested? [7] Victor Shklovsky takes a more rigidly 'Formalist' line than his friend Eikenbaum and denies that prototypes exist. His 'proof' is that different people recognize themselves in the same character and that Tolstoy himself saw Tatyana in the heroine of Mrs Braddon's novel *Aurora Floyd*.[8] Shklovsky seems to think that a prototype claim is an identity claim. But in claiming that Tatyana Kuzminskaya was a prototype of Natasha one need be claiming no more than that Tolstoy's admiration for Tatyana's vitality and youth contributed to his portrait of Natasha, but contributed along with his reading and other experiences. Shklovsky, like a good Formalist, thinks that when Tolstoy entered his study and started to write, he closed the door on the world and on prototypes, and simply became intrigued by such problems as whether it would be a good artistic move to make the gifted young man whom he envisaged having killed in battle into the son of old Bolkonsky. But when Tolstoy published his writings they were no longer confined to his study and Tolstoy did not expect his readers to take exactly the same kind of interest in reading them that he had taken in the problems of composing them *and nothing more*, which is the sort of interest Shklovsky thinks readers *should* take. Eikhenbaum did not intend to imply that *War and Peace* is *identical* with a set of memoirs. He merely wanted to claim that parts of it have an affinity with memoirs in their intimacy of detail and atmosphere, are *memoir-like*. The omniscient stance of the narrator precludes the necessarily limited viewpoint of the memoir writer, but Tolstoy tries to convey details about everything with the easy familiarity that the memoir writer could only have about a limited number of things.

Let us look in more detail at the first paragraph of narration in the novel. It immediately follows Anna Pavlovna Scherer's 'hostessy' outburst to Prince Vasili Kuragin on the subject of Buonaparte as Antichrist. That is a theme to be developed more profoundly later in Pierre's experiences in 1812:

It was in July 1805, and the speaker was the well-known Anna Pavlovna Scherer, maid of honour and favourite of the Empress Marya Fedorovna. With these words she greeted Prince Vasili, a man of high rank and importance, who was the first to arrive at her reception. Anna Pavlovna had had a cough for some days. She was, as she said, suffering from *la grippe*: *grippe* being then a new word in St Petersburg, used only by the *élite*. (I, i, 3)

The 'hostessy' tone of Anna Pavlovna in the speech immediately preceding this (which opens the book *in medias res* so to speak) has already 'placed' her to some degree. How can we take her reference to Buonaparte as Antichrist seriously (though the idea itself is later to become very serious for Pierre) when in the same breath she speaks of an *homme de société* like Prince Vasili as her 'faithful slave'? The narrator steps in with a setting of the scene which is suffused with a sense of complete intimacy with these people and with the well-oiled machinery of their lives. There is no hint, as with supposedly satirical 'high life' novels (one thinks of Thackeray), of a hypocritical pride at moving in the best circles, or being 'where the action is'. On the contrary, the narrator seems to see with a clear vision that all this 'high rank and importance' is mere self-importance. Proust, who knew about such things if anyone did, once wrote:

With Tolstoi, the account of an evening party in high society is dominated by the mind of the author, and, as Aristotle would say, we are purged of our worldliness while we read it: with Balzac, we feel almost a worldly satisfaction at taking part in it.[9]

Elsewhere Proust said that in Balzac's work 'humanity is judged by a literary man anxious to write a great book; in Tolstoi, by a serene god'.[10] In that phrase 'a serene god' he captured much of the tone of the narrator of *War and Peace*.

It would, then, be absurd to take too literally Strakhov's remark that 'the author tells nothing from himself', for *War and Peace* has many passages which give us the narrator's view of things direct, and not just the view of an Andrew or a Natasha. Sometimes the tone in which this view is expressed modulates from the serenity noted by Proust to one of prophetic condemnation as in chapter xxxix of book X with its magisterial survey of the battlefield of Borodino leading in to an attack on war. But Strakhov's remark can, without forcing, be interpreted as meaning that Tolstoy does not draw attention to himself as narrator, but keeps his eye on the object. At the end of that paragraph on Anna Pavlovna Scherer we know what the author thinks of her and of the salon world which she represents, and yet his evident hostility does not make us distrust the details he gives. On the contrary the details somehow seem to have a kind of autonomy of their own and his attitude to them to be entirely fitting.

Let us now look at chapter xx of book I as an example of Tolstoy's art.[11] This chapter gives us a picture of life in the Rostov household. The older members of the family are playing cards. The younger ones are singing round the piano. Natasha goes off to look for Sonya and eventually finds her on the chest in the passage. 'The chest in the passage was the place of mourning for the younger female generation in the Rostov household.' This is a good example of the kind of detail which we associate with the memoir writer, but which comes here from the omniscient narrator. Sonya is upset, as she explains to Natasha, because her cousin Nicholas is going to the war and moreover she fears (quite rightly) that Nicholas's mother, the Countess, thinks her socially beneath him. She is worried that Natasha's starchy sister Vera will reveal the secret of their love to the Countess. Natasha manages to cheer her up and in the course of doing so remarks on how funny the 'fat Pierre' is and how happy she feels. They return to the singing. Then dancing begins and Pierre, who is bored with a conversation he is engaged in about politics, is glad to dance with Natasha who, in turn, is thrilled at dancing with a grown-up and acts the part of a society lady. The older people now join in, and Count Rostov, like some jovial Pickwick, dances the *Daniel Cooper* he had loved in his youth with the awkward Marya Dmitrievna, *le terrible dragon*, to everyone's delight and her exhaustion.

It might seem that all we have here is an account by a narrator who makes no connections, has no sense of composition and leaves us with incoherence. But it is precisely *because* the rapidly moving narrator does not dwell on any single detail as portentously significant, but selects all the details to build up a single impression of a household where old and young (with the possible exception of poor Sonya with her fears) are in harmony, that we have coherence. For example the song Nicholas sings is an album love-song entirely appropriate to the social context and to the atmosphere of calf love that grips all the younger generation. When Nicholas comes to the words

> in this world there's one
> Who still is thinking but of thee

we know that they refer to the love between him and Sonya. The youth/age motif runs through the chapter as a binding thread. Natasha looks forward to being grown up and the Count looks back to 'how we used to dance in our time'. The most unifying element, however, is the narrative tone which arises from the narrator's relation to what he is telling. In this case that relation is one of genial interest and love with a complete absence of spite and irony, and it is consistently maintained throughout the chapter. Tolstoy himself gave us the best clue to the kind of unity which we must look for in his own works in his essay on Maupassant:

The cement which binds any artistic production into one whole and therefore produces the illusion of being a reflection of life, is not the unity of persons or situations, but the unity of the author's own independent moral relation to his subject.[12]

When we go on to set chapter xx of book I into the wider context of *War and Peace* as a whole the unity the narrator has given his material becomes even more astonishing. As John Hagan has pointed out the youth/age contrast in the book is cut across by the more inclusive contrast between 'Real life' and 'Artificial life'.[13] The Rostov household, young and old, in homely traditional Moscow, gives us 'Real life' as contrasted with Anna Pavlovna Scherer's salon in synthetic, westernized St Petersburg which gives us 'Artificial life'. Pierre serves to link the two, for he had been present at the conversations about diplomacy at the salon where, to everyone's embarrassment, he had grown 'unnaturally' heated about them, while here at the Rostovs, by contrast, talk about politics and diplomacy only bores him and he wants to dance with Natasha. Pierre also becomes the link with what follows for there is an immediate transition in the next chapter from the gaiety of the Rostov household to the gloom of the house where his father, the old Count Bezukhov, is dying. That death prompts even the frivolous Prince Vasili to say to Pierre with 'a sincerity and weakness Pierre had never observed before': 'Ah, my friend! . . . How often we sin, how much we deceive, and all for what? I am near sixty, dear friend . . . I too. . . . All will end in death, all! Death is awful . . .' (I, xxiv, 109). The exuberant young life opening out at the Rostovs will have to meet and cope with this very question 'all for what?' which tormented Tolstoy himself to the end of his life. Natasha comes to terms with it by marrying Pierre after nearly falling for 'Artificial life' as embodied in Anatole Kuragin, the son of the very Prince Vasili who speaks the above words to Pierre. Anatole is the brother of the beautiful and dissolute Helene, Pierre's first wife. Natasha is saved from her elopement by Marya Dmitrievna Akhrosimova, *le terrible dragon*, the very same woman who puffs her way through the *Daniel Cooper* with Natasha's father Count Rostov in chapter xx of book I. It is also in this very chapter that Tolstoy has planted a hint of the affinity between Natasha and Pierre which, after many vicissitudes, is to lead to their marriage.

I have spoken of unity of tone and hinted at the use of family connections as a natural and unforced means of building up the plot as opposed, say, to the use of the kind of devices we associate with the 'mystery' novel such as *Little Dorrit* or *Our Mutual Friend*. There is another means by which Tolstoy builds the heterogeneous material of the work into a unity, and this is his articulation of what Proust calls the 'law of reason or unreason' by which human beings try to come to terms with things. Proust writes of *War and Peace*:

This is not the work of an observing eye but of a thinking mind. Every so-called stroke of observation is simply the clothing, the proof, the instance, of a law, a law of reason or of unreason which the novelist has laid bare . . . one feels oneself moving in a throng of laws. . . .[14]

Moreover when we have laid *War and Peace* down we can observe these same laws of which Proust speaks at work in our own lives, played out as they are in a social world that is about as different from that of nineteenth-century Russia as any social world could be. We find something of the same with Proust's own great novel, for although the social world of *la belle époque* which it describes has vanished for ever, Proust's profound understanding of love, jealousy and illusion remains.

R. F. Christian shows how Tolstoy manages to convey a sense of the uniqueness and individuality of every human being while at the same time giving a sense of the predictability of much human behaviour. He writes:

Nobody who has read *War and Peace* carefully could fail to notice the frequency of such words or phrases as, for example, 'peculiar to' (*svoistvenny*), 'simple' (*prostoy*), 'natural' (*estestvenny*), 'as is always the case' (*kak vsegda byvaet*), or 'all this must be so' (*eto dolzhno byt' tak*) . . . The crux of Tolstoy's thought is that every human being has features which mark him off from every other human being—hence the frequency of the word 'peculiar to'— while at the same time human beings in the mass exhibit a sameness, a uniformity, a predictability, an inevitability which is conveyed in Tolstoy's language by the repetition of 'as is always the case', 'as all people do', or 'all this must be so'.[15]

But there is a danger here. The passage might be taken as implying that the 'throng of laws' of which Proust speaks can only be seen at work in the 'swarm life'. It is crucial to note that Tolstoy shows these laws at work in the individual life as well as in life in the mass.

For example: the young Nicholas Rostov is wounded in the cavalry attack at Schön Grabern. Suddenly he realizes that the men in front of him are Frenchmen—enemies:

'Who are they? Why are they running? Can they be coming at me? And why? To kill me? *Me* whom every one is so fond of?' He remembered his mother's love for him, and his family's, and his friends', and the enemy's intention to kill him seemed impossible. (II, xix, 245)

The reader has come to know Nicholas Rostov as a unique individual and yet immediately recognizes that he would feel just as Nicholas does if he were in Nicholas's circumstances and understands at once the fact that 'one single sentiment, that of fear for his young and happy life, possessed his whole being'. Then there is Nicholas's mother Countess Rostov and her thoughts when a letter arrives from Nicholas at the front telling her how he has been wounded and made an officer:

How strange, how extraordinary, how joyful it seemed, that her son, the scarcely perceptible motion of whose tiny limbs she had felt twenty years ago within her, . . . should now be away in a foreign land amid strange surroundings, a manly warrior doing some kind of man's work of his own without help or guidance. The universal experience of ages, showing that children do grow imperceptibly from the cradle to manhood, did not exist for the countess. Her son's growth towards manhood at each of its stages had seemed as extraordinary to her as if there had never existed the millions of human beings who grew up in the same way. . . . (III, vi, 308)

This is one of the countless passages in which Tolstoy makes us perceive what we already know, namely how mothers feel, but brings it home to us with such force and specificity that it seems as if we are grasping it for the first time. We get that combination of the familiar and the new which Dr Johnson saw as the sign of genius.

The most important of the 'laws' which Tolstoy shows at work is the law of self-deception. Whenever we try to grasp the significance of our actions or those of others we distort it in accordance with our interest, or, as Schopenhauer put it, man '*knows* himself in consequence of, and in accordance with, the nature of his will, instead of *willing* in consequence of, and according to, his knowing'.[16] Jacques Rivière once wrote: 'In contact with Proust, we realized to what extent man is an artist in deceiving himself about himself'.[17] The sentence applies even more appropriately to Tolstoy, for whereas we feel Proust sometimes writes merely to *illustrate* a prior theory, we feel that Tolstoy makes use of theory to make intelligible a mass of detail which yet has a kind of autonomy from it. This is true mainly of Tolstoy's dealings with fictional material. He does sometimes distort historical material in the service of his views, as we saw in the last chapter.

Here are some examples from *War and Peace* of man's artistry in self-deception at work. Boris Drubetskoy's mother Anna Mikhaylovna tells the Rostovs that Pierre's father 'remembered everything and everybody at the last and had spoken such pathetic words to the son', and that Pierre 'had been pitiful to see . . .' (I, xxv, 110), because that is how a touching death-bed scene *ought* to be. We feel that she has come to believe this herself either before (or even as) she deceives the Rostovs. The narrator has already told us the truth in the preceding chapter. In fact old Count Bezukhov had been distorted, twitching and incoherent and Pierre had felt terror as well as pity. Natasha Rostov looks into her mirror at Christmas hoping to see her future betrothed as superstition promises. Seeing nothing, she asks Sonya to look, and Sonya, not wanting to disappoint her, says to herself, 'But why shouldn't I say I saw something? Others do see! Besides, who can tell whether I saw anything or not?' (VII, xii, 159). Much later in the book 'what she had invented then seemed to her now as real as any other recollection' (XII, viii, 184). The heiress Julie Karagina really knows that the careerist Boris Drubetskoy is courting her for her money and does not love her, but when she notices that he hesitates to propose 'her feminine self-deception immediately supplied her with consolation, and she told herself that he was only shy from love' (VIII, v, 186).

It is, therefore, not only in the battle scenes that Tolstoy juxtaposes what really happened with the falsifying account, though of course some very striking examples do occur in the battle scenes. The general who meets Bagration at Schön Grabern tells him he met the French with the fire of his whole battalion:

The general had so wished to do this, and was so sorry he had not managed to do it, that it seemed to him as if it had really happened. Perhaps it might really have been so? Could one possibly make out amid all that confusion, what did or did not happen? (II, xxi, 257)

Zherkov then joins in, telling how he saw the Pavlograd hussars break up two squares. Several people present take him seriously because what he is saying redounds to the glory of the Russians 'though many of them knew that what he was saying was a lie devoid of any foundation'. The 'honest' Nicholas Rostov who had fled, as we know, to save 'his young and happy life' (II, xix, 246), speaks of the 'strange frenzy' one experiences during an attack:

If he had told the truth to his hearers—who like himself had often heard stories of attacks and had formed a definite idea of what an attack was and were expecting to hear just such a story—they would either not have believed him or, still worse, would have thought that Rostov was himself to blame since what generally happens to the narrators of cavalry attacks had not happened to him. . . . Besides, to tell everything as it really happened it would have been necessary to make an effort of will to tell only what happened. It is very difficult to tell the truth, and young people are rarely capable of it. (III, vii, 316)

Much later on, when Rostov hears 'how a deed worthy of antiquity had been performed by General Raevski', Tolstoy comments that 'he had experience enough to know that nothing happens in war at all as we can imagine or relate it' (IX, xii, 312).

Robert Scholes has written that realism claimed to be able to look at life 'without filters of any kind'.[18] Tolstoy's realism is in fact predicated on the very opposite assumption, namely that all descriptions are interpretations. He is moreover not only concerned with rendering the sort of external detail that the cinema can convey much better, but also with rendering the interior monologues of his characters—their consciousness.

It is because the narrator of *War and Peace* is so aware of the hypocrisy of consciousness, which arises from the fact that, in Jacques Rivière's words, 'the primary function of our feelings is to lie to us',[19] that we trust him, for we assume that one from whom the secrets of no hearts are hid will not deceive us. Tolstoy's authoritative knowledge over the world of his fiction seemed to those who knew him to extend over the actual world as well. The Tatyana Kuzminskaya whom some have seen as a prototype of Natasha tells an interesting story that illustrates this fact. While staying at Yasnaya Polyana in the summer of 1863 Tatyana went out riding with a friend called Anatoli Shostak. Anatoli delayed her while they were out in order to steal a kiss and when they got back the following incident occurred:

'Why did you lag behind with Anatoly and dismount from your horse?' Leo Nikolayevich asked me directly without any preliminaries. I kept silent. 'Whatever I'll say will be a lie,' I thought. 'My saddle girth got loose,' I said. He looked intently at me, and I felt as if his eyes pierced right through me and read all my innermost thoughts without difficulty.[20]

No doubt it was this sense that he knew the secrets of men's hearts (and not just his striking physical presence) which led people to feel that, in the last words of Gorky's portrait of him: 'This man is like God.'

Nevertheless the analogy of the omniscience of the narrator of *War and Peace* with that of God must not be carried too far for two important reasons. The first is that, as Louis Mink has pointed out,[21] no narrator can ever comprehend his story, past, present and to come, *totum simul*, all at once, in the way that Boethius conceived God as doing. Every narrator can only select the detail of his material *seriatim*, as one item after another, and that is, of course, how he has to unfold it to his hearers or readers. The second is that the Tolstoyan narrator is prepared to create characters with a capacity to attain spiritual insights just as deep as his own. Here he contrasts with Thackeray, say, or even George Eliot, of whom Scholes and Kellogg write: 'Since no character in the novel [*Middlemarch*] can be granted a mind impressive enough to make the kind of moral generalization George Eliot wants made repeatedly in this work, the narrator must perform the task.' [22] Thus, as we have seen, Tolstoy can make the mediocre Rostov (who, unlike Pierre, Prince Andrew and his own wife Princess Mary, is not given to introspection) attain to the important insight that 'nothing happens in war at all as we can imagine or relate it', an insight on which Tolstoy's whole portrayal of reality is founded. Thus, too, Princess Mary can, as we shall see, attain to and express in a letter to a friend a view of Gospel Christianity identical with that of Tolstoy himself,[23] while remaining a completely autonomous character who is not just a mouthpiece for her author's views. The only difference between Tolstoy's insight as narrator and that of his characters is that he, of course, can give us a number of different insights connected together in a narrative *ordonnance*, but this does not affect my point in so far as it concerns the depth and intensity of a single insight.

All this, however, does not alter the fact that Tolstoy could not present *historical* characters and events without seeing them through the filter of his moral presuppositions, his own conception of *normative* laws if you like; and his *historical* characters, unlike his *fictional* characters, were of course stubbornly resistant to such treatment. This was not because their traits and actions were not so ductile to his imagination (it is part of his triumph that he made them so), but because of the inescapable empirical fact that we have alternative sources of information about them—sources which, for all the onslaught on historians that Tolstoy has built into his book, are, in some respects, more trustworthy than Tolstoy. Despite his protests about the primacy of truth he does bend his source materials to his ideological purposes. The godlike omniscient narrator was, in short, 'human all too human' after all, as the intransigent moral absolutism of his later phase will also bring out.

Chapter 11

The Comprehensive Vision

In a letter to his friend Arthur Hugh Clough, written in 1848 or early 1849, Matthew Arnold criticized Keats and Browning with the following remarks:

> They will not be patient, neither understand that they must begin with an Idea of the world in order not to be prevailed over by the world's multitudinousness.[1]

This was Arnold's way of posing what Sir Isaiah Berlin has taught us to see as the hedgehog and the fox problem after Archilochus' fragment which says: 'The fox knows many things, but the hedgehog knows one big thing.' As is well known, Sir Isaiah Berlin sees Tolstoy as a fox who longed to be a hedgehog:

> His genius lay in the perception of specific properties, the most inexpressible individual quality in virtue of which the given object is different from all others. Nevertheless he longed for a universal explanatory principle: that is the perception of resemblances or common origins, or single purpose, or unity in the apparent variety of the mutually exclusive bits and pieces which composed the furniture of the world.[2]

Berlin points out that Tolstoy distorted history to suit his ideological rather than his artistic purposes,[3] but nevertheless gives the most sympathetic account we have of Tolstoy's first-hand wrestling with historical problems, although, in the end, he helps us to our conclusion that Tolstoy's representation of historical characters and actions, however fascinating, is flawed by his capitulation to the historicist comfort of Deistic Providentialism.

But despite the fact that Tolstoy's historicism is unsatisfactory, the extent to which he solved the hedgehog and the fox problem in much of *War and Peace* is extraordinary. The following passage from Scholes and Kellogg's *The Nature of Narrative* should help to show how his use of the convention of the omniscient author helped him, for, as already suggested, Tolstoy combined the reliability of the traditional oral narrator with a wholly 'modern' interest in the details of the inner life:

> God *knows* everything because He *is* everywhere—simultaneously. But a narrator of fiction is imbedded in a time-bound artifact. He does not 'know' simultaneously but consecutively. He is not everywhere at once but now here, now there, now looking into this mind or that, now moving on to other vantage points. He is time-bound and space-bound as God is not. Thus the narrator of the Tolstoyan kind is partly defined by his employment of a variety of separable perspectives, an attribute we may call his *multifariousness*. He is also defined by his resolution of those perspectives into a single, authoritative vision. Whereas, we conceive of God's omniscience and His omnipresence as being functions of an indivisible quality of godliness, we can separate the omniscient narrator in fiction into a multifarious element and a monistic element. The multiple perceptions of the narrator coalesce into a single reality, a single truth.[4]

What is that truth in Tolstoy? Once again Sir Isaiah Berlin has gone the furthest in articulating it. The theodicy which explains and reconciles is the recognition of the need to submit 'to the permanent relationships of things . . . to grasp what human will and reason can do, and what they cannot'.[5] One of the things Tolstoy shows that human will and reason *can* do in individuals made thoughtful and aware by their nature or circumstances, is to achieve an insight into life which at the same time makes them aware that they can never attain, so to speak, to an 'over-view' of life, for to achieve that belongs to the nature of God alone, if he exists. Thus the 'moments of vision' in *War and Peace* are stages in the development of individual *dramatis personae* which are followed by a falling back into the contingencies of time and circumstance. Sometimes further and still more inclusive visions are attained. Sometimes the characters fall back forever into mechanical routine, as Prince Vasili does after his glimpse of reality at the death-bed of old Count Bezukhov.

Tolstoy's vision as narrator 'constitutes' the visions of his characters in such a way as not to obliterate the autonomy of those characters. If he had destroyed that autonomy he would have prematurely collapsed the fruitful tension between multifariousness (the Fox) and monism (the Hedgehog) to which Scholes and Kelloggs's remarks point. Moreover as I have already pointed out Tolstoy gives the thoughtful (and sometimes even the not-so-thoughtful) characters of the novel moments of insight and a capacity to articulate them to themselves, or even at times to others, which are quite equal to any he could attain in his own person. This is why one can claim that the following passage on religion in a letter from Princess Mary to her friend Julie Karagina 'sums up her author's view explicitly': [6]

A thousand thanks, dear friend, for the volume you have sent me and which has such success in Moscow. Yet since you tell me that among some good things it contains others which our weak human understanding cannot grasp, it seems to me rather useless to spend time in reading what is unintelligible and can therefore bear no fruit. I never could understand the fondness some people have for confusing their minds by dwelling on mystical books that merely awaken their doubts and excite their imagination, giving them a bent for exaggeration quite contrary to Christian simplicity. Let us rather read the Epistles and Gospels. Let us not seek to penetrate what mysteries they contain; for how can we, miserable sinners that we are, know the terrible and holy secrets of Providence while we remain in this flesh which forms an impenetrable veil between us and the Eternal? Let us rather confine ourselves to studying those sublime rules which our divine Saviour has left for our guidance here below. Let us try to conform to them and follow them, and let us be persuaded that the less we let our feeble human minds roam, the better we shall please God, who rejects all knowledge that does not come from Him; and the less we seek to fathom what He has been pleased to conceal from us, the sooner will He vouchsafe its revelation to us through His divine Spirit. (I, xxv, 118–119)

This is perfectly appropriate as coming from Princess Mary to such a person on such an occasion and yet it is also an admirable expression of what has been called Tolstoy's 'own brand of Gospel Christianity'.[7]

Many of the linkages in that 'labyrinth of linkages' which constitutes *War and Peace* are made by the close-knit nature of the world which Tolstoy portrays, with its multiplicity of family connections. After sounding the Napoleon theme, so to speak, at her soirée, Anna Pavlovna Scherer goes on to make remarks to Prince Vasili on his sons, such as 'Hippolyte is at least a quiet fool, but Anatole is an active one' (I, i, 7), and to suggest Princess Mary, Prince Andrew's sister, as a match for Anatole. Later on Prince Vasili takes up her suggestion and Anatole humiliates Princess Mary by flirting with her companion, the pretty Mlle Bourrienne (III, v, 301). Later still Anatole ruins her brother Prince Andrew's happiness by turning Natasha's head (VIII, xv, 222). Prince Andrew will forgive him (as his sister Princess Mary had taught him to forgive without his understanding previously) when he sees him a 'miserable, sobbing, enfeebled man' (X, xxxvii, 538) in the operating theatre at Borodino. In the opening scene we observe Prince Vasili angling for a diplomatic post in Vienna for his eldest son Hippolyte and the impoverished Princess Drubetskaya in her turn angling with Prince

Vasili for an appointment in the Guards for her son Boris. Boris, who is at this time flirting with the girlish Natasha, will later dwindle into a cold careerist and marry the heiress Julie Karagina, Princess Mary's correspondent. All this illustrates the close-knit nature of the familial world which Tolstoy describes.

Scholes and Kellogg argue that the Tolstoyan type of narrative is impossible today because the growth of moral relativism has made the moral certainties on the part of the narrator unattainable. While some such growth *may* have taken place I am inclined to think that we overestimate the degree of moral consensus in the past and underestimate its degree in the present. I would argue rather that one of the main reasons why it is impossible to produce a narrative of the Tolstoyan type today is that the complex social structures of our modern industrial meritocracies and their large scale have made it extremely difficult for a single mind to encompass all the social knowledge requisite for portraying them. Paranoiac helplessness and conspiracy theories replace the 'overview'.

The early chapters of *War and Peace* are suffused with a sense of youth setting out on the path of life. Prince Andrew, Pierre, Boris Drubetskoy, Nicholas Rostov, Dolokhov the rake and Denisov the young hussar have all got their careers to make, and over them all, like a risen comet, stands the supreme careerist of them all, Napoleon himself, whom both Pierre and Andrew at this stage greatly admire. Yet Austerlitz, where Napoleon defeats the combined might of the Austrians and Russians, leaves the wounded Andrew disillusioned both with his one-time hero and with the idea of military glory in itself. All these things appear as nothing beside the 'lofty infinite sky' (III, xvi, 369).

Against Andrew's advice, and with the atmosphere of fresh unspoiled love in the Rostov household as a point of contrast, Pierre allows himself to be manœuvred by Prince Vasili into a match with his daughter, the beautiful but trivial Helen. Pierre is tormented by the *prokliatye voprosy* the 'accursed questions' which tormented Tolstoy himself:

What is bad? What is good? What should one love and what hate? What does one live for? And what am I? What is life, and what is death? What Power governs it all? (V, i, 460)

Pierre begins to dabble in Freemasonry, but Tolstoy shows that the mason Bazdeev's seemingly very Tolstoyan remark that God 'is hot to be apprehended by reason, but by life' and his concern with 'the science of the whole' (V, ii, 466) as opposed to particular sciences are a mere simulacrum of the truly comprehensive vision, a misty corner of the very whole they pretend to encompass. Tolstoy the narrator *can* encompass the comprehensive vision not because he is more capable of spiritual insight than a given character at a given moment, but because, as the narrator, he has an 'overview' of other such insights which he has communicated to us or is going to communicate to us. And how, as readers, after entering into the spirit of Natasha's experience at the ball where she guessed what her partner Denisov meant to do 'and abandoning herself to him followed his lead hardly knowing how' (IV, xii, 441), can we take seriously all the hieroglyphics of wisdom 'not cognizable by the senses' (V, iii, 475) with which Freemasonry puzzles a Pierre 'trying to stimulate his emotions' (V, iii, 471)?

Though only Tolstoy and the reader have a spread-out view of the full range of insights and experiences of *all* the *dramatis personae*, Tolstoy is very fond of the method of allowing friends or relations to meet after a period of time and take stock, so to speak, of each other's development and outlook. Pierre, for example, goes to visit his friend Prince Andrew at Bogucharovo. The egoism/altruism problem we have met so many times in Tolstoy comes into focus. Pierre thinks he has found the secret of happiness in living for others (though Tolstoy has shown us that, in fact, he has not helped his peasants nearly as much as he fancies) and Prince Andrew thinks that he has found the secret of happiness in confining his interest to his immediate family who are just the same as himself, a solution Levin is to adopt to some degree in *Anna Karenina*. When Pierre begins to enthuse about the idea of the great chain of being, Andrew comes back to the immediacies of experience, the sort of experience Tolstoy himself had undergone when his brother Nicholas died in his presence on 20 September 1860 in Hyères and which Levin will undergo in *Anna Karenina* when his brother Nicholas dies. Andrew says:

What convinces is when one sees a being dear to one, bound up with one's own life, . . . and suddenly that being is seized with pain, suffers, and ceases to exist. . . . Why? It cannot be that there is no answer . . . it is not argument that convinces me of the necessity of a future life, but this: when you go hand in hand with someone and all at once that person vanishes *there*, *into nowhere*, and you yourself are left facing that abyss, and look in. (V, xii, 515–16)

It is not long since logical empiricists were claiming that such questions as 'what is the meaning of life?' are meaningless. I shall come back to this problem when considering *A Confession*, but at the moment I would suggest that they confused the semantic question of the meaningfulness of propositions with the phenomenological question of how we make sense of our life experiences and of those of others. Tolstoy explores this 'sense-bestowing' activity through interior monologues and through dialogues like those of Pierre and Andrew. These explorations would not have the translucency they do if the question really was meaningless.

Tolstoy is very interested in the phenomenology of those moments of inner experience in which it is forcefully brought home to us that others have an inner life different from our own though, so to speak, running parallel with it. This experience in itself makes us realize that in the nature of things there is much that we cannot comprehend. For example when Prince Andrew visits Otradnoe he is struck by the fact that the gay, unsophisticated Natasha has a 'centre of self' that is just as autonomous, rich and authentic as his own:

that slim pretty girl did not know, or wish to know, of his existence and was contented and cheerful in her own separate—proably foolish—but bright and happy life. (VI, ii, 6)

It is this sort of passage, with its keen insight into the mode of our awareness of other minds, which makes talk about Tolstoy's solipsism so misleading. As he journeys home Prince Andrew passes an old oak tree whose springing into leaf parallels his own inner sense of renewal. He has a comprehensive vision of his whole past:

All the best moments of his life suddenly rose to his memory. Austerlitz with the lofty heavens, his wife's dead reproachful face, Pierre at the ferry, that girl thrilled by the beauty of the night, and that night itself and the moon, and . . . all this rushed suddenly to his mind. (VI, iii, 9)

This passage illustrates the fact that although the characters cannot, of course, have the all-inclusive view of the omniscient narrator, they can be endowed with a capacity for achieving a comprehensive view of their own pasts. The narrator and the re-reader of the book also know the futures of the characters. But the characters themselves can only understand life backwards and live it forwards as we all have to do in our daily lives.

There is another superb comprehensive view of things given to Prince Andrew on the eve of the climactic battle of Borodino, and it is worth quoting in full. It includes recollections of the past and anticipations of the future:

He knew that tomorrow's battle would be the most terrible of all he had taken part in, and for the first time in his life the possibility of death presented itself to him—not in relation to any worldly matter or with reference to its effect on others, but simply in relation to himself, to his own soul—vividly, plainly, terribly, and almost as a certainty. And from the height of this perception all that had previously tormented and preoccupied him suddenly became illumined by a cold white light without shadows, without perspective, and without distinction of outline. All life appeared to him like magic-lantern pictures at which he had long been gazing by artificial light through a glass. Now he suddenly saw those badly daubed pictures in clear daylight and without a glass. 'Yes, yes! There they are, those false images that agitated, enraptured, and tormented me,' said he to himself, passing in review the principal pictures of the magic lantern of life and regarding them in the cold-white daylight of his clear perception of death. 'There they are, those rudely painted figures that once seemed splendid and mysterious. Glory, the good of society, love of a woman, the Fatherland itself—how important these pictures appeared to me, and with what profound meaning they seemed to be filled! And it is all so simple, pale, and crude in the cold white light of this morning which I feel is dawning for me'. The three great sorrows of his life held his attention in particular: his love for a woman, his father's death, and the French invasion which had overrun half Russia. 'Love! . . . that little girl who seemed to me brimming over with mystic forces! Yes, indeed I loved her. I made romantic plans of love and happiness with her! Oh, what a boy I was!' he said aloud bitterly. 'Ah me! I believed in some ideal love which was to keep her faithful to me for the whole year of my absence! Like the gentle dove in the fable she was to pine apart from me. . . . But it was much simpler really. . . . It was all very simple and horrible. When my father built Bald Hills he thought the place was his, his land, his air, his peasants. But Napoleon came and swept him aside, unconscious of his existence, as he might brush a chip from his path, and his Bald Hills, and his whole life fell to pieces. Princess Mary says it is a trial sent from above. What is the trial for, when he is not here and will never return? He is not here! For whom then is the trial intended? The Fatherland, the destruction of Moscow! And tomorrow I shall be killed, perhaps not even by a Frenchman but by one of our own men, by a soldier discharging a musket close to my ear, as one of them did yesterday, and the French will come and take me by head and heels and fling me into a hole that I may not stink under their noses, and new conditions of life will arise, which will seem quite ordinary to others and about which I shall know nothing. I shall not exist.'

He looked at the row of birches shining in the sunshine with their motionless green and yellow foliage and white bark. 'To die . . . to be killed tomorrow . . . That I should not exist . . . That all this should still be, but no me. . . .' (X, xxiv, 479–80)

The use of this sort of summation passage given to a character is one way in which Tolstoy as narrator brings together the 'war' and 'peace' sections of his book and gives the wide range of material he has included coherence and unity.

The bounds of the comprehensive vision, not just of the characters in Tolstoy's narrative, but of Tolstoy himself as omniscient narrator

(as contrasted, say, with Dante as narrator of the *Divina Commedia*)
show a remarkable congruence with 'the bounds of sense' as set out
by Immanuel Kant in his *Critique of Pure Reason*. Tolstoy, in short,
does not apply concepts and judgements outside the empirical world
which is the world of all of us. We have already seen Tolstoy's
scepticism about mystical wisdom 'not cognizable by the senses'
in the sections of *War and Peace* dealing with Freemasonry, and
Princess Mary's expression of religion within the limits of reason
alone which anticipates Tolstoy's later somewhat Kantian religious
views, where the 'spiritual' is at times even identified with the
'rational'.

Tolstoy's treatment of death is very important in connection with
this question of the bounds of sense. Death is a subject which haunts
him in *Childhood* and the Sevastopol sketches, *Three Deaths*, *War and
Peace* itself, *Anna Karenina* (where the only chapter with a title is
headed 'Death'), *The Death of Ivan Ilych*, *Master and Man* and the
later conversations and diaries. He explores the coming to terms
with death in *War and Peace* through the experiences of Pierre and
Prince Andrew. Pierre witnesses the apparently meaningless death
of the young factory worker at the hands of the French soldiers:

Though he did not acknowledge it to himself, his faith in the right ordering
of the universe, in humanity, in his own soul and in God, had been destroyed. . . . He felt that it was not in his power to regain faith in the meaning
of life. (XII, xii, 197)

It is Pierre's disorientation and doubt that we experience the most
strongly. The peasant Karataev who functions as a sort of *deus ex
machina* to help him (and Tolstoy) resolve them seems too much a
piece of wishful thinking on Tolstoy's part—a synthetic concoction
of wise saws and solemn instances from proverb books and diction-
aries of folklore and a world away from the peasants Tolstoy portrayed in *A Landlord's Morning* and *Polikushka*. A merely 'illustrative'
figure like this fits uneasily into a 'representational' work. More
impressive is Pierre's inner wrestling with the problem of freedom
and necessity and his eventual finding that the secret of happiness,
of 'peace and inner harmony', lies in those very privations of his
which have made him conscious of the bliss inherent in the mere
'absence of suffering' (XII, xii, 258–9), a bliss that custom usually
dulls. Truly, as Lear discovered, 'The art of our necessities is strange,/
And can make vile things precious'.

In the case of Prince Andrew's coming to terms with suffering
and death, Tolstoy attempts something even more daring. He
accompanies Andrew's consciousness to the very edge of that death

which cannot be lived through, for, in the words of Wittgenstein's profoundly Kantian remark at the end of the *Tractatus*: 'Death is not an event in life: we do not live to experience death.' [8] By making Andrew dream that he has died Tolstoy gives us the momentary illusion that death *has* been lived through:

He was seized by an agonizing fear. And that fear was the fear of death. *It* stood behind the door . . . Once again *it* pushed from outside . . . *It* entered, and it was *death*, and Prince Andrew died.
But at the instant he died, Prince Andrew remembered that he was asleep, and at the very instant he died, having made an effort, he awoke.
'Yes, it was death! I died—and woke up. Yes, death is an awakening!' And all at once it grew light in his soul and the veil that had till then concealed the unknown was lifted from his spiritual vision . . . (XII, xvi, 219–20)

Even Konstantin Leontiev, who criticized Tolstoy's resorting to 'obscure and not particularly successful allegory' in his portrayal of the death of Anna and of Ivan Ilych, wrote of the *it* behind the closed door: 'Here we have poetry, accuracy, reality, and elevation!' [9] It is some days before Andrew really dies and then Tolstoy leaves us with an experience which *can* be lived through, the perennial experience of mourners who ask themselves: 'Where has he gone? Where is he now? . . .'(XII, xvi, 221). Andrew's own speculations on the eve of his death—'Love is God, and to die means that I, a particle of love, shall return to the general and eternal source'—seem to us, as to him, 'only thoughts' and 'not clear . . . too one-sidedly personal and brain-spun' (XII, xvi, 219). They go beyond 'the bounds of sense'.

It is natural enough to end a work—particularly a tragedy—with the death of the hero; but *War and Peace* is not a tragedy. It is a complex narrative which does not have a single hero, and Tolstoy ends it, as Dickens ends *David Copperfield*, with an account of the subsequent fates of the characters. He takes us seven years on, from 1812 to 1819. Pierre and Natasha are married; and by that natural use of family links for plot motivation characteristic of Tolstoy, Natasha is visiting her brother Nicholas who has married the dead Prince Andrew's sister Princess Mary. Denisov, Nicholas's old hussar comrade, is also, perfectly plausibly, a guest at Nicholas's. Nicholas and Mary look after Prince Andrew's orphaned son, little Nicholas, whom Nicholas Rostov does not really like. Pierre returns from St Petersburg and the assembled party talk about the unsettled state of things in Russia where Arakcheev, the Tsar's minister, is imposing a more and more dictatorial rule. Little Nicholas overhears Pierre's plans for a society of right thinking men (Tolstoy is, of course, hinting at the Decembrists here) and witnesses the clash it provokes with his rather conservative guardian, Uncle Nicholas:

> When they all got up to go in to supper, little Nicholas Bolkonski went up to Pierre, pale and with shining, radiant eyes.
>
> 'Uncle Pierre, you ... no ... if papa were alive ... would he agree with you?' he asked.
>
> And Pierre suddenly realized what a special, independent, complex and powerful process of thought and feeling must have been going on in this boy during that conversation, and remembering all he had said he regretted that the lad should have heard him. (*First Epilogue*, xiv, 475)

In his excitement the boy has broken the sealing wax and pens on his Uncle Nicholas's table and Nicholas represses his vexation with difficulty. The whole complex work is to end, as it began, with youth dreaming of the future, as little Nicholas thinks of doing something with which even his father (whose own youthful dreams of fame we had lived through at the beginning of the book) would be satisfied.

Thus Tolstoy's comprehensive vision bears within itself an acknowledgement of its own essential human incompleteness. Life goes on. The vision of a participant in that life can never be complete. *War and Peace* belongs to that kind of work of art which Kant prized supremely in his *Critique of Judgement* when he spoke of the genius which so conceals contrivance that we feel we are contemplating not art, but nature.

Chapter 12

Tragedy, Contingency and the
Meaning of Life in *Anna Karenina*

F. R. Leavis is right, I think, in recognizing *Anna Karenina* rather than *War and Peace* as Tolstoy's 'supreme masterpiece', and in scotching once and for all (one hopes) Matthew Arnold's notion that what the novel 'loses in art it gains in reality'. He points to the fact that it 'is wonderfully closely worked', a triumph of art, even in its seeming artlessness.[1] In his reading of the book Arnold sometimes seems to have been influenced by the sterile neoclassicism which occasionally overcame him. He pounced on the incident of Levin's delay in getting to church for his wedding saying that it was 'introduced solely to give the author the pleasure of telling us that all Levin's shirts had been packed up'.[2] This is to put the cart before the horse. Tolstoy does not make use of the delay in order to tell us of the shirts, but tells us of the shirts in order to motivate the delay. The delay itself is a retardation device that builds up a tension and excitement suitable to the occasion, first in the characters, and then in the reader. One suspects that the neoclassicist in Arnold looked down on such detail as trivial and low. He did not see that, to quote Tolstoy's diary, 'There is a novelist's poetry: (1) in the interest of the arrangement of occurrences . . . (2) in the presentation of manners on an historic background . . . (3) in the beauty and gaiety of a situation . . . (4) in people's characters . . .' [3]

There are several reasons why *Anna Karenina* is a more integrated work of art than *War and Peace*. It does not have the peculiar relation to history we have noted as constituting a real problem in the case of the latter. Then in *Anna* Tolstoy is dealing with *contemporary* life, so we do not get the somewhat idyllic 'distanced' tone which characterizes his portrayal of the life of the Rostovs, charming as that is. In *Anna*, too, Tolstoy abandons the element of 'romance' plotting still evident in *War and Peace*: as in Nicholas Rostov being on hand to rescue Princess Mary from her peasants, Prince Andrew and Anatole Kuragin finding themselves in the same operating theatre after Borodino, and Natasha meeting the wounded Prince

Andrew during the evacuation from Moscow. The plot of 'romance' depends on mystery, intrigue and coincidence, as in *Little Dorrit*, *Our Mutual Friend* and Shorthouse's *John Inglesant*. This is replaced in *Anna* by a motivation of plot linkages through family ties which is so unforced and natural that one is apt to make the mistake of viewing the work as plotless. Thus a central theme in the novel—family life—enters into the very structure of the book as a constitutive element. This element also motivates that intimacy of detail which is part of the peculiar poetry of Tolstoy.

Much of this is illustrated by the very opening of the novel which must be one of the best first chapters in literature. First we get the chaos of the Oblonsky household which is caused by Oblonsky's wife Dolly having discovered that he is having an affair with the governess. This chaos prepares us for a certain apparently careless ease in the presentation of detail. But the connection of this detail with the animation of the scene is reminiscent of one of the most interesting passages in Tolstoy's later, somewhat cantankerous, *What is Art?*

Once when correcting a pupil's study, Bryulov just touched it in a few places and the poor dead study immediately became animated. 'Why, you only touched it a *wee bit*, and it is quite another thing!' said one of the pupils. 'Art begins where the *wee bit* begins,' replied Bryulov, indicating by these words just what is most characteristic of art.[4]

The detail of Oblonsky stretching out his hand 'from nine years' habit' for his dressing gown and then suddenly remembering why he had been banished to his study from the bedroom, the detail of the 'enormous pear' (I, i, 2) he recollects bringing home for his wife the night before, the detail of the 'Liberal paper' he takes that 'expressed the opinions of the majority' but on this particular morning 'did not give him the quiet, ironical pleasure it usually did' (I, iii, 7–8)—all this detail is only apparently superfluous. Tolstoy was not being falsely modest when he had asked a decade before 'Are the Peasant Children to Learn to Write from Us?', for he had learned from the story by the peasant boy Fedka that a 'carelessly dropped artistic feature during an action which has already begun among persons totally unfamiliar to the reader'[5] acquaints the reader with those persons much more than pages of description. Tolstoy crystallizes the atmosphere of disharmony in the Oblonsky household beautifully by means of a simple but fitting analogy: 'They all felt that there was no sense in their living together, and that any group who had met together by chance at an inn would have had more in common than they' (I, i, 1). What more natural, then, that Oblonsky's sister Anna should have been asked to come from St Petersburg to Moscow to reconcile husband and wife? It is not a far-fetched coincidence that Anna should share a compartment with Vronsky's mother; and, given that, what again more natural than that she should while away the journey by talking about her son Serezha, from whom she is parted for the first time, much to her anxiety? Equally naturally Vronsky has come to the station to meet his mother. He is present when she says to Anna: 'But please don't fret about your son, you can't expect never to be parted' (I, xviii, 71). What an ominous ring that perfectly ordinary sentence has when we re-read the book!

But just as Oblonsky has a sister (Anna), so, too, does Dolly (Kitty). Oblonsky knows that his countrified friend Levin, sincere but awkward, has come up to Moscow in order to propose to her. But Kitty's head has been turned (naturally enough) by the handsome young guards officer Vronsky who, Tolstoy is careful to tell us, had never known that family life which it is Levin's dream to realize, and who even regards it (and husbands) as 'alien, hostile, and above all ridiculous' (I, xvi, 64). This rivalry of Levin and Vronsky is both thematically important and dramatically gripping. When they meet at the formidable Countess Nordston's we are given a picture of Vronsky through Levin's eyes which enhances both men in our estimation, for Levin is magnanimous enough to see what is 'good and attractive' (I, xiv, 57) in his rival. Moreover, when Vronsky's enemy can recognize his merits, we can more easily sympathize (*pace* Matthew Arnold) with Anna's allowing herself to be attracted by him. Every incident in this book tells upon some other incident in it. This is what Leavis meant by its close working.

The importance of the contrast between Oblonsky and Levin should not, however, be underestimated because of that between Vronsky and Levin. Indeed it is easy to underestimate the importance of Oblonsky in the book as a whole through regarding him as too 'light' a character to be invested with any. The remarkable thing is the lack of tendentiousness with which he is portrayed. His faults, and especially the suffering he causes Dolly, are not glossed over, but his fundamental decency and his joy in the natural pleasures of life, food, exercise and conversation, are rendered with a fullness of sympathy and a lack of censoriousness which strike us as all the more remarkable for coming from the mind which produced *The Kreutzer Sonata* and which was attacked by the late Victorian rationalist J. M. Robertson for its narrowness.[6]

In *Anna Karenina* Tolstoy's vision is still comprehensive enough to 'place' moral rigorism by distributing the tensions it sets up in himself between the easy-going Oblonsky and the serious Levin:

'Well, of course,' said Oblonsky. 'The aim of civilization is to enable us to get enjoyment out of everything.' 'Well, if that is its aim, I'd rather be a savage.' 'You are a savage as it is. All you Levins are savages.' Levin sighed. He remembered his brother Nicholas and frowned, feeling ashamed and distressed. (I, x, 40)

Oblonsky, moreover, is intelligent, and he has a real problem: 'What am I to do? Tell me, what am I to do? My wife is getting old, and I am full of vitality.' But Levin is right to see that when Oblonsky says 'What are you to do? How are you to act? It is a terrible tragedy' (I, xi, 46–7) he is, so to speak, stepping out of his role; for he is essentially cut out to be a figure in the *comédie humaine* rather than, like his sister Anna (who with an older husband and a vital lover faces the same problem as he does in reverse), to take life tragically. Anna's love is (to use Levin's classification) neither completely spiritual, nor merely a matter of physical appetite, but an unhappy amalgam of the sensuous will and the ethical will.

What we have here, in fact, is Isaiah Berlin's hedgehog and fox dichotomy again, though limited to the question of ethics in personal relationships rather than, as in *War and Peace*, expanded over wider questions of God, the cosmos and history. In encompassing both Oblonsky and Levin in his imaginative grasp Tolstoy shows us that it is a dichotomy he can resolve artistically. This comes out in the remarks he gives to Oblonsky apropos Levin's wish for everything in the moral life to be all of a piece:

'It is both a virtue and a fault in you. You have a consistent character yourself and you wish all the facts of life to be consistent, but they never are. For instance you despise public service because you want work always to correspond to its aims, and that never happens. You also want the activity of each separate man to have an aim, and love and family life always to coincide—and that doesn't happen either. All the variety, charm and beauty of life are made up of light and shade.' (I, xi, 47)

Tolstoy could well be carrying on a colloquy with himself here.

Later on Oblonsky has an important role to play as a go-between in Anna's efforts to persuade Karenin to a divorce. Oblonsky's Moscow 'honesty' contrasts with Karenin's Petersburg 'rectitude' as Oblonsky also takes the opportunity to angle with the influential Karenin for a better post for himself. It is evident that all Karenin's animation now goes into his official work. He shows only weariness as soon as Oblonsky turns the conversation to Anna (VII, xviii, 328). But Tolstoy uses Oblonsky's essential sanity to 'place' the false religiosity of the atmosphere around Countess Lydia Ivanovna, who is carrying on an *amitié amoureuse* with Karenin. Countess Lydia

Ivanovna is shown as too easy on herself in despising fasting and self-denial as the result of 'the barbarous opinions of our monks' and in thinking that a devout life consists of reading English tracts like *Safe and Happy, or, Under the Wing,* of endorsing the complacency of her friend Mary Sanina's ability to thank God for the death of her only child, and of dabbling with clairvoyants (VII, xxi, 342–343). Tolstoy despises this religion of the comfortable, and he puts a brake on his censoriousness by allowing all these things to be reflected in the interior monologue that runs through Oblonsky's muddled, but decent brain:

Mary Sanina is glad that her child is dead. . . . I should like to have a smoke. . . . To be saved one need only have faith; the monks don't know how to do it, but the Countess Lydia Ivanovna knows. . . . And what is so heavy in my head? Is it the brandy, or is it because all this is so very strange? (VII, xxii, 344)

Passages like this bear out Socrates' contention in *The Symposium* that the master of tragedy can also show himself a master of comedy.

Tolstoy has cross-linked the Levin/Kitty, Vronsky/Anna material with great skill, and it reaches its climax in Levin's visit to Anna (at Oblonsky's suggestion), after his realization at the *Zemstvo* meeting that he and Vronsky 'had nothing to say to one other' (VII, ix, 294), and shortly before Anna's suicide. Levin and Anna have a conversation about truth in art in which Levin attacks French naturalism in the novel and Levin feels pity for Anna and fears 'that Vronsky did not fully understand her' (VII, x, 303). This dialogue in itself (like the sections on the painter Mikhaylov, in V, vii–xiii, 25–49) shows the intimate relationship between life and art in the Tolstoyan world where art has a 'natural' role to play in the lives of the characters. Tolstoy devises a characteristically true-to-life touch, however, when he makes Levin realize as soon as he mentions his visit to Anna to his wife Kitty that 'he should not have gone there' (VII, xi, 305). In Kitty's presence his visit seems quite different from what it did to him at the time. But Kitty herself is to be given a chance to see Anna before the latter's suicide by the perfectly natural circumstance that Anna, wrought up by Vronsky's absence, should go to Dolly's for comfort and find her there. As soon as Kitty sees Anna, her hostility is swallowed up in pity (VII, xxviii, 369).

Any reading of the book (which in early drafts Tolstoy thought of calling *Two Marriages* or *Two Couples*) [7] that emphasizes the Levin/Kitty side or the Vronsky/Anna side at the expense of the other is bound to go astray. D. H. Lawrence, for example, seems to have been more intensely drawn to the Vronsky/Anna side even when he first read the book around the age of seventeen along with E. T. (Jessie Chambers).[8] His subsequent relationship to Frieda, which was not unlike that of Vronsky and Anna, seems to have led him to blame Tolstoy for not allowing Vronsky and Anna to achieve what he was proud that he and Frieda had achieved. For him *Anna Karenina* should have been a *Lady Chatterley's Lover avant la lettre*. But Lawrence does not seem to have seen the close parallel between *Anna Karenina* and his own *Women in Love* in that both books reject *l'amour-passion* as an adequate basis for worthwhile happiness. Vronsky and Anna parallel Gerald and Gudrun while Levin and Kitty parallel Birkin and Ursula.

But Lawrence's misreading of the book has at least the virtue of intensity. Much more annoying is the rather conventional reading in which Levin's story is seen as an 'anticlimax' and Levin dismissed as 'an amiable bore'.[9] This view seems to be rooted in nothing more than the notion that ordinary men cannot be seriously concerned with the problems of God, freedom and immortality and that the portrayal of family life (as opposed to 'high life') is *ipso facto* bound to be dull; and it completely obscures the fact that the artistic miracle of *Anna Karenina* lies in Tolstoy's unrivalled ability to treat serious philosophical problems in novelistic terms, so that we get ideas in a novel rather than a novel of ideas. Again Tolstoy gives us a clue to his concern in *What is Art?* when he writes: 'The business of art lies just in this: to make that understood and felt which in the form of an argument might be incomprehensible and inaccessible'.[10]

Tolstoy makes marriage, which often constitutes the happy ending to a novel, into a problematic beginning instead—a mixture of disillusionment and enchantment which helps to keep Levin from being a bore to us. Moreover he links marriage directly to his philosophical theme, for marriage emerges, along with the family life of which it is a condition, as a realization of the possibilities of creativeness and order in a baffling universe. The social world is a world in which good and evil are inextricably intermingled, good actions sometimes producing evil and evil actions, good. Only in the intimate sphere of family relationships, for all their tensions, cruelties and even tyrannies, can man find a clue to what is good and evil. Even when our causes seem good our efforts in the wider social sphere are only too often a product of self-deception and weakness. Karenin's concern for the subject peoples masks his failure in personal relations and his careerism. Vronsky's philanthropy masks his boredom. Levin's brother Nicholas and his half-brother Koznyshev smother their inner hollowness by nihilism in Nicholas's case and 'social concern' and Panslavism in Koznyshev's. For Levin family life becomes a kind of touchstone whereby the true is separated from the false. Nicholas is too unbalanced for it. Koznyshev, who poses as an altruist, is too egotistical to propose to Kitty's friend Varenka when the crucial moment arises (VI, v, 147–149). (Arnold mistakenly considers this relevant and masterly little drama superfluous.) The comic and apparently harmless flirt, Vasenka Veslovsky, whom Vronsky tolerates (though Anna—as Dolly perceives—resents his familiarities, VI, xxii, 225), is thrown out by Levin, not just from jealousy at Veslovsky's attentions to Kitty, but from a genuine sense that the sanctity of the home has been outraged (VI, xv, 192). Tolstoy is reported to have compared Veslovsky's offence with that of a tourist who interrupts mass to admire the icons.

Tolstoy brings the problem of the hedgehog and the fox into *Anna Karenina* not just by giving us Oblonsky as a contrast to Levin, but by putting the problem into Levin's own mind. Levin himself is tormentedly aware of the irreducibility of the contrasts and complexities of life to any single formula. At the same time he thirsts for (to borrow Schopenhauer's words) 'the correct and universal understanding of experience itself, the true interpretation of its meaning and content'. Thus a tension is set up in Levin which reflects the tension in Tolstoy between the awareness of multitudinousness and of the need of an 'idea' so as not to be prevailed over by it. Leavis gives an excellent formulation of the problem:

What Tolstoy has to guard against is the intensity of his need for an 'answer'. For the concern for significance that is the principle of life in *Anna Karenina* is a deep spontaneous *lived* question, or quest. The temptation in wait for Tolstoy is to relax the tension, which, in being that of his integrity, is the vital tension of his art, by reducing the 'question' into one that *can* be answered—or, rather, one to which a seemingly satisfying answer strongly solicits him: that is, to simplify the challenge life actually is for him and deny the complexity of his total knowledge and need.[11]

Leavis goes on to suggest that one of the temptations to which Tolstoy is subject is the wish to make the simple belief of the peasants 'the central reality' of Levin's life, although the force of the whole work makes against this as a 'desperately simplifying' situation. But did Tolstoy really succumb to this temptation? I think that Leavis is reading back into the book his knowledge of Tolstoy's own subsequent development into a sage and a prophet. There *was* a narrowing of vision in Tolstoy after *A Confession* (1879) and it was not always compensated by an intensification either. I agree that it is impossible to ignore this fact and even that it is almost impossible to avoid seeing Levin in the light of it and yet I think that to allow ourselves to do so is to ignore the integrity of what we have in the novel. Levin himself put his Rousseauistic dream of *becoming* a peasant behind him in the scene where, after having spent the night out on the hay, he sees Kitty going by in a coach (III, xii, 315), a scene which Leavis himself discusses very well. The conversation with the peasant Theodore (VIII, xi, 411) at the end of the book simply illuminates for him the problem in ethics which has been tormenting him; and the fact that the illumination comes from a peasant serves to show that the problems of what Kant called the 'practical reason' and the ability to solve them are common to all thinking men and not just confined to the educated. It can and should be dissociated from any simplifying idyllicism. Moreover, the problem which has been tormenting Levin has also teased such philosophically sophisticated minds as those of Kant, Schopenhauer and Wittgenstein and is, in fact, *the* cardinal problem of ethics. This is the conflict between duty and inclination and the concomitant problem of the relation between goodness and happiness.

Tolstoy sees the problem in this way. We all strive for happiness and the purely sensuous man like Oblonsky finds it in the satisfaction of his desires, like Kirilov the innkeeper who 'lives for his belly'. The highest good is the union of goodness and happiness, but the good man cannot be good in order to be happy as the sensuous man can satisfy his desire in order to be happy, for goodness and happiness are not causally related in a means/ends consequential way like sensuous fulfilment and happiness. As Levin puts it (VIII, xii, 413): 'If goodness has a cause, it is no longer goodness; if it has a consequence—a reward, it is also not goodness. Therefore goodness is beyond the chain of cause and effect.' Wittgenstein's position at the end of the *Tractatus* is identical with this:

It is clear, however, that ethics has nothing to do with punishment and reward in the usual sense of the terms. . . . There must indeed be some kind of ethical reward and ethical punishment, but they must reside in the action itself.[12]

So when Levin wonders whether he has found 'the solution of everything' as he strides along the dusty road, his elation is not entirely misplaced, for he *has* come to terms with the cardinal question of ethics which is certainly central to every thoughtful conception of life. He has reached a solution in which he sets aside the question 'does it pay to be good?' as one which arises from a misunderstanding of the nature of goodness, while at the same time he can sympathize with those who ask it. This sympathy arises from the fact that Tolstoy himself, as we saw at the very beginning of the book, was engaged right from his childhood in the quest for the secret of happiness which his brother Nicholas said he had written on the green stick. Tolstoy has no rigorous Kantian or Schopenhauerian objection to the idea of happiness *per se*, and he makes the sympathetic and essentially good Dolly ask herself the question 'does it pay to be good?' in certain moods (see VI, xvi, 195–7 and VI, xx, 213). Levin's solution (and Tolstoy's) is not the Schopenhauerian one of scorning every wish for happiness as stemming from the will and *ipso facto* evil, but nearer to Kant in that he sees that the happiness of the good man is as dependent on chance as that of any other man, but that *only goodness is worthy of happiness*. At the same time, of course, the rigourism, abstraction and touch of pharisaism in Kant are absent in the artist's concern with particularities and with the role the inner emotional life plays in ethics, a role always neglected or distorted by analytic philosophers. Tolstoy dramatizes the dependence of happiness on contingency when at the end of the book Kitty and her baby are caught in a storm and Levin stumbles blindly towards them 'senselessly' praying that they should not be struck by an oak that has already fallen at the lightning's stroke (VIII, xvii, 431).

Levin is perfectly rational in seeing the limitations of reason. His rejection of the Panslavism of Koznyshev should also prevent us from seeing him as a man who has adopted (to use Leavis's phrase) a 'peasant solution' to his moral problems, for it is rooted in a perfectly rational view of the social question. I do not know whether it has been remarked that Levin's rejection of Koznyshev's Panslavism is also, by implication, a rejection of the serious revolutionary movements of the day, in so far as such movements claimed to speak for the will of the people. When Koznyshev claims that on the question of the Serbian war he can appeal to the people's direct expression of its will [13] Levin's rejoinder runs:

'That word *people* is so indefinite. . . . Clerks in district offices, schoolmasters, and one out of a thousand peasants, may know what it is all about. The rest of the eighty millions . . . not only don't express their will, but have not the least idea what it is they have to express it about! What right have we then to say it is the will of the people?' (VIII, xv, 426)

As Koznyshev and Katavasov proceed with their arguments Levin finds himself wanting to ask them 'why, if public opinion is an infallible judge, is a Revolution and a Commune not as lawful as the movement in favour of the Slavs?' (VIII, xvi, 430). Levin's distrust of those who claim to speak for 'the people' is not that of a man who has adopted a *simpliste* solution to life's problems.

There *is* an unacceptably *simpliste* passage concerning Levin's inner discoveries, but it occurs at the end of chapter x of book VIII and thus *precedes* the revelation which the peasant Theodore's words bring, which is not described till the chapter following. The passage I find unacceptable turns on Levin's doubts about whether he is acting well or ill (he feels guilty about exploiting the peasants)— so far so good, but then we get:

> Thinking about it led him into doubts and prevented him from seeing what he should and should not do. But when he did not think, but just lived, he unceasingly felt in his soul the presence of an infallible judge deciding which of two possible actions was the better and which the worse . . . (VIII, x, 408)

Here Tolstoy as omniscient narrator falters, for he is undoubtedly endorsing an infallibility of judgement to which man can no more attain when he acts on impulse than when he takes thought. It is here, and not in Levin's reflections after his conversation with the peasant Theodore, that we have a 'desperately simplifying' solution.

Levin, in fact, comes to a mature realization at the end of the book that goodness is a matter of decision. He realizes that he has the power to invest life with a meaning. But he also realizes that this power will not necessarily make him happy, or stop him being irritable, or prevent differences of view between himself and Kitty on important matters. This is hardly oversimplification. In fact a good case could be made out for the view that Tolstoy gave Levin a balance of tensions that, tragically, he himself could not maintain in his own life so that he was driven to the painful ethical absolutism of his later years.

Tolstoy also deals with the problem of the merely contingent relation between goodness and happiness in his masterly portrayal of Oblonsky's wife Dolly. The power of chance comes out in Tolstoy's casual remark that Levin might well have fallen in love with her as the eldest sister rather than with her sister Kitty if Oblonsky's courtship had not intervened (I, vi, 25). How different her life with the family-loving Levin would have been, one reflects. As it is she is harassed because Oblonsky really takes no interest in family life and the children. When she is tired she is often tempted to think that those who put their sensuous pleasures first may have the right of it after all, and, in effect, to ask 'does it pay to be good?' Tolstoy enters into her situation with powerful sympathy. On the way to Vronsky's from Levin's she recalls her talk with a young peasant woman:

> In answer to the question whether she had any children, the good-looking young peasant wife had cheerfully replied:
> 'I had one girl, but God released me. I buried her in Lent.'
> 'And are you very sorry?' asked Dolly.
> 'What's there to be sorry about? The old man has plenty of grandchildren as it is. They're nothing but worry. You can't work or anything. They're nothing but a tie . . .'
> This answer had seemed horrible to Dolly, despite the good-natured sweetness of the young woman's looks, but now she could not help recalling it. In those cynical words there was some truth. (VI, xvi, 196)

And how different is this freshness and openness, one reflects, from the religious hypocrisy with which Countess Lydia Ivanovna surrounds the death of Mary Sanina's only child!

But to return to Dolly. When she reaches Vronsky's she cannot help noticing Anna's uneasiness amid the splendour and Western European luxury with which Vronsky has surrounded her, and the falseness and lack of spontaneity in Anna's relationship to her daughter by Vronsky. Neither can she help contrasting the sense of fulfilment and creativeness in the Levin household with the sense of futility and parasitism that fills the Vronsky estate. Tolstoy presents the moral dilemma that faces Anna (including the question of birth control) *as a woman like Dolly would see it*, though it is true that his own condemnation of birth control *per se* can be felt in the superb scene between the two women. Dolly's essential goodness, however, comes out in her pity for Anna's unhappiness, and her refusal to judge Anna. But after Anna's tension and morphine addiction it is perfectly natural that 'Recollections of home and her children rose in her imagination with a new and peculiar charm' (VI, xxiv, 235).

What then of Karenin and the tragic heroine Anna herself? Leavis quite rightly sees D. H. Lawrence's view of Anna and Vronsky as cowards before society as a misreading and puts the position in a nutshell when he writes: 'Though Karenin is insufferable, she has done wrong' and draws attention to her son Serezha as the focus of the 'dreadful contradiction' [14] embodied in her dream in which he has two fathers. But I think that he is himself guilty of an oversimplification when he comes to consider the scene in which Karenin returns to the house and finds Vronsky at the bedside of an Anna they both think is dying after having given birth to Vronsky's child. This is the scene of which Matthew Arnold wrote: 'Karenine has words of forgiveness and kindness only. The noble and victorious effort transfigures him, and all that her husband gains in the eyes of Anna, her lover Vronsky loses.' On this Leavis comments:

—who would divine from that the disturbing subtlety of the actual present-ment? The state of feeling actually produced in us is very different from that which Arnold suggests. . . . The way we take the scene, its moral and human significance for us, is conditioned by all that goes before, and this has estab-lished what Karenin is, what Anna is, and what, inexorably, the relations between them must be. We know him as, in the pejorative Laurentian sense, a purely 'social' being, ego-bound, self-important, without any spontaneity of life in him and unable to be anything but offended and made uncom-fortable by spontaneity of life in others.[15]

That no doubt is how D. H. Lawrence would have portrayed him, one is tempted to reply, but then D. H. Lawrence is—and it is no shame to him or any other novelist—no Tolstoy! For can any reader who looks at the forgiveness scene with an open mind and unin-fluenced by Laurentian presuppositions, fail to recognize that Arnold's reaction is the natural one and the one which the author intended the reader to have? Karenin is no Laurentian Rico or Mr Massy.[16] It is Tolstoy's very point that in this scene, and in this scene alone, Karenin reaches a height of self-transcendence that he never attained before and will never attain again. To some degree the issue here turns on the very question of ethics and of means and ends which I have just been discussing apropos Levin, for Karenin is par excellence the Kantian man of rigour and duty who by mak-ing his own will to virtue into a goal corrupts morals into pharisaism. Now though Tolstoy agrees with Kant that the happiness of the good man is just as much a matter of chance as that of the purely sensuous man, he does *not* agree with Kant that one can make the good will an end in the sense that one sets it up as something one ought to pursue and then feels justified self-approval at one's own rectitude. This is to confuse the means with the end, for the good will is only a means to various particular ends. Nevertheless Tolstoy's emphasis in *this* scene falls on Karenin's unwonted spontaneity, the very spontaneity Leavis denies him:

He was not thinking that the law of Christ, which all his life he had wished to fulfil, told him to forgive and love his enemies, but a joyous feeling of forgiveness and love . . . filled his soul. (IV, xvii, 468)

For the only moment in his life Karenin has abandoned the letter for the spirit, has, to adapt some words of Kitty to Varenka, ceased to live by 'principles' and started to live from the 'heart'.

Tolstoy's close friend Strakhov saw Anna herself as pursued pitilessly by Tolstoy right up to the moment of her suicide whereas Arnold, though he speaks of Flaubert as being 'cruel, with the cruelty of petrified feeling, to his poor heroine' Emma Bovary, implies that this was not the case with Tolstoy's treatment of Anna. It is interesting that when a visitor to Yasnaya Polyana once said that Tolstoy had been too hard on Anna by letting her be run over by a train, Tolstoy replied:

Pushkin once said to some friends: 'What do you think has happened to my Tatyana? She has gone and got married! I should never have thought it of her!' So it was with my Anna Karenina; in fact, my heroes and heroines are apt to behave quite differently from what I could wish them to do! [17]

What Sir Karl Popper has called the 'logic of situation' is very important in Tolstoy, but it is a 'logic of situation' which, unlike the sociological analysis posited by Popper, involves the mental and even physical states of the persons involved. Tolstoy shows that the events which Anna and Vronsky have set in motion by their free choices bring about situations which greatly restrict the possibilities of choice, and force them into roles which they only half-willingly sustain, Vronsky as the philanthropist and lover and Anna as one the sole purpose of whose destiny, the meaning of whose life, is to be the object of that love. Those situations seem to have a certain autonomy *even from the wishes of the author*, as well as from those of the characters themselves.

Boris Eikhenbaum saw *Anna Karenina* as Tolstoy's victory over the Western love novel, but he makes it sound too much as though this was just a question of a formal *literary* struggle with a sort of battle of the genres from which Tolstoy emerged as conqueror. But *Anna Karenina* is far more than an intra-literary phenomenon, it is a demonstration, through literary fiction, of the extra-literary truth that *l'amour-passion* is not a sufficient basis on which to build a good life of creative fulfilment, a demonstration that, as Leavis puts it:

The spontaneity and depth of Vronsky's and Anna's passion for one another may be admirable, but passion—love—can't itself, though going with estimable qualities in both parties, make a permanent relation. [18]

The claim that the largesse of human life in the book includes eating, dancing, hunting, racing and farming, but that there is an 'absolute silence on the fundamental human activity of sex' [19] seems to me completely mistaken. It mistakes reticence for rejection. Tolstoy makes it quite clear that Oblonsky hungers for women just as he hungers for food, and that when Anna undresses to go into

Karenin's bedroom because of Karenin's 'significant smile' the fire in her is 'quenched or hidden' (I, xxxiii, 127) whereas Vronsky's caresses fulfil a 'bewitching dream of happiness' (II, xi, 168). Tolstoy *does* sometimes give an impression of disgust with physical love-making (though not always), but he nowhere overlooks the power of physical desires. What he rightly sees, however, is that sexual activity cannot be seen as *just* on a par with eating (except by a feat of epicurean abstractionism) because it commonly involves at some stage so many more aspects of the human beings involved than the satisfaction of a physical appetite.

The dreadfulness of the high-pitched feeling with which Anna becomes Vronsky's mistress arises not because Tolstoy condemns physical love-making *per se* (as in *The Kreutzer Sonata* or *Father Sergius*) but because this is the moment at which Anna clearly (and rightly) realizes her total dependence on her relationship of *l'amour-passion* to Vronsky to give meaning to her life. 'I have nothing but you left. Remember that' (II, xi, 169). Tolstoy has a Proustian insight into the deception of self and others to which *l'amour-passion* inevitably leads, but expresses it with a clarity and concision foreign to Proust. Vronsky has to hide from Anna his disappointment at his ruined career. He has to humour her wish to defy society, though he knows the unhappiness it will bring. When he wants to keep Oblonsky's telegram which says that there is little hope of a divorce from Anna, she immediately thinks: 'In the same way he may hide and is hiding from me his correspondence from women' (VII, xxv, 355). Some kind of *immanent* justice seems to be at work here. Vronsky has got his desire, possession of Anna, but now her jealousy and possessiveness have become a torment to them both. As Tolstoy says of Vronsky when they are in Italy:

He soon felt that the realization of his longing gave him only one grain of the mountain of bliss he had anticipated. That realization showed him the eternal error men make by imagining that happiness consists in the gratification of their wishes. . . . Soon he felt rising in his soul a desire for desires —boredom. (V, viii, 32)

Morris Weitz is right to see that the theme 'that human beings are not to blame for their actions and hence should not judge one another' cannot be identified as the main theme of the novel. He continues:

For, if it is, the philosophy of *Anna Karenina* constitutes a denial of morality altogether, which clearly conflicts with much of the novel, especially Anna's shame and self-destruction. Furthermore, to accept this theme as central necessitates its application to all experience, not only Anna's affair, but all the hypocrisy, frigidity, and vacuity which are actually deplored in the novel. Finally, such a reading of the novel demands that Oblonsky become its true spokesman, forever pleading for the attitude of laissez faire in human life, and thus reduces the novel to a moral mockery.[20]

There is no doubt, however, that the idea 'judge not' is *one* of the main themes of the book. Weitz misses the point that there is a kind of moral paradox here akin to Sir Karl Popper's paradox of tolerance.[21] The hypocritical, frigid and vacuous society that condemns Anna is itself open to condemnation precisely for the reason that it judges. Moreover Anna herself judges too. Her last wish is the moralistic wish to punish Vronsky. No, not quite her last wish, for even as she throws herself under the train she is horrified and prays for forgiveness (VII, xxxi, 380). That is why Strakhov is not quite right in saying that Tolstoy pursues her pitilessly to the very end.

The tragic situation is a situation from which there is no escape except by the death of the protagonist, whereas it is the essence of comedy that there is always a way out. This point is dramatized in the following discussion between Anna and Oblonsky:

'No, Stiva,' said she, 'I am lost, quite lost! And even worse than lost. I am not lost yet; I cannot say "all is finished": on the contrary, I feel that all is not yet finished. I am like a tightly-strung cord which must snap. But all is not yet finished . . . and it will end in some dreadful manner.'
'Oh no! One can loosen the string gently. There is no situation from which there is no escape.'
'I have been thinking and thinking. Only one. . . .'
Again he understood from her frightened face that she considered death to be the only escape, and did not let her finish. (IV, xxi, 483–4)

This dialogue comes about half-way through the novel shortly after Anna has recovered from her illness in giving birth to Vronsky's child. But what about the 'dreadful manner' in which it does end? It is interesting to contrast Tolstoy's portrayal of Anna's death with Flaubert's portrayal of Madame Bovary's. Flaubert throws all the emphasis on the sensuous aspects of Emma, on 'the soles of the feet, that once had run so swiftly to the assuaging of her desires, and now would walk no more.' [22] He savours Emma's sensuous disintegration as he had once savoured her sensuous ecstasies. The touch of the voluptuary is inescapable. But Tolstoy allows Anna a clear *moral* consciousness of her situation and dilemmas right to the end. Her interior monologues on the way to her suicide contain one of the most potent negative visions in the whole of literature: 'Are we not all flung into the world only to hate each other, and therefore to torment ourselves and others?' (VII, xxx, 375). She wishes to punish

Vronsky, as we have seen, until her last 'God forgive me everything!' as the railway truck strikes her. Her original dilemma had been painful, to yield to Vronsky or to continue to be stifled by Karenin. She had committed herself to Vronsky. But then she had found herself demanding a full commitment from him and placing both in a situation from which there was no way out except by her death. We do not feel that Tolstoy indulged her and then got satisfaction out of punishing her. Her fate has a contingency and yet a pattern that bears the marks not of the author's vindictiveness, but of the poetic inevitability we associate with tragedy. Even with her descent into hysteria and morphine addiction Anna is never denied the protection of that aura of dignity with which tragedy always invests its protagonists.

But Tolstoy's comprehensive vision is a vision of the whole truth, and the whole truth is wider than the artistically shaped contingencies of poetic inevitability, encompassing contingency in the raw so to speak. It includes a world in which the real most emphatically is not the rational, a world in which women suffer from pregnancy-sickness and shattered heroes from toothache, and in which a man's whole happiness and everything that makes life meaningful to him may be subject to something as chancy and as artistically non-tragic as a stroke of lightning—the world, in short, of us all. And yet we, like Levin, have the power to invest this meaningless world of chance with the meaning of goodness; for that is its challenge, and our perhaps unique privilege.

Chapter 13

Death, *A Confession* and *Ivan Ilych*

Tolstoy portrays himself in *A Confession* as a man like Levin in *Anna Karenina*. He tells us that he was 'favoured by fortune', with a good wife and good children in good circumstances, physically fit, and yet subject to such depressions that he ceased to go shooting in case he might be tempted to commit suicide. He had become conscious of the reality of 'death which destroys all things, including my work and its remembrance' with an intensity that he had never experienced before, and this consciousness had prompted him to ask what is in fact the central question of *A Confession*, namely, 'Is there any meaning in my life that the inevitable death awaiting me does not destroy?' [1] That Tolstoy's attitude to death is not an inevitable one, or, indeed, even the only natural one, is illustrated by the following remarks of Santayana's:

That the end of life should be death may sound sad: yet what other end could it have? The end of an evening party is to go to bed; but its use is to gather congenial people together so that they may pass the time pleasantly. An invitation to the dance is not rendered ironical because the dance cannot last forever; the youngest of us and the most vigorously wound up, after a few hours, has had enough of sinuous stepping and prancing. The transitoriness of things is essential to their physical being and not at all sad in itself; it becomes sad by virtue of a sentimental illusion, which makes us imagine that they wish to endure, and that their end is always untimely; but in a healthy nature it is not so. What is truly sad is to have some impulse frustrated in the midst of its career and robbed of its chosen object; and what is painful is to have an organ lacerated or destroyed when it is still vigorous, and not ready for its natural sleep and dissolution. We must not confuse the itch which our unsatisfied instincts continue to cause with the pleasure of satisfying and dismissing each of them in turn. [2]

What Santayana says is logically unexceptionable, and yet, can one fail to detect in the way he says it a fatal note of complacency? He is a comfortable man, a man who assents to the proposition that he is mortal in the sense that Tolstoy's Ivan Ilych assented to the proposition 'That Caius—man in the abstract—was mortal' while really believing that it did not apply to 'little Vanya, Ivan Ilych, with all my thoughts and emotions'.[3] This fatal note is, despite the elegance of Santayana's expression, the result of a lack of imagination, for it takes a Shakespeare (Claudio's speech in *Measure for Measure*) or a Dostoevsky (the account in *The Idiot* of what it feels like just before one's execution) or a Tolstoy (as in *Ivan Ilych*) really to bring home to one *in the concrete* what the apprehension of death is like.

Santayana's privileged, spectatorial position comes out in his analogy of life with a dance. He is willing to admit that those (like Tolstoy's Moscow poor) whose wish to 'dance' has been frustrated may suffer; but as one who personally has 'had enough of stepping and prancing' he himself is perfectly ready for a rest. True, Tolstoy does not deny that he has had more than his share of the 'dance' of life; but the whole point for him is, of course, that death is not a rest, as the facile analogy has it, for one wakes up from a rest. It is *annihilation* that Tolstoy fears, however irrational this might be. It is, of course, the very point of Santayana's analogy that it quite plays down the horror of death, just as it is the point of Tolstoy's Eastern fable of the man hanging by a twig over a well with a hungry dragon at the bottom, to bring that horror home to us.[4]

It is sometimes thought that in *A Confession* Tolstoy is simply advancing the proposition that because we must die everything in our life is devalued. As a matter of fact *A Confession* as a whole is designed not to advance such a proposition, but precisely to rebut it, and to do so on the grounds of Tolstoyan Christianity. Tolstoy is not so much trying to advance a logical proposition in the early pages of *A Confession* as to bring home to us his psychological state and, in particular, his pessimistic mood and his fear of death. I agree that Tolstoy mixes up psychological and logical questions, and makes some logical howlers,[5] but in a curious way this only contributes to the artistic and spiritual effect and the sincerity of the work as a whole.

It may be true that Tolstoy comes near to developing 'a mystique of the masses' in the argument that the 'arrest of life' from which he suffers is confined to members of the educated upper class like himself and not found among peasants. But when we take account of the strong Christian tradition of exalting the humble, combined with the heritage of Slavophil populism and the fact that Tolstoy was a guilt-tormented man trying to awaken the conscience of his own class, we may be rather more inclined to make excuses for this than to use it as a stick with which to beat him. After all there would be no sense in running down the peasants, workers and atheist

Narodniks to people all too ready to despise them. Moreover Tolstoy does not believe that the peasants possess a 'theoretical' knowledge of the meaning of life denied to their social superiors. The idioms Tolstoy uses—'irrational knowledge', 'faith', 'strength of life' and 'Christian faith'—are hardly suggestive of 'theoretical knowledge'.[6] For all his cult of the people, Tolstoy does not hesitate to go on and say that this faith of theirs is mixed up with much regrettable absurdity and superstition. He does not use the wretched Pascalian argument that we should take holy water and stupefy ourselves if we want to find faith. On the contrary, his whole effort in his religious works is to make a bold attempt to separate the essential truths of the faith he sees around him from the igorance and superstition in which they are embedded. He dislikes the ritual and dogma of both the learned and the ignorant.

Tolstoy's whole endeavour in *A Confession* is to try to show that he and those like him are mistaken in supposing that there is 'some evil irony in the fact that we suffer and die'. This is particularly difficult for him as he has an incomparably more concrete grasp than Santayana of what suffering and dying involve, and therefore cannot be quite so resigned in his dismissal of these things as Santayana is. Tolstoy is careful to point out, however, that he was in error in assuming that what applied to his own life (a feeling of meaninglessness) applied to 'life in general'. But when he tries to give us the positive side of his religious discoveries things become very difficult because, as Kant has shown (and as Tolstoy agreed), the existence of God cannot be proved. Tolstoy knows that the fact that he can conceive of God does not entail that God really exists. What he leaves us with, in the end, is an overwhelming feeling of his need for God to exist and his sense that many among the people possess an enviable faith in the reality of that existence which he himself lacks. Since he nevertheless sees that much unnecessary ritual, dogma and false belief go along with the faith of the people,[7] he embarks with fervour on the task of going to the Gospels themselves to see what is truly essential to faith.

The Death of Ivan Ilych is Tolstoy's attempt to bring home to us through the art of fiction the view he had already expressed in *A Confession*, namely that death is most terrible to those who have never really learned how to live. The story is, in fact, far more about Ivan Ilych's life than about his death. It has absolutely nothing in common with the absurd quest for an ontology of death conducted by some existentialist.[8] Tolstoy was too rational to suppose that death (as opposed to dying) can be experienced and would have agreed with Wittgenstein's remark: 'Death is not an event in life: we do not live to experience death'.[9]

The story opens with Tolstoy revealing what the death of Ilych means to his colleagues. It awakens first the universally thankful and complacent feeling 'it is he who is dead and not I', and secondly thoughts, for example, of possible promotion. Then we learn about Ilych's life which 'had been most simple and most ordinary and therefore most terrible'. On graduating from law school Ilych bought a fine set of fashionable clothes and hung a medallion enscribed *respice finem* on his watch chain, but as with all of us *finem* (the end, death) was precisely what he forgot. Ilych has married reasonably well and prospered in his career, in which, indeed, he feels happier than in his domestic life where his wife's need for money leads to friction. This friction lessens when he gets a still higher post, but at about the same time he becomes ill from an apparently trivial fall which occurs while he is directing the decoration of a lavish new house. As the pain gets worse he grows more and more irritable and feels that the doctor treats him just as he himself treats an accused person. The central theme of the story is, then, that of our need to be loved, even when we are unlovely and unlovable. Ilych even becomes physically repulsive to himself, let alone to others. He cannot stand his own smell. His life is morally poisoned, too, and he feels that he is poisoning the life of others. He needs a pity and love that none can give and he grows resentful. Above all he comes to feel a 'real' rather than 'notional' assent to the fact that he must die:

The syllogism he had learned from Kiezewetter's Logic: 'Caius is a man, men are mortal, therefore Caius is mortal', had always seemed to him correct as applied to Caius, but certainly not as applied to himself. That Caius—man in the abstract—was mortal, was perfectly correct, but he was not Caius, not an abstract man, but a creature quite, quite separate from others. . . . 'Caius really was mortal, and it was right for him to die: but for me, little Vanya, Ivan Ilych, with all my thoughts and emotions, it's altogether a different matter. It cannot be that I ought to die. That would be too terrible'.[10]

Tolstoy's inexorable matter-of-fact narration of this unique case which is, at the same time, the case of us all, prevents any over-emphasis on self-pity or unfocused emotion. Ilych's daughter Lisa, 'strong, healthy, evidently in love', and 'impatient with illness', will one day meet the same fate, though now no thought is more remote from her than that. As the pain grows worse Ilych utters the terrible Job-like cry against the cruelty of God: 'Why hast Thou done all this? Why hast Thou brought me here? Why, why dost Thou torment me so terribly?' [11] But Ilych's situation is worse than Job's; for God enters into a long colloquy with Job and restores him to health and riches, while for Ilych there is only 'the cruelty of God, and the absence of God', and one is not sure how much the absence is part of the cruelty. Tolstoy wants to convey artistically the conclusion he had reached in *A Confession* that death is most fearful to those who have not discovered the meaning of life and who, consequently, 'see some evil irony in the fact that we suffer and die'. What he succeeds in conveying is, however, not so much that, as the awful passivity of the process of dying. He wants to show that the screaming mass 'in the hands of the executioner' achieved a spiritual insight and even 'joy' in the instant before death, but I think artistic success eludes him here, as it eludes him in Brekhunov's sudden conversion from egoism to altruism in *Master and Man* (1895). A Karataev-like unreality breaks in. Tolstoy's grasp of the phenomenal world is sure, but, at the moment in both stories when, so to speak, the noumenal world is meant to intersect with it, that grasp falters. The mode of connection between the two worlds is vague, motiveless and uncertain, and it is a feeble justification to retort that that is just the point. I am not claiming that it is impossible to depict an attitude of Christian acceptance of death in fiction successfully, but I think that Tolstoy falters in this particular case.[12] The story emphasizes the emptiness of Ivan Ilych's life with a thoroughness that makes it very difficult for us to accede to the fact that Ilych received at the end of it an illumination we are far from certain Tolstoy himself, with all his struggles, ever achieved.

Although *The Death of Ivan Ilych* is not marred by self-pity or unfocused emotion, there are passages which have an unacceptable note of too much censoriousness towards the weakness of humanity; and these passages, together with the failure of the conclusion, prevent the story from being the supreme masterpiece it is often taken for. True, it is supposed to have inspired Bunin's famous story of a death, *The Gentleman from San Francisco*. True, it is often cited as the supreme illustration of Heidegger's existentialist thesis that 'inauthentic' existence consists of submerging oneself in what everyone does. Nevertheless, if it had not been by the author of *War and Peace* and *Anna Karenina* neither the admirers of Bunin, nor those of Heidegger, would have been so keen to extol its merits. The very fact that it is not a work of pure imagination centred in itself, but too overt an illustration of a moral standpoint outside itself, so to speak, makes it both fatally tempting as a demonstrative touchstone and inferior to Tolstoy at his best.

Tolstoy is a little too eager in *Ivan Ilych* to convict mankind of trivial pleasures and petty complacencies, whether these consist of a desire for promotion or too great a fondness for furniture. Ilych, for example, wants to possess 'all the things people of a certain class have in order to resemble other people of that class' and yet 'to him it all seemed quite exceptional' (Chapter III). What is he guilty of, conformity or standing apart? The fact that only 'a clean, fresh peasant lad' (Chapter VIII), Gerasim, and not, say, a member of his own class, like his wife, can adapt to the unpleasant task of removing Ilych's excretions (as his bowel cancer requires), somehow falls in a little too neatly with Tolstoy's social message during the 1880s. Moreover is it not more likely that a man in Ilych's situation would understand and even be grateful for the fact that the others pretended he was not fatally ill, than that he would expect them to obey his exclamation: 'Stop lying!' (Chapter VII)? But even if we accept this exclamation as showing Ilych's desperate need for others to realize his real situation, it must also be conceded that Tolstoy as narrator uses Ilych's suffering in order to disparage the satisfactions a normal healthy body can enjoy.

When Tolstoy suggests that the only truly happy moments of Ilych's life occurred in his childhood (Chapter IX), he does not really evoke these as he had done in other works, and one gets the feeling that a Tolstoyan 'theme' is being sounded somewhat automatically, that the master is repeating himself. Ilych the careerist is a Karenin *redivivus*, but portrayed more externally than Karenin, whose complex relationships with wife, son and colleagues, and whose inner fears and weaknesses are conveyed with fuller particularity and a concomitantly fuller insight and sympathy. Even the set-piece of Ilych's death is pale beside the masterly rendering of the death of Levin's brother Nicholas in *Anna Karenina* (V, 20), and Levin's own despair at life and fear of annihilation.

Tolstoy has shown us Ilych's anxieties before his illness and his despair during it, so what warrant is there for his claim in Chapter XII that Ilych is hindered from coming to terms with death 'by his conviction that his life had been a good one'? Is it really true that to have insight into good and evil makes physical pain and degradation more easily conquerable at the end, as seems to be the implication? Tolstoy goes out of his way to stress that, in so far as we belong to the phenomenal world, these are just things that happen to us as helpless victims. Yet he wants to suggest is *Ilych* that we can transcend them by the mental act of pronouncing 'Death is finished', to ourselves. The unmitigated horror of death and the impossibility of understanding its meaning are more honestly expressed in the account of the death of Nicholas.

Chapter 14

Tolstoy, the Gospels and Jesus:
Christian Ethics and *Hadji Murad*

There is no getting around the fact that *A Confession* (1879) marks a dramatic break in Tolstoy's life and work. The comprehensive vision he had achieved in *War and Peace* and *Anna Karenina* narrows its scope, and this narrowing is not always compensated by an increase in intensity. Instead of working through many themes (death, sexual conflict, social oppression and war) in a single long work, each theme is now confined to a single short work (e.g. *Ivan Ilych*, *The Kreutzer Sonata* and *Hadji Murad*). The many-sided questing figure disappears (the Nekhlyudov of *Resurrection* is 'thin' in this respect when compared with Pierre, Prince Andrew and Levin) perhaps because Tolstoy now feels that he is, in a sense, in possession of the truth.

At the same time it is important to emphasize that Tolstoy greatly exaggerates in *A Confession* his lack of concern with ethical, metaphysical and religious problems in the early years of his marriage when he was at the height of his literary creativeness. He also appears to forget the fact that he delivered a bitter attack on the 'religion of progress' in *Lucerne* (1857), and in his educational articles in the early sixties—the very time when *A Confession* claims that he was a convinced adherent of that very 'religion'. The fact is, of course, that ethical and religious problems are essential constituents of his work at all periods. In both the Sevastopol sketches and *War and Peace*, for example, the condemnation of war sometimes takes on an oratorical-charismatic tone that is in complete harmony with his later teaching of non-resistance. One has only to recall the diary entry for 1853, in which Tolstoy spoke of a reading of Karamzin having reminded him that 'morality' is the one aim of literature, to realize the importance of the continuities between the early and the late Tolstoy. In fact it could be said that Tolstoy's whole conscious enterprise from *A Confession* onwards was to carry out that 'great, stupendous, idea' which he had conceived as early as March 1855, and which he described then in his diary (as quoted above,

p. 13) as 'the founding of a new religion corresponding to the present development of mankind'.[1] Tolstoy's *The Gospel in Brief*, *What I Believe*, *The Kingdom of God is Within You* and *What is Religion and Wherein Lies its Essence?* [2] can rightly be seen as his attempt to state 'the religion of Christ . . . purged of dogmas and mysticism', in short to carry out the intention formulated in 1855.

Nor can it be claimed that with 1879 Tolstoy stopped being an artist and began to be a preacher. He had always been something of a preacher in his art and did not cease to be an artist in his preaching. It is not so much a matter of discontinuity as of a shift of emphasis. We can focus the problem of looking again at that passage (partially quoted above, p. 36) from a letter written in 1865 when he was in the middle of *War and Peace*:

The aims of an artist are incommensurate (as the mathematicians say) with social aims. The aim of an artist is not to solve a problem irrefutably but to make people love life in all its countless and inexhaustible manifestations. If I were to be told that I could write a novel whereby I might irrefutably establish what seemed to me the correct point of view on all social problems, I would not even devote two hours work to such a novel; . . . [3]

Suppose, it might be said, we substitute the word 'religious' for the word 'social' in the above sentence, would that not show that all Tolstoy's work after 1879 vitiates his own principle in that it all strives to do what he says the artist is not interested in doing, namely 'irrefutably establish . . . the correct point of view'? But even here when one reflects on Tolstoy's actual works the antithesis becomes blurred. Certainly *War and Peace* awakens a joy in life; but that does not mean that we love Helene herself, for example, although we may love Tolstoy's portrayal of her as a manifestation of art, and so as a part of life. In fact Tolstoy does try to establish the correct point of view on certain ethical (normative) and historical (factual) questions in *War and Peace*; and although it might be claimed that the latter enterprise leads to artistic flaws, this is certainly not the case with the former. At the same time *A Confession* and *What I Believe* can be seen as not just trying to establish the correct point of view (though it is true that they try to do that), but also as trying to *awaken* the educated classes to a lively sense of the realities of life and death, and of the demands of the Christianity that many of them outwardly profess. Tolstoy is just as concerned with a *metanoia* or a 'change of heart' as with a 'correct point of view'.

We have seen that the whole artistic striving of Tolstoy was to achieve a comprehensive vision, a synoptic view of life, a striving, that is, towards the ideal but unattainable overview that Boethius saw his God as having: a view of everything that was, is and will be the case, *totum simul*, all at once. The questions of God, freedom and immortality greatly exercise those thoughtful characters in Tolstoy's works who come nearest to achieving the breadth of vision of Tolstoy himself—Pierre, Prince Andrew, Princess Mary and Levin. In *A Confession* Tolstoy can no longer hold these questions at a distance, but, as it were, steps into the role of one of his characters. He now asks *in propria persona* the questions they had asked, in particular the question, 'Is there any meaning in my life that the inevitable death awaiting me does not destroy?' Now in the past the great religions of the world have had an answer to this question. In the case of Judaism and of Christianity the answer lay in what Professor Hick [4] calls *fiducia*, 'a trust, maintained sometimes despite contrary indications, that the divine purpose towards us is wholly good and loving'. Professor Hick points out that in the Bible

The reality of the divine Being is assumed throughout as a manifest fact. For within the borders of living religion the validity of faith in divine existence, like the validity of sense perception in ordinary daily life, is simply taken for granted and acted upon. The biblical writers are not conscious of their belief in God as being itself an exercise of faith but only of their confidence in his promises and providence.[5]

It should be immediately evident that this biblical 'validity of faith' was not and could not be taken for granted by Tolstoy who wrote:

Though I was quite convinced of the impossibility of proving the existence of a Deity (Kant had shown, and I quite understood him, that it could not be proved), I yet sought for God, hoped that I should find Him, and from old habit addressed prayers to that which I sought but had not found.[6]

As Professor Hick goes on to say, faith as trust (the *fiducia* we find in the Bible) logically presupposes faith as cognition of the object of that trust (*fides*), and it is the very possibility of that cognition which has become problematic for Tolstoy (as for us) in a way that it never was for the people of whom the Bible speaks.

We can be certain that Tolstoy thought that science and philosophy had not rendered a religious view of life superfluous, and indeed that he wrote his later works to show that such a view is a *necessity* for man; but it is not at all clear (despite all Tolstoy's clarity and avoidance of mystery-mongering) how far Tolstoy was committed to a transcendent theism as opposed to what is ultimately a religious naturalism. This is partly because Tolstoy said different things at different times and partly because of the difficult nature of the problems themselves. After all, a man committed to transcendent theism may well believe that we can only apprehend 'the supernatural in and through the natural',[7] and that the Kingdom of God is our concern not 'in its eventual universal form', as the new Jerusalem in heaven, but 'in its already operative, though fragmentary, earthly existence'.[8]

When we take Tolstoy's simple, parable-like story *God Sees the Truth, but Waits*,[9] we find a moving account of the central dilemma of life for every thinking person whether theist or atheist. Why is it that so often in life the innocent suffer while the guilty prosper? A merchant, Aksenev, is framed by Semenich, the murderer and robber of a fellow merchant, and sent away from his wife and children to Siberia. He says to himself: 'It seems that only God knows the truth; it is to Him alone we must appeal and from him alone expect mercy.' Twenty-six years later Semenich comes to the same prison. Aksenev finds out Semenich was the real murderer and is deeply troubled. One day he comes across Semenich digging a tunnel. When the tunnel is discovered the prison governor, who trusts Aksenev, asks him who the culprit is. Aksenev's enemy has been delivered into his hands. Aksenev thinks:

Why should I screen him who ruined my life? Let him pay for what I have suffered. But if I tell they will probably flog the life out of him, and maybe I suspect him wrongly. And, after all, what good would it be to me?

Semenich's hard heart is softened at this and he comes to Aksenev and begs forgiveness saying that he will confess to the old crime of murdering the merchant. Aksenev sobs and says, 'God will forgive you! . . . Maybe I am a hundred times worse than you.' Semenich goes ahead and confesses, but by the time Aksenev's pardon arrives Aksenev is dead. There is no suggestion that he, like Lazarus, goes to Abraham's bosom while Semenich goes to Gehenna. The ethic is an immanent one. Semenich's remorse is his hell and Aksenev's refusal to judge ('God will forgive you') is his heaven. This is deeply moving, but does it go far enough? What if Semenich had remained unrepentant to the end and mocked Aksenev for being soft-hearted?

Some critics have felt that Tolstoy is too much of a dry eighteenth-century rationalist really to understand religion; and they see his extraction of five commandments or rules from the Sermon on the Mount as a narrow legalism which is further evidence for this.[10] It seems to me that nothing is further from the truth than such a view; and it is one that might well commend itself to a romantic pietist of the type Tolstoy witheringly portrayed in Mme Stahl and Countess Lydia Ivanovna. It is quite true that Tolstoy's whole enterprise is rational, but only a mystic obscurantist should object to that. Tolstoy wants to find out what Jesus taught, whether what Jesus taught is true, and, if so, what obedience to it involves. The truth of the teaching is the all important thing. In the face of that it does not matter what the historical Jesus taught, or even if he existed, though it is evident that Tolstoy would like to think that he did and that what he taught was the truth. Tolstoy makes it clear that obedience to the true teaching involves far more than mere legalism. It requires (this is explicit in the teaching itself) a *metanoia* or a change of heart.[11] The emphasis on the five commandments he sees in the Sermon on the Mount—and, in particular, on the commandment 'Resist not him that is evil' [12]—is Tolstoy's way of bringing home to people that one cannot be obedient to the teaching of Jesus and simply carry on as before. Jesus's claims as he sees them are absolute and total. The whole history of Christianity has shown how those claims have been vitiated by a compromise with 'the world'. Tolstoy would have had no truck with any such dubious conception as an 'interim' ethic, if he had become aware of it. According to those who hold this conception (which became widespread after the publication of Albert Schweitzer's *The Quest for the Historical Jesus*), Jesus made such uncompromising claims on men because he and his followers believed that the end of the world was at hand; consequently those claims are no longer binding on us (who no longer hold such a belief) to such a degree. Tolstoy would have distrusted this argument, as he distrusted all 'historicist' type assumptions. At any rate his whole endeavour is to bring home to his contemporaries the absolute nature of the demands of Jesus as addressed, not to others, but *to them*, and to remind them of the fact that temporal life always stands under the imminent judgement of the eternal. Why, it may be asked, should one obey the demands of Jesus? We have seen from our very first chapter that Tolstoy's lifelong quest was for 'the message which would destroy all evil in men and give them universal welfare', the secret his brother Nicholas claimed to have written on the green stick. It now seemed to him that Jesus had revealed that message to men. The reason why one should obey the demands of Jesus is the perfectly rational one that only by doing so can one find true happiness. Tolstoy is not afraid of any Kantian rigourist accusing him here of *eudaemonism* or too much concern with happiness as a goal, for he thinks, and surely he is right, that Jesus himself promises that goodness will be rewarded by happiness in the end. After all, as Schopenhauer pointed out, Kant's rigorous notion of an unconditional *ought* that does not imply reward or punishment is absurd.[13] A sort of paradox is involved. Jesus promises happiness as a reward for goodness and yet we can only be truly good by putting goodness before happiness. We cannot *know* that we will win in the end. It is a case of the biblical *fiducia* again. Is not this the meaning implicit in the sublime paradox: 'He that findeth his life shall lose it: and he that loseth his life for my sake shall find it' (Matthew X: 39)?

Tolstoy's religious writings of the 1879–84 period were intended to consist firstly of an account of his life and of the thoughts which led him to the conviction that Jesus's teaching contains the truth (*A Confession*), secondly an examination of the teaching of the Churches, and of the true teaching as independent of the interpretation of the Churches (*The Gospel in Brief*), and thirdly an exposition of the real meaning of that teaching (*What I Believe*). We have already considered *A Confession* in the previous chapter and must now go on to look at the other works in the sequence.

Tolstoy's religious quest is a noble endeavour, and one which arguably brought him nearer to exercising the charismatic function of the prophet than any other 'Western' man in modern times. His 'rationalism' is not that of a dry legalist. On the contrary, it is inspired by a fervent turning from the dogma and fetishism of priests and the egoism of mystics to the old prophetic message of the centrality of doing justice and loving mercy and walking humbly with God. The crucial difference between Tolstoy and the biblical prophets is that for them every natural appearance of cloud, sea or storm, and every historical occurrence, bore the marks of the immediate handiwork of the Lord; whereas he was the son of a critical age who had written that a return to a belief in the direct intervention of the Deity in human affairs is impossible, and who, for all his hostility to historicism, could use a phrase like 'corresponding to the present development of mankind'.[14] No biblical prophet could have spoken as Tolstoy does in the following remark to Goldenveizer: 'God ... is a necessary hypothesis or, more truly speaking, the only possible condition of a right, moral life. . . .'[15] Tolstoy is not like the biblical prophets who were living within a commitment to transcendent theism so unquestionable that it is difficult for a critical age to conceive of it. In those times it was truly a fool who said in his heart 'There is no God', whereas in ours we are more likely to regard as fools those who say there is one. As has been shown, even the modern attempts to reformulate Anselm's ontological argument for the existence of God have only in the end succeeded in showing that, logically, God is a being whose non-existence cannot be simply a matter of fact; what they have not proved is that He exists.[16]

Once more we come back to that central passage from Gorky on Tolstoy:

I was struck by a strange saying in the diary he gave me to read: 'God is my desire'.

When I returned it to him to-day, I asked him what he meant.

'An unfinished thought,' he said, screwing up his eyes as he looked at the page. 'I must have wanted to say—God is my desire to realize him. . . . No, not that. . . .' He laughed, rolled the notebook up and thrust it into the wide pocket of his smock. His relations with God are indefinite, sometimes they make me think of 'two bears in one lair'.[17]

'God is my desire to realize him . . .'. It is a profoundly ambiguous phrase, but it is not the sort of thing that could have been said by Amos or Micah.

In his letter to M. A. Engelhardt (1882), Tolstoy says that his religious writings are 'only the refutation of a false understanding of the Christian teaching and an explanation of its real meaning',[18] rather than a new preaching. Tolstoy's whole endeavour is to substitute a 'real' Christianity for a 'nominal' one, and he admits to Engelhardt that he himself does not fulfil what he sees as Jesus's commands. This brings out, I think, the irrelevance of the common criticism of Tolstoy for compromising and living at Yasnaya Polyana in comparative ease and luxury instead of forsaking wife and family for an ascetic life (a criticism which often goes along with the view that Jesus's commands, as Tolstoy saw them, are impracticable). Tolstoy is first and foremost addressing contemporary positivists and secularists and saying, in effect, 'Can you, in the face of suffering and death, endow life with meaning?' His answer to this, unlike that of Santayana, is that they cannot. I suggest that it deserves respectful consideration not primarily because of the quality of his arguments (though these are not always poor) but because of the quality of his sensibility.

As to his concern with the Gospels, Tolstoy cannot merely be dismissed as one more example of a thinker who succumbed to the now-discredited, old-style Liberal quest for the historical Jesus, for two main reasons. First of all he himself subjects the nineteenth-century continental Liberal ideology, and in particular its 'religion of science', to a far more withering attack than that of many twentieth-century thinkers. It is, moreover, much more impressive than theirs because it lacked the benefit of hindsight. He explicitly condemns Strauss and Renan for regarding Jesus as one who would not have been able to 'rise high enough to understand all the wisdom of our civilization and culture',[19] and attacks them for selecting from Jesus's teaching only what will suit that modern 'civilization'. Secondly Tolstoy does not try to write a 'life' of Jesus, Strauss or Renan style, but sets about the task of finding out what the actual Jesus of Nazareth taught as opposed to what the Churches claim he taught and to what the Gospel texts themselves say he taught. Granted Tolstoy does not realize the enormity and pitfalls of the task, not just for an amateur like himself, but even, perhaps, for any single mind however well endowed. But who can deny that it is a task which needs to be undertaken? The following comparison between the views of a modern biblical scholar, Norman Perrin, on the ethics and teaching of Jesus, and those of Tolstoy, may help to clarify the problems involved.

Perrin in his book *Rediscovering the Teaching of Jesus* advances the view that it is erroneous to assume that there is in the teaching of Jesus 'a Christian ethic as there is a Socratic or humanistic ethic'. He writes that there is nothing in that teaching 'about standards of conduct or moral judgements, there is only the urgent call to recognize the challenge of the proclamation and to respond to it'.[20] He sees 'the parables, the Kingdom teaching and the Lord's Prayer' as the areas in which it is possible to reconstruct the actual teaching of Jesus most accurately.[21] This helps his case to some degree as ethical teaching *per se* is hardly to be expected in a prayer and is implicit rather than explicit in a parable, though one would have thought that ethical presuppositions and even an ethical teaching are nevertheless present in, say, the story of the Good Samaritan. But what about the Sermon on the Mount, central for Tolstoy, and an area in which it has also been argued that it is possible to get back to the actual teaching of Jesus in its original setting? [22] It is instructive to see what Perrin makes of Matthew 5: 39–41 :

But if anyone strikes you on the right cheek, turn to him the other also ; and if anyone would sue you and take your coat let him have your cloak as well ; and if anyone forces you to go one mile, go with him two miles.

Perrin writes :

True, a man could accept insult in this spirit—so long as he was living in a community which recognized the dignity of the individual and therefore could be touched by the spirit of the act. Again, a man could respond to military imposition in this spirit and it would be effective—with some armies and some soldiers. But the 'coat/cloak' saying is, literally taken, ridiculous. A man acting in that manner would soon be back before the court on a charge of indecent exposure! If we may accept the axiom that Jesus knew what he was talking about, then we must recognize that these are not specific commandments and that they were never meant to be taken literally. What we have here are illustrations of a principle. The illustrations are extreme, and in the one instance so much so as to approach the ridiculous; but that is deliberate. . . . In light of the challenge of God and of the new relationship with one's fellow man one must respond in a new way, in a way appropriate to the new situation. What the specifics of that new way are is *not* stated; these sayings are illustrations of the necessity for a new way rather than regulations for it. But the implication of these sayings is, surely, that if one approaches the crisis in this spirit, and seeks the way in terms of the reality of one's experience of God and the new relationship with one's fellow man, then that way can be found.[23]

It seems to me that Perrin is quite right to see that Jesus is commanding what, in a sense, cannot be commanded. This is probably because Jesus wants us to carry out these seemingly impossible tasks not in the spirit of *mere obedience to a rule*, but in the spirit which arises from the *metanoia* or change of heart that has come about in us. But the challenge is felt (and here surely Tolstoy's more straightforward reading of the passage is right) because the specifics of the new way *are* stated, and stated so uncompromisingly. Perrin differentiates the approach of Jesus from 'the prudential morality of an Epictetus',[24] but then himself goes on to argue in such a way as to imply that Jesus must have known that we could only 'turn the cheek' in a community that recognizes the dignity of the individual and so could not have intended his story as an example for conduct. In doing this Perrin is, of course, imputing a prudential consideration to Jesus, the very sort of consideration he says Jesus took no account of, unlike Epictetus. Perrin ignores the following problem, which must surely strike every evaluator of the case as he presents it. What is the point of teaching by examples rather than rules if they are examples which we need not follow? It is here that Tolstoy's simplicity scores.

When we turn to Tolstoy's account of Jesus's teaching two main problems face us. The first (which I have already touched on apropos Perrin) is the nature of the mode of obedience which Jesus asks of his followers. The second is the difference between what Jesus believed about God and what Tolstoy believed about Him.

The first problem can be focused for us by the following passage from *Anna Karenina*:

The perturbation in Karenin's soul went on increasing and reached a point where he gave up struggling against it. Suddenly he felt that what he had taken for perturbation was on the contrary a blissful state of his soul, bringing him joy such as he had never before known. He was not thinking that the law of Christ, which all his life he had wished to fulfil, told him to forgive and love his enemies, but a joyous feeling of forgiveness and love filled his soul. (IV, xvii, 468)

Does not Tolstoy's approach in *What I Believe* and his other religious writings put him in the position of Karenin? Tolstoy, too, is constantly thinking about the law of Christ, while, at the same time, he wants to be in the position of fulfilling that law from a feeling of spontaneous love such as filled Karenin's soul only on that one occasion? Still, this problem seems to arise from the very nature of Jesus's commands, which seem to be somewhat like G. E. Moore's 'ideal' rules,[25] that is commands which, like 'Love thy neighbour', enjoin feelings rather than being concerned, like 'Thou shalt not steal', with the sphere of action alone.

The second problem is that Jesus, like the prophets, but, as we have seen, unlike Tolstoy, was most probably a practical (as opposed to a theoretical) transcendent theist in that the reality of God would not have been susceptible of theoretical doubt for him. In fact the modern biblical scholar Joachim Jeremias's establishment of the uniqueness of Jesus's use of the familiar Aramaic term *Abba* [26] (the term a child used of his father, though not with quite the same feeling-tone as our 'daddy') in addressing God brings out Jesus's intense sense of the nearness and reality of God. One feels that Tolstoy in his interpretation of the Gospels sometimes plays down this sense of God as a person because (though he is not consistent on the matter) he himself is attracted at times to an impersonal quasi-pantheistic conception of God.

There is a striking affinity between the Palestine of Jesus and the Russia of Tolstoy. This is the presence of intense revolutionary activity in both. In the case of Palestine this was directed by Jewish nationalists against a foreign power (the Romans), whereas in Russia it was directed against a Caesaropapist state controlled by rulers of the same nationality as the revolutionaries. Tolstoy was far more condemnatory of the rulers and the state power (what he called the 'patriotic Conservative Christians') than of the revolutionaries (whom he called 'Revolutionary Atheists'); but he felt he had to condemn the latter also, for 'Neither these nor those wish to abandon the right to resist by violence what they consider evil'.[27] Even so there is an interesting difference of direction between the pacifist teaching of Jesus as we have it in the Gospels and that of Tolstoy, although Tolstoy himself sincerely believes that the direction of both, so to speak, is identical. Tolstoy thinks that the doctrine of non-resistance is addressed primarily to the State and its agents (police, tax-collectors, jurymen, etc.) and to us in so far as we act as its agents. He contends, that is, that it is the State which has taken it upon itself to resist evil (in the form of criminals, etc.) and thus disobeyed Jesus's commandments. It is we, therefore, who must resist the State's resistance, so to speak, though only by nonviolent means. Now Jesus, at any rate as presented in the Gospels, directs the command of non-resistance not to the agents of the State, but to those who wish to resist the State, presumably to the Zealots and their sympathizers. Despite his own intense hostility to the State Tolstoy is honest enough in his own translation of the Gospels to make Jesus say that if tax is demanded it should be paid 'because you must not resist evil',[28] even though it cuts across his own doctrine.

Notwithstanding his deep commitment to the doctrine of non-resistance Tolstoy turned in the last decade of his life to a celebration of the courage and tenacity of the warrior in his 'archaizing' epic narrative *Hadji Murad*.[29] This work seems to have been a favourite of Wittgenstein's, despite the fact that Wittgenstein was deeply moved by Tolstoy's version of the teaching of Jesus. Wittgenstein wrote of Tolstoy: 'It seems to me his philosophy is most true when it's *latent* in the story'.[30] Yet what philosophy is latent in this story other than the philosophy of defiance? Does the conclusion not celebrate the vitality of a revengeful, proud, defiant warrior who once, as we learn in an aside, 'ordered twenty-six prisoners to be killed'? [31] It would seem so. Yet is not Hadji Murad only admirable relative to the withering portrait of the complacent and cruel Nicholas I and the careerist and predatory Russians? Is it not significant that the words 'He is a great man', 'another Napoleon', 'He died like a hero', 'a valiant head', are spoken in chapter IX by those same Russians to flatter Hadji's captor, their commander, Vorontsov, and not by the narrator? The vitality was admirable, yes, but its uses and fate were not so.

Hadji Murad opens with a symbolic introduction in the form of a brief apologue, or story illustrative of a truth, in which the narrator describes how, when returning home after the hay harvest, he had seen a 'Tartar' thistle which he had only been able to pick after a struggle. Further along, in a ploughed field, he came across another which was surviving even though crushed by a cart. This tenacity of life amid destruction reminds him of the Caucasian episode of the Tartar Hadji Murad's death during the tribesmen's struggle with the Russian invader at the beginning of the 1850s.

The story proper begins with Hadji Murad's *kunák*, or comrade, Sado, swearing loyalty to his friend even though their chief Shamil has exiled Hadji. Shamil is engaged in a struggle with the Russians. The third chapter moves to the Russian fort at Vozdvizhensk and the commander Prince Vorontsov. The announcement that Hadji Murad has arranged to meet the Prince brings some welcome excitement to the monotonous life of the fortress. The Russians, who have just lost General Sleptsov (whose death in battle they typically romanticize), in no way regard their old enemy Hadji as an ally, but treat him as a prisoner.

The Viceroy's aide-de-camp, Loris-Melikov, comes to question Hadji who tells him about past battles among the Tartars, and, in particular, about the quarrel of his own family with Shamil. But Hadji has now simply become a pawn in the hands of Russian officials engaged in an internal struggle for power. The war minister, Chernyshov, a parvenu, dislikes Vorontsov and is jealous of what he sees as the Emperor's favour towards him. Nicholas is portrayed as a corpulent senile sensualist who smells rebellion everywhere and thinks of himself as a great strategist. He approves of Vorontsov's treatment of Hadji and orders a further expedition against the tribesmen which takes place in January 1852. Chapters XVI and XVII describe the fighting, in part through the eyes of a soldier, Butler. Butler is, in some ways, cast in the role Olenin had played in *The Cossacks*; but Tolstoy cannot make his consciousness sufficiently interesting, partly because he vacillates between Butler and Hadji Murad himself as the true centre of the story.

Eventually Hadji, wearied by the Russians' inactivity about getting his family released from Shamil's hold, decides to escape. He is caught and killed; and Butler, who had begun to admire Hadji and 'the poetry of warfare' (which Tolstoy presents in a more ironic and disillusioned way than he had done in *The Cossacks*), is presented with his head by Kamenev in the presence of the horrified Marya Dmitrievna (the major's wife with whom Butler had somewhat coarsely flirted) who tells them that they are all cut-throats. Kamenev tells Butler the story of Hadji's death. But here an ambiguity enters in; for Kamenev's narrative itself romanticizes war, seeing Hadji's end as epically heroic, and yet the narrative does not seem to be put in ironic quotation marks, as were the earlier remarks by the Russians in chapter IX about Hadji, who had killed twenty-six prisoners, being 'a great man', 'another Napoleon'. On the contrary, the sympathetic account of Hadji Murad's last stand against the Russians (an account which is a curious mixture of high romance and laconicism) seems to come directly from Tolstoy himself. Hadji is portrayed as defiant so long as he has any strength left, an instance of pure physical courage. Even his apparently dead body rises up and makes those who are approaching stop short. The beheading of his body by a tribesman in the Russian service takes on an almost ceremonial quality. This is not quite the 'cut-throat' atmosphere Marya Dmitrievna had envisaged, but a more 'equivocal' one of sportsmen around a noble animal they have killed. Russian 'civilization' has crushed a primitive thistle-like beauty which itself had a strain of cruelty to which Tolstoy could not define his attitude.

Chapter 15

Tolstoy the Ascetic? *The Kreutzer Sonata, Father Sergius, Resurrection*

Aylmer Maude points out that the views approving marriage which satisfied Tolstoy in 1884 when he wrote *What I Believe* no longer satisfied him in 1889 when he wrote *The Kreutzer Sonata*.[1] This can be brought out by considering Tolstoy's remarks on Jesus's teaching on sexual conduct in the Sermon on the Mount and his translation in *The Gospel in Brief* (1883) of Jesus's teaching on celibacy in the later passage in Matthew (19: 10–12). Let us first take Jesus's teaching on sexual conduct in Matthew 5: 27–32, part of the Sermon on the Mount:

> You have heard that it was said, 'You shall not commit adultery'. But I say to you that every one who looks at a woman lustfully has already committed adultery with her in his heart. If your right eye causes you to sin, pluck it out and throw it away; it is better that you lose one of your members than that your whole body be thrown into hell. And if your right hand causes you to sin, cut it off and throw it away; it is better that you lose one of your members than that your whole body go into hell.
>
> It was also said, 'Whoever divorces his wife, let him give her a certificate of divorce'. But I say to you that every one who divorces his wife, except on the ground of unchastity, makes her an adulteress: and whoever marries a divorced woman commits adultery.[2]

In *What I Believe* (1884) Tolstoy takes this passage as implying that 'Men and women, knowing indulgence in sexual relations to lead to strife, should avoid all that evokes desire'.[3] He shrewdly questions the *caveat* that Jesus allowed divorce on the grounds of adultery. I say shrewdly, because it appears that this caveat was not spoken by Jesus, but added by the Church.[4]

In the passage in Matthew on celibacy, the disciples had evidently been worried by the teaching forbidding a man to divorce his wife, particularly after some Pharisees had pointed out to Jesus that Moses had allowed such divorce. The disciples themselves said to Jesus, 'If such is the case of a man with his wife, it is not expedient to marry.' To this Jesus replied:

Not all men can receive this precept [presumably the precept that it is not expedient to marry], but only those to whom it is given. For there are eunuchs who have been so from birth, and there are eunuchs who have been made eunuchs by men, and there are eunuchs who have made themselves eunuchs for the sake of the kingdom of heaven. He who is able to receive this, let him receive it.[5]

Tolstoy's version in *The Gospel in Brief* (1883) runs:

And his pupils said to Jesus: It is too hard to be always bound to one wife. If that must be, it would be better not to marry at all.

He said to them: You may refrain from marriage but you must understand what that means. If a man wishes to live without a wife, let him be quite pure and not approach women: but let him who loves women unite with one wife and not cast her off or look at other women.[6]

It is clear that Jesus is primarily concerned to establish the spiritual superiority of celibacy to marriage for those who are 'called' to it and that Tolstoy's 1883 version interestingly shifts the emphasis to the marriage side of the issue. There is no hint in it that Tolstoy himself wishes to emphasize the importance of celibacy. But in 1889 when he wrote *The Kreutzer Sonata* he had come to see celibacy as the ideal and implicitly advocates it in that story. In 'An Afterword to *The Kreutzer Sonata*' [7] in the following year, though he does not rule out marriage, he certainly sees it as a kind of fall compared with the ideal of perfect chastity. Aylmer Maude is surely right in explaining this change of view on Tolstoy's part as the result of the intensification of the conflict between him and his wife Sonya over his wish to renounce his property and over his other principles.[8] The beginnings of that conflict, it is true, go back to 1881, and in May of that year Tolstoy recorded, 'To abandon one's family is the second temptation.' At the same time he added, 'Serve not the family, but the one God.' [9] On 26 August 1882 Tolstoy suddenly exclaimed that his most passionate wish was to go away.[10] This deeply upset Sonya, who made her first, but not her last, attempt at suicide. Again in June 1884 after a bitter quarrel over his principles with Sonya in the final stages of pregnancy Tolstoy stalked out even as she was starting to go into labour, but turned back as feelings of guilt overcame him.[11] This was the incident of which Shaw was so critical in his review of Maude's biography. About the change of view between 1883 and 1889 there is *no* doubt. In 1883 he could still write in *What I Believe* that the union of marriage was 'holy and obligatory'. By

1890 in the 'Afterword to *The Kreutzer Sonata*' he is calling 'sexual love, marriage . . . from a Christian point of view, a fall, a sin'.[12]

Tolstoy's moral dilemma was to know how much, in this sudden wish to break free from marriage (the stages of which we have traced above), he was following a selfish wish for freedom (such as in many others ends in the very divorce he condemned) under the cloak of an avowed wish to serve God before his family.

What, then, are we to make of *The Kreutzer Sonata* (1889) and of 'An Afterword to *The Kreutzer Sonata*' (1890)? The first thing to be said is that Tolstoy's wife, family and first readers identified Pozdnyshev's views in the story with those of Tolstoy himself. The fact that Pozdnyshev says 'I am a sort of lunatic'[13] could hardly deter them, for they sometimes regarded Tolstoy as a sort of lunatic. It is no wonder, then, that Sonya recorded in December 1890 her terrible fear of becoming pregnant, 'for everybody will hear of the disgrace and jubilantly repeat the recent Moscow joke: "Voilà le véritable postscriptum de la Sonate de Kreutzer"'.[14] On 6 March 1891 Sonya recorded in her diary one of the bitterest and most telling comments on the work: 'At tea we talked about . . . the vegetarianism which Lyova advocates. He said he saw a vegetarian menu in a German paper which was composed of bread and almonds. I expect the person who wrote the menu practises vegetarianism as much as the author of *The Kreutzer Sonata* practises chastity. . . .'[15] And, after all, were not Sonya and the work's first readers right in identifying Pozdnyshev's views with Tolstoy's? A recent student of the question, G. W. Spence, writes in his book *Tolstoy the Ascetic*:

Pozdnyshev's theory is not just Pozdnyshev's: it is not contradicted by Tolstoy in anything that was written after *The Kreutzer Sonata*, and not only is the statement of the ideal of complete celibacy or perfect chastity repeated in the *Afterword* to *The Kreutzer Sonata* and in *The Kingdom of God is Within You*, IV, but also the doctrine of general suicide by means of chastity is the logical outcome of the despairing last pages of the *Confession*.[16]

I agree with everything here except the last remark. There is no *logical* connection between *A Confession* and Tolstoy's later extreme asceticism, but at most a psychological one. Moreover, that claim obscures the fact that whatever the stresses and strains (and, as some have postulated, illness) behind *A Confession* the overt purpose of the work is to show that the view that life is 'senseless and evil' (which had also been Anna's view before her suicide) is *mistaken*. In *A Confession* Tolstoy is not putting forward the view (as some criticisms are apt to leave the impression he is) that life is meaningless, but repudiating that view. Thus if a sense of the meaninglessness of life and even of life-hatred is present in *The Kreutzer Sonata* then that work does not endorse Tolstoy's thesis in *A Confession* but undermines it, or at least leaves us merely with the psychological mood of negation and bafflement *A Confession* was designed to leave behind.

The central subject of *The Kreutzer Sonata* is not so much an attack on the physical side of sex (though that is the aspect of *The Kreutzer Sonata* which everyone remembers) as the burning wish to be free of being tied to any woman, the wish which I have suggested Tolstoy could not acknowledge to himself in the case of his own wife Sonya save in the devious disguise of an ascetic moralism. Pozdnyshev delivers tirades against tight-fitting jerseys, bustles and copulation ('our *swinish* connection') [17] not primarily in themselves, but because they are the agents of bondage to a woman. Pozdnyshev is hopelessly confused. One moment he speaks of pregnancy as 'this sacred work' and the next he speaks of virginity as the 'highest state'.[18] But it is very difficult to decide how much this contradictoriness was intended by Tolstoy, as artist, to be dramatically expressive of the highly-wrought state of the mind of his protagonist and how much it arises from Tolstoy's own utter bewilderment. It must be admitted that the remark which Maude quotes as having been made by Tolstoy apropos *The Kreutzer Sonata* ('The indispensable thing is to go beyond what others have done, to pick off something fresh, however small . . .') [19] is the remark of a man who seems to have thought he was in artistic control. Be that as it may, Pozdnyshev's jealousy of the musician Trukhachevski's playing of the Kreutzer Sonata with his wife (the whole thing seems almost to become a metaphor for intercourse) is not so much jealousy as normally understood as a deliberate inflammation of the sexual bondage to her which he feels, an inflammation which at the same time affords the excuse of breaking that bondage by murder.

Pozdnyshev's twisted attack on sexuality parallels Tolstoy's own tormented attempts to convince himself that he was following the teaching of Jesus in putting God before his family, when all the time he inwardly suspected that what he was trying to do was merely to escape from them for all the world like any *roué*. What better way than to stigmatize marriage (as he does in the 'Afterword to *The Kreutzer Sonata*') [20] as the 'service of self' when what he feared was that it might really be selfishness which underlay his own passionate desire for freedom?

Tolstoy well understood the problem of mixed motives. This in fact is the central subject of *Father Sergius*, [21] begun in the same year in which *The Kreutzer Sonata* was published (1890) but not completed and published till 1898—although once again it is the motif of sexual desire which looms most in the memory rather than the central subject proper, because of the striking, climactic temptation scene. Kasatsky's decision to become a monk after a dissolute life in the court circles of Nicholas I in the 1840s is only partly motivated by 'a sincere religious feeling'.[22] There is also present in it aristocratic pride, ambition and a contempt for others that he can exercise in the very act of showing how different from them he is. This was a temptation which the independent minded landowner in Tolstoy knew very well and for which his cousin Alexandra (who, however, erred too much in the direction of the 'conformism' of the courtier) had often rebuked him. Kasatsky's Abbott recognizes that Kasatsky (now Father Sergius) did not renounce vanity for God's sake, but for reasons of worldly pride. He agrees that Sergius should go to live at the Tambov hermitage in order to quell this. Here Sergius suffers both from doubt in the existence of God and from sexual lust. One day a bored society *divorcée* comes to his cell to tempt him, just for a prank. He has to let her in from the cold and he hears her dress rustling and her bare feet on the floor at the other side of the partition (very telling details these!) [23] and is sorely tempted. He recalls the saint who laid one hand on an adulteress and thrust the other into a fire. One is reminded, too, of the incident in the Archpriest Avvakum's autobiography in which a peasant girl's confession of the sins of the flesh awakened 'a lecherous fire' [24] in him so that he thrust his right hand into a burning candle. Sergius chops off his left forefinger with an axe rather than sin. The woman—Makovnika —repents at this and eventually enters a convent. Sergius becomes oppressed by his fame as a remarkable man and wants 'to go away and hide'—a feeling Tolstoy understood well. He feels that he has 'neither love nor humility nor purity' within. One day he is tempted by the feeble-minded though sensual twenty-two-year-old daughter of a merchant and this time, with a kind of resignation, succumbs. Gorky reports that when Tolstoy read this 'ruthless scene' to himself and Suler the latter remarked that it was too cruel, 'just like Dostoevsky', and spoke of 'pancake-like breasts' asking why Sergius couldn't have sinned 'with a beautiful, healthy woman'. Tolstoy replied: 'That would have been a sin with no justification—this way his pity for the girl could be pleaded—nobody else would take her, poor thing'.[25] This reading was perhaps from a variant of the scene, for there is no indication of 'pancake-like breasts' and of the 'infernal' motivation of Sergius's action in the version of the story as translated by Maude. After this incident Sergius despairs, feeling that there is no God and that he must end it all. Then he suddenly remembers a childhood playmate Pashenka whom they had all made fun of, and who had eventually made an unhappy marriage.

She is now a poor widow with a daughter, a weak son-in-law and five grandchildren whom she helps to support by giving music lessons. He goes to her and she takes him in. He realizes that Pashenka is what he ought to have been, but failed to be: much as the peasant Efim, who, in the story *Two Old Men* (1885),[26] makes a pilgrimage to the physical Jerusalem, realizes when he gets back that his friend Elisha who stopped behind to help some sick peasants had been in the spiritual Jerusalem all the time.

Tolstoy once remarked to Gorky:

A man goes through earthquakes, epidemics, the horrors of disease, and all sorts of spiritual torments, but the most agonizing tragedy he ever knows always has been and always will be—the tragedy of the bedroom.[27]

He had already portrayed something of that tragedy in his account of Anna's relations with Karenin and with Vronsky. It is probably the scenes of sexual torment in *The Kreutzer Sonata, Father Sergius* and the artistically weaker *The Devil* [28] that we remember, in spite of the fact that these stories can be seen without forcing as directed *against* the *willed* ascetic stance their protagonists (and author) adopt. Sex also haunts many of the pages of the late novel *Resurrection* published in 1899. The circumstances of the composition and publication of *Resurrection* must be among the strangest in literature.[29] Tolstoy began the book in 1889 (the same year that he finished *The Kreutzer Sonata*) and worked on it intermittently during the following ten years. While the work was still unfinished he became interested in a Russian religious sect called the Doukhobors, or spirit wrestlers, whom he saw as victims of persecution by the Orthodox Church and by the state. One of the things which had got them into trouble was their refusal to do the compulsory military service which had long been a feature of Russian peasant life. This refusal strongly appealed to Tolstoy who saw it as putting his crucial doctrine of non-resistance into practice. Tolstoy entered into correspondence with Peter Verigin, one of the Doukhobor leaders, and although, as we shall see in the next chapter, he was to become aware that there was an aggressiveness and intransigence in this spokesman for pacifism which he could not approve, Tolstoy never abandoned his efforts on behalf of the sect.

He decided that the best way he could help them was to further a scheme for their emigration to Canada so that they would be out of the clutches of the Tsarist church and state. In order to help finance this emigration he took up the manuscript of *Resurrection* and worked on it during 1898, completing it in the following year. Most of the proceeds from the book were devoted to financing the emigration. Aylmer Maude, Tolstoy's friend and, later, his biographer, was involved in many of the practical negotiations all this necessitated.

The germ of the plot of *Resurrection* was an incident in Tolstoy's own youth back in 1849 when he had seduced one of the maids of his aunt Tatyana Ergolskaya, a girl called Gasha.[30] Whereas Gasha subsequently did reasonably well for herself, however (she became a maid to Tolstoy's sister Marya), Tolstoy was haunted by the image of a Gretchen brought to misery by being seduced (he told his biographer Biryukov quite inaccurately that Gasha 'perished'). In 1887 a friend called Koni who was a lawyer told Tolstoy about the case of a seduced girl who became a prostitute, was charged with theft and was recognized at her trial by her seducer who by the strangest of coincidences was serving on the jury and who, struck with remorse, passionately wanted to marry her.[31] Here was an alternative to the fate of Gretchen. He would make his heroine Katyusha-Maslova enter the world of prostitution, get accused of a sordid theft and murder and be recognized at her trial by his 'hero' Prince Nekhlyudov, her seducer, now a juryman, just as in Koni's story.

As he worked on the book, Tolstoy wanted to incorporate a wider range of material than the theme of sexuality afforded (though this theme remains central) and, in fact, to turn it into a repository for his views on the grim state of things in contemporary Russia with its huge army, its police, its prisons, its grinding poverty amid an expanding state capitalism, and its idealistic (but, to Tolstoy, mistakenly atheistic) revolutionaries. His overriding efforts to get so much about the contemporary social situation into the book make *Resurrection* into a tendentious social-problem novel which has somewhat dated in a way that *War and Peace* and *Anna Karenina* have not. Katyusha-Maslova's imprisonment, in particular, enabled Tolstoy to deal with the whole world of the administration and enforcement of 'justice' in an oppressive state and with the political prisoners who opposed it.

Resurrection begins with an account of Maslova in the dock. Tolstoy tells us that the aristocratic ladies who had adopted her had treated her as 'half servant, half young lady' and so it is not surprising that when they turn her out she sinks into the life of a prostitute rather than adopt the life of 'misery and hardship' led by the town workers in sweated industries. The third chapter introduces Prince Nekhlyudov with much emphasis on the pampered luxury of his surroundings and on his sexual immorality. The reader familiar with *Anna Karenina* may well feel that the old master is repeating himself when he makes Nekhlyudov a failed dilettante artist like

Vronsky and, like Levin, unable to convince his peasants that he cares for their interests.

After Nekhlyudov has recognized Katyusha-Maslova in court, Tolstoy recounts in chapter XII the story of their early relationship as Nekhlyudov remembers it. One of the most spontaneous chapters in the book is chapter XV in which Tolstoy describes spring, the Easter service and the exchange of the Easter kiss with Katyusha. Much of *Resurrection* is spoiled by a tendency to confuse the condemnation of happiness bought at the price of another's misery with a condemnation of happiness as such; but in this chapter, and in chapter XVII, with its description of the last snow, the breaking ice and Katyusha's rejection of Nekhlyudov with her words while all her being says she is his, the artist in Tolstoy overcomes the ascetic moralist. Tolstoy's wife Sonya actually wrote of her distress that 'an old man of seventy should be describing scenes of adultery between an officer and a maid with particular relish, like a gastronome savouring a tasty dish'.[32]

The rest of the first book of *Resurrection* (and some of the second) is taken up with an account of Katyusha-Maslova's trial, her sentence to penal servitude (which is in part brought about by the jury's failure to stress that they did not believe her killing of the merchant had been intentional) and Nekhlyudov's efforts to get the sentence quashed. Tolstoy attacks the way religion is used to sanction the very punishment he hates by giving a bitterly sarcastic account in chapter XXXIX of a religious service in the prison. This account led his wife Sonya to write in her diary: 'I am revolted by his intentionally cynical description of the Orthodox mass . . . it is nothing but a crude attack on those who have faith and it disgusts me'.[33] Tolstoy combines an attack on the association of Church and State (prayers for the Tsar, for example) with savage ridicule of the symbolism of the Eucharist which, he claims in chapter XL, consists of 'meaningless much-speaking and . . . blasphemous incarnation' of a sort Jesus had expressly forbidden. The two issues are, in fact, separable although Tolstoy runs them together. One can well conceive of the historical Jesus condemning the use of his beliefs for purposes of state (a use Nekhlyudov's friend Selenin in II, xxiii, 312–15, resigns himself to) while being tender towards the turning of objects like bread and wine into symbols which so outraged Tolstoy.

Nekhlyudov is both partly afraid of the trouble his association with Katyusha-Maslova might bring upon him, and genuinely sorry for her. She in her turn both wants to 'use' him and gets spontaneously angry with him. At one point she cries: 'You've got pleasure out of me in this life, and want to save yourself through me in the life to come. You are disgusting to me— . . .' (I, xlviii,

183). Katyusha-Maslova's imprisonment brings her and, through her, Nekhlyudov, into contact with the revolutionaries. I mentioned in the last chapter Tolstoy's division of Russian society into 'patriotic Conservative Christians' and 'Revolutionary atheists' and *Resurrection* contains mordantly satirical portraits of both. The first revolutionary that Tolstoy portrays is Vera Bogodukhovskaya, Dukhova in Louise Maude's translation (there is perhaps some irony in the fact that the elements of her name contain the words God and spirit), who is pitiable in the way she considers herself a heroine and shows off. He also mentions Mary Pavlovna, a general's daughter who out of altruism took the blame for the firing of a shot which mortally wounded a gendarme who had come to search the apartment she shared with conspirators (I, lv, 202–4). In Book II Tolstoy also shows us some of the 'patriotic Conservative Christians' such as Tóporov, who really 'believed in nothing' (II, xxvii, 331) but used the Church as an instrument of state (this was a satirical portrait of a very important official, the Procurator of the Holy Synod Pobedonostsev, who was to support the excommunication of Tolstoy in February 1901), and Nekhlyudov's brother-in-law Rogozhinsky, who cannot accept Nekhlyudov's view that the courts are purely an instrument of class oppression (II, xxxiii, 359).

The final book, however, brings us back to the political prisoners to whose company Nekhlyudov manages to get Katyusha-Maslova transferred, and so to the 'Revolutionary atheists' once more. Katyusha begins to worship the altruistic and beautiful Mary Pavlovna who 'knew and was even pleased to know that she [Mary] was beautiful' and yet feared and hated the effect her appearance had on men and 'had an absolute disgust and fear of all falling in love' (III, iii, 411). The two girls feel united 'by the repulsion both felt from sexual love' (III, iii, 412), and there is no indication that the guilt-produced ascetic in Tolstoy does not sanction their repulsion. Yet not even Tolstoy the ascetic can forego love interest in his novel. Simonson, a thoughtful, self-taught revolutionary, falls in love with Katyusha. Simonson stands outside the category of 'revolutionary atheist' in the sense that he has worked out a mystical cosmic religion of his own which has led him to a Tolstoyan vegetarianism and to an adoption of the view that celibacy is a higher state than marriage. His love for Katyusha-Maslova is purely Platonic. He is portrayed as a crank who even heats a stove in accordance with a special theory of his own (III, iv, 412–15). Hitherto Nekhlyudov had regarded the revolutionaries with contempt, particularly after the assassination of Alexander II, but now their cruelty, secrecy and overbearing self-assurance are less prominent for him than their self-control, hard-living and idealism. The best of them stand far higher than the average level of morality while the worst in their untruthfulness, hypocrisy and arrogance sink far below it. Nekhlyudov becomes particularly fond of a consumptive revolutionary called Kriltsov who tells of the cruel execution of a seventeen-year-old Polish Jew Rozovsky merely for an escape attempt which injured no one (III, vi, 419–24). Nekhlyudov can understand how such a thing has driven Kriltsov himself to cruelty. However, the celebrated revolutionist Novodvorov (the elements of the name ironically suggest the words 'new court'), who loves to be unpleasant, awakens Nekhlyudov's dislike. Nabatov, a peasant revolutionary (a kind of touchstone for Tolstoy), significantly disapproves of Novodvorov's views which involve altering 'the fundamental forms of the life of the people', whereas the Marxist Kondratyev, a factory hand who is basically an egotist, indifferent to his comrades and contemptuous of women, regards Novodvorov's arguments as 'irrefutable truths' (III, xii, 441–3). Novodvorov is contemptuous of the masses as beasts and power-worshippers and has no self-doubts, but is really motivated by vanity. Nekhlyudov contrasts him unfavourably with Simonson though the latter is undoubtedly cranky and, moreover, Nekhlyudov's rival for Katyusha's love. Mary Pavlovna tells Nekhlyudov that she sees Simonson's love for Katya as ordinary sexual feeling with 'the same nastiness' underneath as in Novodvorov's love for his mistress Grabets (III, xvii, 455). It is not at all clear whether Tolstoy disapproves of Mary's somewhat priggish view or shares it and this indicates that Tolstoy's control over his use of irony is much less assured than in *Anna Karenina*.

In the end Katyusha-Maslova renounces Nekhlyudov for Simonson not so much out of love for the latter as out of a wish to free Nekhlyudov from the burden of his concern for her. Tolstoy was surely not entirely purged of feelings of vanity and self-regard when he imagined such a resolution for his hero. As Maude observed, Tolstoy does not really know what to do with his hero at the end of the book. He allows him to meet a mysterious sectarian on a ferry who regards the powers of this world (including the law) as Antichrist, and to undergo a kind of conversion as he reads the Sermon on the Mount and, in Maude's words, 'notes the injunction not to resist him that is evil, and decides on a new life'.[34] But as with the regeneration of Raskolnikov at the end of *Crime and Punishment* we are dubious at being left to take that new life on trust. Dostoevsky had written that the spritual rebirth of Raskolnikov at the end of *Crime and Punishment* 'might be the subject of a new story'. It was a story neither he nor Tolstoy ever succeeded in writing, perhaps because the novel as a form does not take kindly to transcendental transformation.

Chapter 16

The Prodigal as Prophet

Far from being a shallow rationalist unable to comprehend the real essence of religion (as Shestov and others have suggested) Tolstoy was a man for whom *a religious comprehension of life as a whole* was an absolute necessity. Religion could not be made a matter of dogma, or ritual, or sensitiveness to figurative language (as Redpath in his nevertheless most sympathetic account of Tolstoy's views seems to me to come near to making it [1]), nor something to be left to spiritual *virtuosi*, whether magicians, priests or poets. Nevertheless Tolstoy after 1879 ran into two great difficulties. The first is that he knew that he was 'privileged' and thought he was not suffering as thousands around him were suffering. This was no doubt one of the driving forces behind his asceticism, though at the same time he may have had an obscure feeling that asceticism helped to establish the *charisma* of a moral teacher, an aspect of it which Max Weber was later to draw attention to.[2] Whatever the motivation, this drive for a kind of self-punishment sometimes led him into an almost hysterical wish to suffer as in *I Cannot Be Silent* (1908) in which his desire to share the fate of some executed peasants and feel 'the well-soaped noose' tighten round his 'old throat' borders on self-indulgent fantasy.[3]

The second great difficulty, which we have already touched on, is that he found himself preaching principles which he wanted obeyed not *as principles* but with Rousseauistic spontaneity, or, to use his own distinction in 'An Afterword to *The Kreutzer Sonata*', followed as 'ideals' rather than as 'rules'.[4] This difficulty as to the mode in which principles are to be followed is a much more severe difficulty than the standard one of the conflict between principles and practice. Thus the most cutting remark in Sonya's diary is not so much the one about the author of *The Kreutzer Sonata* not practising chastity as the following: 'There is so little genuine warmth and kindness about him; his kindness does not come from the *heart*, but merely from *principles*.' [5] This is reminiscent of passages from Tolstoy's own work, for example his judgements of Sonya in *War and Peace* and of Varenka and Karenin in *Anna Karenina*. I do not present Sonya's remark as a fair one; they were irritated with each other as a result of discussing their children's education. I present it as a remark which, whatever its justification, or lack of it, focuses an important problem. Later in her diary Sonya writes of Tolstoy's 'terrible coldness', adding: 'And his excuse for this gulf between us is always the same: "I live a Christian life and you refuse to recognize it; you spoil the children, etc., etc."' Nevertheless (and it says something for Tolstoy) she goes on: 'I still love this frigid Christian so much that it breaks my heart wondering what to do.' [6] It is true that candid witnesses not unsympathetic to the Countess such as Aylmer Maude (who disliked her enemy Chertkov) and Bulgakov, have shown that Sonya was not an easy woman to live with. She was certainly jealous, suspicious and possessive. Nevertheless it must be admitted that there is sometimes an unpleasantly self-conscious element in the way Tolstoy fell back on using his 'convictions' (and fads like vegetarianism) in his conflict with her. After all this was the same man who in the 1860s had written the withering sentence: 'The expression "honest convictions" is, in my opinion, absolutely meaningless: there are honest habits, but not honest convictions' [7] and who in *War and Peace* and *Anna Karenina* had celebrated those who speak and act 'not from conviction, but unconsciously'.[8]

In fact Tolstoy knew that the very thing one must not do if one was to follow his teaching was to become a 'Tolstoyan'. He would ironically remark:

I shall soon be dead, and people will say that Tolstoy taught men to plough and reap and make boots; while the chief thing that I have been trying to say all my life, the one thing I believe in, the most important of all they will forget.[9]

In November 1899 he noted in his diary:

Talked with Dushan. Since he has involuntarily become my representative in Hungary, he asked my advice about the attitude he should adopt. I took this opportunity to clarify the matter for myself, and to say that to speak of a Tolstoyan teaching, and to come and ask my advice, is a grave mistake. There is neither a Tolstoyan sect nor a Tolstoyan teaching. There is only one unique teaching, that of truth—that universal and eternal teaching so perfectly expressed, for myself no less than for others, in the Gospels. This teaching calls man to recognize his sonship to God, and to realize, according to his understanding, both his freedom and his service, since in freeing himself from the influence of the world he enters the service of God and His will. And as soon as a man has understood this teaching, he enters into free communication with God and has nothing more to ask from anyone.[10]

When, during the 1905 revolution, a friend called Postupayev re-marked that it was every man's duty to work on the land (which seems a piece of unexceptionably Tolstoyan doctrine) Tolstoy made the kind of remark he is not remembered nearly often enough for making:

It is not everyone who would be willing to do so. There are people who manufacture concertinas and dislike working on the land. Christ and His apostles were not farm-labourers. It does not do to suppose that manual labour is the duty and the only way of salvation for everyone. That would be slavery. One man, for instance, prefers to sing songs; another is not able to work.[11]

Maude points out that when Tolstoy started to help the persecuted Doukhobors he met in their leader Peter Verigin a fanatic who, so to speak, out-Tolstoyed Tolstoy and who attacked books and print-ing in the sort of way Tolstoy himself had done on some occasions, saying that the labour devoted to them ought to go to food production and to building shelters for those in need. To this sort of thing Tolstoy, of all people, actually replied: 'To speak frankly, your stubborn contention against books seems to me a peculiarly sectarian method of defending a once adopted and expressed opinion. And such a peculiarity does not accord with the conception I had formed of your intellect, and especially of your candour and sincerity'.[12] This leads Maude to reflect on Tolstoy's constant tendency to take a contrary line or (to borrow Kenneth Burke's *mot*) 'to do when in Rome as the Greeks'. Maude writes:

Reading these letters one regrets that so many people (including myself) often urged Tolstoy to be more moderate and to recognize the good side of existing institutions. Had he but been surrounded by people who played in another octave and outran him in the adoption of extreme conclusions, we might have had from him many more letters like these, full of sound prac-tical sense and showing an appreciation of things as they are.[13]

It is not true, as Shaw (who, by the way, was succinctly character-ized by Tolstoy as 'clever-foolish')[14] claimed in his review of Aylmer Maude's biography, that Tolstoy was incapable of laughing at himself. We have a very good example of his ability to do just this in an anecdote which his son Sergey tells about one of the entertain-ments at Yasnaya during the 1880s, a difficult period for Tolstoy. Anybody in the household who wanted could drop a piece of paper with a description of something amusing into the so-called Yasnaya Polyana 'pillar-box' and this would later be read out loud in the family. Here is Tolstoy's character sketch of himself as given by Sergey, his son:

Of sanguine temperament. Is to be ranked with the 'quiet' ones. The patient is suffering from a mania called by German psychiatrists *weltbesserungswahn*, the mania of world improvement. The core of the patient's sickness is the patient's belief that his message can alter other people's lives. *General symptoms :* discontent with the existing order, criticism of everyone except himself, an irritable verbosity, disregarding his audience. Switches often from anger to tearful sentimentality. *Individual symptoms:* occupations with unsuitable and superfluous labours, like making shoes, cutting grass, etc. *Cure :* total indifference on the part of his audience to his speeches, and occupations of a character that would absorb the patient's energy.[15]

But there is a lot in Shaw's view that much in Tolstoy's stance can be accounted for by the fact that 'he had never been obliged to do a real job of real work, and do it for his living'. It is significant that when Tolstoy wrote to Peter Verigin that he would have been glad to have worked in a mine or a factory in his youth to show his 'spirit' he added, 'provided the work were not compulsory'.[16] Shaw's view is in fact expressed in a more temperate way throughout Maude's biography which Shaw himself rightly put 'among the great biographies of our literature' and which is a neglected masterpiece that ought to be kept in print. No-one has subjected Tolstoy's later doctrines to a more sympathetically critical examination than Maude. He is one of the best products of the English nineteenth-century middle-class culture we associate with men like Mill, T. H. Green, and Henry Sidgwick, a culture of whose worse side Tolstoy painted a scornful picture in *Lucerne*, but of whose better side, he, like many so-called radicals today, had no grasp. Maude's criticism of Tolstoy is really far sounder than that of the apparently profound but basically rather flashy Shestov.

There is much that we can gratefully accept in the moral and religious teachings of the later Tolstoy, but his doctrine of non-resistance (which is, in fact, an aristocrat's doctrine of resistance to the state), and even his periodical aspirations to fly from his wife and family take on a different colouring when one sees them as partly conditioned by the life and temperament of an aristocratic *pomeshchik*, or landowner, who had never known what it is to be the underdog, and who prized his freedom and independence before anything else. As we saw at the very beginning of this book Tolstoy's first memory was, significantly enough, of a struggle to break free of his swaddling clothes. There is even something in Shaw's caricature (in part borrowed from Sonya [17]) of him as 'a baby that must be nursed and coddled and petted and let go his own way in spite of all the wisdom of governesses and schoolmasters'. Although I agree with Tolstoy's views on violence (particularly salutary at a time when the concept has become the plaything of 'intellectuals') rather than with those of the exiled revolutionary who wrote the following lines summarized in Bulgakov, I have to admit that the revolutionary shows a fearful, telling (and, as it turned out, prophetic) penetration:

No, Lev Nikolayevich, I am by no means in agreement with you that human relations are improved by love alone. Only the well-educated and those who have always been well-fed can talk like that. But what is to be said to a hungry man with children, a man who has suffered all his life under the yoke of tyrants? He will combat them and try to liberate himself from bondage. And now, before your own death, I say to you, Lev Nikolayevich, that the world is still battening on blood, that again and again men will fight and kill, not only the masters, men and women alike, but even their children, so that we shall not have to look forward to evil from them too. I regret that you will not live to see it with your own eyes and be convinced of your mistake. I wish you a happy death.[18]

Truly this terrible letter points to 1917 and beyond! It shows shrewdness in the way in which it accounts for much in Tolstoy's opinions and attitudes by reference to his social status. But who, in the end, was wrong as to the futility of violence? Did the world cease to batten on blood when the masters and their children had been killed?

Here is Maude's judicious and penetrating view of the way in which Tolstoy's radical self-perfectionism was rooted in the soil of his aristocratic background:

The detachment from the real business of life in which young Russians grew up and the comparative isolation in which they lived on their country estates, explain the extremely radical conclusions often arrived at by those of them who wished to make the world better. . . the less a man is involved in practical work the easier and pleasanter it is for him to take up extreme positions. . . .

It is partly because he grew up in a detached and irresponsible position that the state of his own mind and soul were to him so much more important than the immediate effect of his conduct on others, and the same cause led him to remain in ignorance of lessons every intelligent man of business among us learns of necessity. . . .

Contrasting his moral attitude with that of a young Englishman anxious to do right in our day, I should say that Tolstoy had no adequate sense of being a responsible member of a complex community with the opinions and wishes of which it is necessary to reckon. . . .

He thus came to see things in a way we do not see them, while he remained blind to some things with which we are quite familiar. That is one reason why he is so extraordinarily interesting. . . .[19]

Maude had experience of the Doukhobors and of the Tolstoyan community at Purleigh in Essex. Out of this and out of his own insight came such a remark as the following:

When speaking of the simplification of life, Tolstoy once said to me: 'There is one thing I cannot do without—I must have a quiet room to work in.' This was a most reasonable and modest demand, but one that like *any* demand, runs fundamentally counter to his doctrine, that man must hold himself ready to yield up all he possesses to anybody who likes to take it.[20]

Strakhov wrote that '*War and Peace* presents us with a complete picture of human life',[21] and certainly such a comprehensive vision of life has hardly been reached in any other literary work; but even on this issue Maude has interesting things to say. He rightly points out:

What Tolstoy does not show is what he did not know—the middle-class world: the world of merchants, manufacturers, engineers and men of business. . . .

Of certain important types of humanity he had hardly any conception. Of the George Stephenson type, for instance, which masters the brute forces of nature and harnesses them to the service of man—doing this primarily from love of efficient work—he knows nothing; nor does he know anything . . . of the best type of organizers in our great industrial undertakings. . . . He made a sharp contrast between the predatory and the humble types, and there is much truth in his presentation. He is right that life is supported by the humble and rendered hard by the predatory types, but he has omitted from his scheme of things the man of organizing mind: the man who knows how to get his way and generally gets it (or a great deal of it) but does this mainly from worthy motives. . . .[22]

Maude was struck by how much in the world goes awry from faulty management and organization; and although these things may be clichés to our ears, and although the Tolstoyan virtues are perhaps more needed by many in the Western world, it may be that they are clichés whose validity we are apt to forget for that very reason. Actually Tolstoy himself seems to have been very efficient in helping to organize work in famine relief in the bad years of 1891 and 1892, at least according to Maude's account.[23] But as far as the management of the Doukhobor affair was concerned, Maude (who was involved) could not help remarking that of the people he had to deal with the most efficient and expeditious were the businessmen of the Canadian Pacific Railway, while the least efficient were the Tolstoyans.[24]

As to other important questions touched on by Tolstoy, Maude was convinced (rightly I think) that there exists a rational basis for national feeling of a non-malevolent kind,[25] and that Tolstoy's doctrine of non-resistance does not obviate hypocrisy, spiritual bullying and bad motives in general.[26] His critical and scrupulous weighing-up of all Tolstoy's arguments on this matter is one of the most inter-

esting, moving and praiseworthy parts of his excellent book. He
pointed out, as we have seen, that Tolstoy's peculiar kind of 'radi-
calism' owed a lot to the fact that he had never really had to undergo discipline in his aristocratic youth and thus was used to getting
his own way.[27] He wrote forcefully to Tolstoy himself saying that he
thought that Tolstoy was too anti-political and put it to him that
'in general the attempt the Western world has made at Constitu-
tional Government . . . was not an ignoble effort and has not utterly
failed . . . and . . . may yet lead on to a juster and kindlier society
than the world has yet seen'.[28] Nevertheless no one saw the good
elements in Tolstoy's teaching more strongly than Maude, and no
one did more than he did to spread that teaching by translation and
commentary throughout the English-speaking world. He devoted
his whole life to the task. And it was Maude who claimed (rightly
again) that 'those from Turgenev downwards, who expressed regret
that Tolstoy occupied himself with religious, moral and social
questions, show their own limitations by doing so'. He continued
eloquently:

Even his novels owe much of their value to that craving for truth and longing for brotherhood which characterized him from childhood to old age, and
only those who are attracted by *What Then Must We Do?* can really appreciate what there is in *War and Peace*.[29]

A technical and managerial society like ours has more need of
attending to the sort of truths Tolstoy emphasized than the pre-
dominantly agricultural and patriarchal society for which he wrote.
Tolstoy can offer no help in solving our technical and economic
problems, but life is not just a matter of techniques and of economics,
and Tolstoy's teaching in both novel and tract has much to offer us
as individuals who have to face the perennial facts of time, bereave-
ment and death.

And what of Tolstoy's flight and death? The circumstances have
been movingly described by Alexandra (Sasha) his daughter in
'Tolstoy's Home-Leaving and Death', which can be read in Maude's
collection *Family Views of Tolstoy*. We have seen that this was not
the first time Tolstoy had seriously contemplated the plan of leaving
Yasnaya Polyana; but Shaw's reference to his 'trick of suddenly
leaving the house' is maliciously inaccurate. He had expressed a
passionate *wish* to leave in August 1882.[30] Then in June 1884, after
a quarrel just as Sonya was about to go into labour with Alexandra,
he did stalk out, only to return overcome by guilt.[31] This was the
incident which shocked Shaw, who seems to have been surprised
to discover that authors are human; but as far as I can recall it was

the only time Tolstoy actually left home until the final departure on 28 October 1910. Still, restiveness there was, and I think it was due to that wish to assert his freedom which was naturally marked in a man unaccustomed to being crossed. After the 1884 attempt to leave he recorded ominously: 'It was a mistake not to go away, I think it will be bound to happen sooner or later.' [32] Thirteen years later, in June 1897, he made a more measured decision to leave home and wrote a letter to Sonya (which was, in fact, not handed to her until after his death) in which he asked her forgiveness, but said that he had decided to go away because of his longing for 'peace, solitude, and if not for complete harmony, at least to avoid glaring discord between my life and my conviction and conscience'.[33] Here we can see that the wish to leave Yasnaya was prompted not so much by an urge to renunciation as by a desire for certain concrete, if 'intangible' goods. He wanted happiness. He did not, however, put the contemplated measure into effect at this time.

The final flight from Yasnaya on 28 October 1910 [34] was precipitated not so much by a hope for happiness as by a desperate wish to escape unhappiness. The conflict over his will and copyrights between Sonya and his 'disciple' Chertkov had poisoned the atmosphere at Yasnaya. As he noted pathetically in his diary for 30 July: 'Chertkov has drawn me into a struggle, and this struggle is painful and repellent to me. I shall try to carry it on with love (it is terrible to say how far I am from it).' [35] On October 27th he woke to find Sonya hunting through his room for papers. At this all the proud aristocratic wish for privacy and independence, that wish on which Maude was to remark, rose up in him. He felt 'an uncontrollable aversion and indignation' [36] and this increased when Sonya returned to his room later and pretended, in effect, that she had not been there before. He had to resist, but the only possible resistance was flight!

The extent to which Tolstoy's life and work are all of a piece is illustrated by the similarity between the reflections on God which he dictated to Alexandra (Sasha) from his death-bed at Astapovo and those of Pierre and Prince Andrew in *War and Peace*. Prince Andrew's reflections ran:

Love hinders death. Love is life. . . . Love is God, and to die means that I, a particle of love, shall return to the general and eternal source. (XII, xvi, 219)

Pierre reflects that:

Life is everything. Life is God. Everything changes and moves and that movement is God. . . . To love life is to love God. . . . God is in the midst, and each drop tries to expand so as to reflect Him to the greatest extent. (XIV, xv, 330–1)

And Tolstoy dictated to Alexandra:

. . . . God is that unlimited All of which man is conscious of being a limited part.

Only God truly exists; man is His manifestation in matter, time, and space. The more the manifestation of God in man (life) unites with the manifestations (lives) in other beings, the more alive man is. This union of his life with the life of others is accomplished by love.

God is not love, but the more love a man has the more he manifests God —the more he really exists.

We are conscious of God only through consciousness of His manifestation in ourselves. All we deduce from that consciousness, as well as the guidance based upon it, yields man entire satisfaction, both as to the consciousness of God Himself and as to the guidance for life based on that consciousness.[37]

In a television biography of Tolstoy the schoolmistress of Yasnaya Polyana said: 'We all have our weaknesses and Tolstoy's weakness was God.' Yet there is much truth in Max Scheler's powerful dictum: 'man believes either in a God or in an idol' [38]—as a century which has seen race, nation, economic growth, and an absolute (and contentless) 'freedom' idolized, has good cause to know. Tolstoy has nothing to say to us on economic problems *per se*. He greatly underestimated the importance of good institutions as opposed to good men. But in the realm of the personal and individual life he is supreme. In so far as religious and metaphysical questions trouble us in that life his work should be far more valuable than that of pan-logicists like Hegel, paradox-mongers like Kierkegaard, and disappointed rationalists like Sartre and the Absurdists whose 'thought' in this area has received far more attention. He rightly saw the crucial problem as being that we must somehow recognize the limitations of reason in the face of these questions without becoming what Socrates called *misologists*, haters of reason. He rightly felt that there is an eternal and absolute, before which the temporal and relative are subject to judgement. Perhaps, after all, the true secret of happiness is simply to be, as Tolstoy was, a seeker after that God whom from the moral point of view we have to create in order to worship, if we are not to worship an idol unworthy of Him. As Tolstoy said to Bulgakov: 'Pitiful are those who do not seek, or who think that they have found.' [39]

Notes

All references to Tolstoy's works are to the Aylmer Maude translations in the World's Classics edition published by the Oxford University Press, with the exception of *The Private Diary, Pedagogical Articles* and 'The Meaning of the Russian Revolution'.

INTRODUCTION

1 Nettl (J. P.), *Rosa Luxemburg* (London, 1966), vol. 2, p. 668.
2 *Lucerne* is printed in *The Snow Storm and Other Stories*, p. 249.
3 See the Preface to Von Polenz's novel *Der Butternbauer* in *What is Art?*, p. 322.
4 Revel (Jean François), *On Proust*, trans. Martin Turnell (London, 1972), p. 174.
5 *Recollections and Essays*, p. 19.
6 *The Porcelain Doll* is printed in *The Kreutzer Sonata, The Devil and Other Tales*, pp. 371–375.
7 A diary entry for November 1899 quoted in Leon (Derrick), *Tolstoy: His Life and Work* (London, 1944), pp. 240–241.

CHAPTER ONE

1 Maude (Aylmer), *The Life of Tolstoy* (World's Classics 2 vols. in 1 edn; London, reprinted 1953), vol. I, p. 10. (Afterwards referred to as *Life*.)
2 For this, and for the quotations immediately following on the ant brotherhood and the green stick, see *Life*, I, pp. 17–19.
3 The quotation on the soul is from Sir Karl Popper, *The Open Society and its Enemies* (London, reprinted 1969), vol. 1, p. 190.
4 Nietzsche (Friedrich), *The Twilight of the Idols* . . . trans. R. J. Hollingdale (Penguin Books, Harmondsworth, reprinted 1969), p. 23.
5 Dostoevsky (Fyodor), *Notes from Underground* . . . trans. Andrew R. MacAndrew (A Signet Classic, New York and Toronto, 1961), ch. VII, pp. 105–106.
6 *The Diaries of Leo Tolstoy*, trans. from the Russian by C. J. Hogarth and A. Sirnis, 'Youth', 1847–1852 (London, 1917), p. 30. (Afterwards referred to as *Diaries, 1847–1852*.)
7 *The Private Diary of Leo Tolstoy*, 1853–1857, ed. Aylmer Maude and trans. Louise and Aylmer Maude (London, 1927), p. 114. (Afterwards referred to as *Diary, 1853–1857*.)

8 Quoted in Ivanov-Razumnik's *Lev Tolstoi* (St Petersburg), [n.d.], p. 108.
9 *Lucerne* in *The Snow Storm and Other Stories* (London, reprinted 1966), p. 248.
10 For an allegation of Tolstoy's impurity of motives in his dealings with the poor see Shestov (Lev), 'The Good in the Teaching of Tolstoy and Nietzsche', trans. Bernard Martin, in *Dostoevsky, Tolstoy and Nietzsche* (Ohio University Press, 1969), p. 30. Shestov ignores Tolstoy's awareness that the sort of charity which merely consists of 'getting rid of the sufferer' has something suspect about it. See *What Then Must We Do?*, trans. Aylmer Maude (London, reprinted 1960), p. 82. The notion that God should be identified with the good was too banal for Shestov whose spiritual digestion required stronger meat. No wonder Tolstoy thought him an 'intellectual dandy', a 'daring barber' of thought. For Tolstoy on Shestov see Gorky (Maxim), *Literary Portraits*, trans. Ivy Litvinov (Moscow, n.d.), p. 61.
   For an interesting study of Shestov's thought and his bizarre biblical interpretations see Wernham (James C. S.), *Two Russian Thinkers: An Essay in Berdyaev and Shestov* (Toronto 1968).

CHAPTER TWO

1 *Diaries, 1847–1852* (London, 1917), pp. 57–58.
2 *Diary, 1853–1857* (London, 1927), p. 46.
3 *Ibid.*, pp. 43–44.
4 *Ibid.*, p. 45.
5 Eikhenbaum (Boris), *Lev Tolstoi*, Nachdruck der Ausgabe Leningrad 1928/31, Wilhelm Fink Verlag, München (2 t. in one), t. 1, pp. 150–151. (Afterwards referred to as Eikhenbaum (Boris), *Lev Tolstoi*.)
6 *Diary, 1853–1857*, p. 34.
7 *Diaries, 1847–1852*, p. 129.
8 Pascal (Blaise), *Pensées*, ed. H. T. Barnwell, trans. John Warrington (Everyman's University Library; London, reprinted 1973), no. 93, p. 31.
9 *Diaries, 1847–1852*, p. 190.
10 *Diary, 1853–1857*, p. 47.
11 *Pensées*, no. 84, p. 29.
12 Wittgenstein (Ludwig), *Notebooks, 1914–1916*, ed. G. H. Von Wright and G. E. M. Anscombe (Oxford, 1969), p. 74e.
13 Santayana (George), *Scepticism and Animal Faith* (Dover edn, 1955), p. 252.
   See also chapter 5, 'Psychology', of *Reason in Science* (Collier

Books, New York, 1962), pp. 93–117. Ortega Y Gasset's reflections on what he calls 'imaginary psychology' in his 'Notes on the Novel' (in *The Dehumanization of Art* (New York, 1956)) are also interesting in this connection.

14 *Diaries*, 1847–1852, pp. 88–89.

15 Vygotsky (Lev), *Thought and Language*, ed. and trans. E. Hanfmann and G. Vakar (Cambridge, Mass., 1962), p. 149.

16 Tolstoy told V. G. Chertkov and P. I. Biriukov that Tiutchev was his favourite poet, and recited 'Silentium' to them from memory in December 1886. See Gusev (N. N.), *Letopis Zhizni i Tvorchestva Tolstogo*, 1828–1890 (Moskva, 1858), p. 650. (Afterwards referred to as *Letopis*.)

17 *What is Art?* ch. V, p. 123.

18 This passage, like the section on Plato and myth in chapter one, is indebted to J. A. Stewart's stimulating book *The Myths of Plato* (London, 1905), p. 44 *et alia*.

CHAPTER THREE

1 Gusev, *Letopis*, p. 42.

2 Eikhenbaum (Boris), *Lev Tolstoi*, t. 1, p. 35.

3 *Diaries*, 1847–1852, p. 112.

4 *Ibid.*, p. 181.

5 *Ibid.*

6 I am indebted for this analysis to Eikhenbaum (Boris), *Lev Tolstoi*, t. 1, p. 88.

7 *Diary*, 1853–1857, pp. 58 and 60.

8 For the preceding facts see *Diary*, 1853–1857, p. 58; letter to Nekrasov in *Diaries*, 1847–1852, pp. 210–211; Gusev (N. N.), *Letopis*, pp. 76, 124.

9 Gusev (N. N.), *Letopis*, p. 91,

10 *Diary*, 1853–1857, p. 18.

11 Maude (Aylmer), *Life*, vol. 1, p. 175.

CHAPTER FOUR

1 See *Recollections and Essays*, p. 245.

2 See the introduction to *Tales of Army Life*, p. xi, and *Life*, vol. II, p. 440.

3 The question of whether courage diminishes with intelligence and education is debated, in *Meeting a Moscow Acquaintance in the Detachment* (1856), with Guskov, a Dostoevskyan *humilié* who has been reduced to the ranks.

4 *Diary*, 1853–1857, p. 7.

5 *Ibid.*, p. 1.

6   Maude, *Life*, vol. I, pp. 107–109.
7   For dates and quotation see Gusev, *Letopis*, pp. 82–83.
8   *Ibid.*, p. 85.
9   Maude, *Life*, vol. I, p. 115.
10 Gusev, *Letopis*, p. 84.
11 For preceding dates, *ibid.*, pp. 90 and 93.
12 For the monologue see *Tales of Army Life*, pp. 139–141. On Chernyshevsky as originating the term 'inner monologue' see Struve (Gleb), '*Monologue Intérieur: The Origins of the Formula*', P.M.L.A., vol. 69, no. 5 (Dec. 1954), pp. 1101–1111.
13 Eikhenbaum has a good analysis of this aspect of the story in *Lev Tolstoi*, t. 1, p. 170.
14 For dates see Gusev, *Letopis*, pp. 97–98 and 104.
15 For Eikhenbaum's comments on *Sevastopol in August 1855* as a transitional story see *Lev Tolstoi*, t. 1, pp. 237–238.

CHAPTER FIVE

1   Tolstoi (Lev), *Sobranie Sochinenii*, t. 17, *Pisma (Letters)*, 1845–1886 (Moskva, 1965), pp. 176–177.
2   *Diary*, 1853–1857, p. 34.
3   Quoted in Christian (R. F.), *Tolstoy's 'War and Peace': A Study* (Oxford, 1962), p. 179.
4   For dates see Gusev (N. N.), *Letopis*, pp. 111–112, 138–139, 176–178.
5   Benjamin Goriely advances this theory in his *Léon Tolstoi: Lettres* (Paris, 1954), t. 1, pp. 322–323.
6   See Eikhenbaum (Boris), *Lev Tolstoi*, t. 1, pp. 243 and 296.
7   Gusev (N. N.), *Letopis*, p. 197.
8   Maude (Aylmer), *Life*, vol. I, p. 203.
9   Weber (Max), *The Sociology of Religion*, trans. Ephraim Fischoff, (reprinted 1966), p. 83.
10 *Ibid.*, p. 84.
11 'The Meaning of the Russian Revolution' (1906) is printed in *Russian Intellectual History: An Anthology* (New York, 1966), ed. Marc Raeff.
12 *Recollections and Essays*, p. 52.
13 *Diaries*, 1847–1852, p. 202.
14 Maude (Aylmer), *Life*, vol. I, p. 150. For Tolstoy and the peasants in May 1856, see pp. 151–152.
15 Lampert (E.), *Sons Against Fathers* (Oxford, 1965), p. 13.
16 *Diary*, 1853–1857, p. 31.
17 *A Landlord's Morning* is printed in *The Snow Storm and other Stories*, pp. 151–217.

18 *Polikushka* is printed in *The Snow Storm and Other Stories*, pp. 311–388.
19 Gusev (N. N.), *Letopis*, p. 290.
20 Maude (Aylmer), *Life*, vol. I, p. 295.
21 See Gusev (N. N.), *Letopis*, pp. 227 and 288.

CHAPTER SIX

1 See *Diaries*, 1847–1852, pp. 114–115; and *Diary*, 1853–1857, pp. 44–46, 52, 161–162, 232–233 and 240.
2 Gusev, *Letopis*, pp. 285 and 287. Eikhenbaum, in *Lev Tolstoi*, t. 2, pp. 140–143, suggests that *The Cossacks* as we have it is incomplete. He thinks that Tolstoy had originally intended to write a second part, but had abandoned the idea. As it is the piece ends appropriately with Olenin's leaving Eroshka and Maryanka.
3 *The Cossacks* is printed in *Tales of Army Life*, pp. 267–464.
4 *Diary*, 1853–1857, p. 37.
5 *Ibid.*, p. 149. The entry runs: 'Yes, the means to gain true happiness in life is, without any rules, to throw out from oneself in all directions like a spider an adhesive web of love, and to catch in it all that comes: an old woman, a child, a girl, or a policeman.
6 *Diary*, 1853–1857, p. 240. The full quotation runs: 'I cannot write without an idea. But the idea that good is good in every sphere, that the same passions exist everywhere, and that a savage condition is good, is not sufficient. It would be well enough were I penetrated by the latter conception.'
7 Eikhenbaum (Boris), *Lev Tolstoi*, t. 1, pp. 343–344.
8 *Strider* is printed in *The Snow Storm and Other Stories*, pp. 391–439.
9 Victor Shklovsky, 'Art as Technique', pp. 13–18, in *Russian Formalist Criticism: Four Essays*, trans. Lee T. Lemon and Marion J. Reis (Lincoln, Nebraska, 1965), pp. 5–24. See also Shklovsky's *Material i Stil v Romane Tolstogo 'Voina i Mir'* (Moskva, 1928), p. 174.
10 Maude (Aylmer), *Life*, vol. I, pp. 73–74.
11 *Family Happiness* is printed in *The Kreutzer Sonata, The Devil and Other Tales*, pp. 3–108.
12 For the above see *Diary*, 1853–1857, pp. 163–165.
13 *Ibid.*, pp. 174 and 178.
14 *Ibid.*, p. 243.
15 See *Tolstoy's Love Letters with a Study* . . . by Paul Biryukov, trans. from the Russian by S. S. Koteliansky and Virginia Woolf (Richmond, 1923).
16 *Tolstoy's Love Letters*, pp. 38–39.
17 Eikhenbaum (Boris), *Lev Tolstoi*, t. 1, p. 360.

CHAPTER SEVEN

1   See Goldenveizer (A. B.), *Talks with Tolstoy*, trans. S. S. Koteliansky and Virginia Woolf (Richmond, 1923), p. 23.
2   See Maude (Aylmer), *Life*, vol. 1, p. 48, and his remarks on Tolstoy and Dickens in his preface to *Family Views of Tolstoy*, ed. Aylmer Maude (London, 1926), pp. 8–13.
3   For this theme in Strakhov's works see Gerstein (Linda), *Nikolai Strakhov: Philosopher, Man of Letters, Social Critic* (Cambridge, Mass., 1971), pp. 102–146.
4   Maude (Aylmer), *Life*, vol. I, pp. 227–228.
5   On the Petrashevsky circle and Dostoevsky, see Venturi (Franco), *The Roots of Revolution*, trans. from the Italian by Francis Haskell (London, 2nd impression, 1964), pp. 79–80.
6   Goldenveizer, *op. cit.*, p. 87.
7   Gorky (Maksim), *Literary Portraits*, trans. Ivy Litvinov (Moscow, n.d.), p. 23.
8   Goldenveizer, *op. cit.*, p. 14.
9   Maude (Aylmer), *Life*, vol. I, p. 183.
10 Herzen (Alexander), *My Past and Thoughts*, trans. Constance Garnett (London, 1924), vol. III, p. 142.
11 Tolstoi (Léon), *Lettres, . . . traduites . . . par* Benjamin Goriely (Paris, 1954), t. I, pp. 288–289. The letter was not actually sent to Botkin. See Tolstoy (Lev), *Sobranie Sochinenii*, t. 17, *Pisma (Letters)* (Moskva, 1969), p. 163.
12 *Lettres* (Paris, 1954), t. I, pp. 175–176, and *Pisma* (Moskva, 1969), pp. 98–99.
13 *Lettres* (Paris, 1954), t. I, p. 195, and *Pisma* (Moskva, 1969), p. 105.
14 *Lucerne* is printed in *The Snow Storm and Other Stories*, pp. 221–251.
15 Eikhenbaum (Boris), *Lev Tolstoi*, t. I, p. 311.

CHAPTER EIGHT

1   Popper (Sir Karl), *The Poverty of Historicism* (London, reprinted 1969), p. 41.
2   H. A. L. Fisher's remarks on p. vii of vol. I of his *History of Europe* are quoted by Popper in *The Poverty of Historicism*, p. 109.
3   *The Poverty of Historicism*, p. 54.
4   Tolstoy (Leo), 'Progress and the Definition of Education' in *Pedagogical Articles . . .*, trans. Leo Wiener (London, 1904), p. 159.
5   *Ibid.*, p. 163.
6   *Ibid.*
7   *What is Art?*, p. 140.

8   'Progress and the Definition of Education', in *Pedagogical Articles*, pp. 153–154.
9   *Ibid.*, p. 158.
10 *Ibid.*, p. 163.
11 Maude (Aylmer), *Life*, vol. I, p. 225.
12 Eikhenbaum (Boris), *Lev Tolstoi*, t. 2, pp. 325–378.
13 Goldenveizer (A. B.), *Talks with Tolstoy* (Richmond, 1923), pp. 148–149.
14 The above quotations come from the Second Epilogue of *War and Peace*, ch. III, p. 500 and ch. V, p. 510.
15 *War and Peace*, XV, iv, 359.
16 *Ibid.*, X, xxviii, 498.
17 *Ibid.*, X, xxxviii, 540.
18 Hook (Sidney), *The Hero in History* (London, 1945), pp. 56–57. Hook has the historicism of Hegel and Spencer in mind.
19 'The School at Yasnaya Polyana', in *Pedagogical Articles*, p. 330.
20 *War and Peace*, XV, v, 363.
21 *Ibid.*, XIII, xvii, 277.
22 Berlin (Sir Isaiah), *The Hedgehog and the Fox* (London, reprinted 1954), pp. 28–29.
23 Maude, *Life*, vol. II, p. 322.

CHAPTER NINE

1   *Diary*, 1853–1857, p. 55.
2   Maude (Aylmer), *Life*, vol. I, p. 38.
3   Tolstoy (Leo), *Pedagogical Articles* . . ., trans. Leo Wiener (London, 1904), p. 316.
4   Geyl (Pieter), *Napoleon For and Against* (London, revised edn, 1964), p. 55.
5   *Ibid.*, pp. 448–449.
6   Elton (G. R.), *Political History: Principles and Practice* (London, 1970), p. 53.
7   Laqueur (Walter), 'Literature and the Historian', *The Journal of Contemporary History*, vol. 2, no. 2 (April, 1967), p. 5.
8   Popper (Sir Karl), *The Poverty of Historicism*, p. 149.
9   Myshkovskaya (L. M.) points out the closeness of Tolstoy's views to those of Von Clausewitz in her *Masterstvo L. N. Tolstogo* (Moskva, 1958), p. 186.
10 Watkins (J. W. N.), 'Imperfect rationality', in *Explanation in the Behavioural Sciences*, ed. Robert Borger and Frank Cioffi (Cambridge, 1970), pp. 541–558.
11 Dragomirov (Mikhail Ivanovich), *Étude du Roman 'La Guerre et La Paix' . . . Au Point de Vue Militaire* (Paris, 1896), p. 77.

12 Christian (R. F.), *Tolstoy's 'War and Peace': A Study* (Oxford, 1962), p. 108.

13 Berlin refers to Norov and Vitmer in *The Hedgehog and the Fox*, p. 6. I have consulted at first hand A. Vitmer's *1812 God v Voine i Mire* (Sankt peterburg, 1869).

14 Shklovsky (Viktor), *Material i Stil v Romane 'Voina i Mir'* (Moskva, 1928), pp. 180–181.

15 *War and Peace*, X, xix, 460.

16 Von Clausewitz, *The Campaign of 1812 in Russia* (London, 1843), pp. 148–149.

17 *War and Peace*, X, xix, 460–461. See also Dragomirov (M. I.), *Étude du Roman 'La Guerre et La Paix'* . . . (Paris [1896]), p. 89 onwards.

18 *War and Peace*, X, xxvii, 496. H. B. George thought that Napoleon's plan was 'well conceived, but not successfully executed'. He wrote of Poniatowski's failure: 'Two more divisions might have turned the scale.' This shows that George did not believe the plan could not have been executed. See George (Hereford Brooke), *Napoleon's Invasion of Russia* (London, 1899), p. 199.

19 See *War and Peace*, X, xxvii, 497; X, xxxiv, 522 and 526.

20 *Pedagogical Articles* . . . (London, 1904), p. 158.

21 For the following points see Dragomirov (Mikhail Ivanovich), *Étude du Roman 'La Guerre et La Paix'* . . . (Paris [1896]), pp. 100, 96, 97, 94–95.

22 Sorel (Albert), 'Tolstoi Historien', *Revue Bleue* (Paris, 1888), p. 468. Sir Isaiah Berlin's *The Hedgehog and the Fox*, p. 55, drew my attention to Sorel's article.

23 Maude (Aylmer), *Life*, vol. I, p. 225.

24 Quoted in Christian (R. F.), *Tolstoy's 'War and Peace': A Study*, p. 178.

25 Assessments vary, but all are high. Von Clausewitz quotes Boutourlin's assessment of 50,000 as the Russian losses, but himself prefers an assessment of 30,000. (*The Campaign of 1812 in Russia* (London, 1843), p. 153). The approximate assessments I use are those of Brigadier P. Young in his account in Chandler (David), *A Reader's Guide to the Battlefields of Europe* (London, 1965), vol. 2, pp. 167–171.

26 For the atypicality of Borodino see Duffy (Christopher), 'Borodino', *The Listener*, vol. 88, no. 2269 (21 September 1972), pp. 369–371, and his book *Borodino and The War of 1812* (London, 1972).

27 Poggioli (Renato), *The Phoenix and the Spider* (Cambridge, Mass., 1957), pp. 9–11. Poggioli thinks this is true of nineteenth-

century Russian fiction in general, with the possible exception of Dostoevsky.

28 For Pierre's experiences see *War and Peace*, XII, x, 191 and XII, xi, 195. For Vereshchagin and Rostopchin, see *War and Peace*, XI, xxv, 91–100.

29 e.g. by John Bayley in his *Tolstoy and the Novel* (London, 1966), pp. 136–138. Bayley to my mind overstresses the 'class' connection between Davout and Pierre. He cannot accept the humanitarian thesis implicit in Tolstoy's presentation of the scene.

30 Wilson (Sir Robert T.), *General Wilson's Journal*: 1812–1814, ed. Antony Brett-James (London, 1964), p. 71.

31 Shklovsky (Viktor), *Material i Stil v Romane Tolstogo 'Voina i Mir'* (Moskva, 1928), p. 68, says that such an incident was noted by Mikhailovsky-Danilevsky.

32 *Diary*, 1853–1857, p. 31.

33 *Ibid.*, p. 242.

34 Maude (Aylmer), *Life*, vol. I, pp. 326–327.

35 Christian (R. F.), *Tolstoy's 'War and Peace': A Study*, p. 111.

36 Nietzsche (Friedrich), *Twilight of the Idols . . .*, trans. R. J. Hollingdale (Harmondsworth, reprinted 1969), p. 30.

37 Berlin (Sir Isaiah), *The Hedgehog and the Fox* (London, reprinted 1954), p. 35. In the seventh of the St Petersburg dialogues, Joseph de Maistre wrote: 'At the exact moment brought about by men and prescribed by justice, God comes forward to exact vengeance for the iniquity committed by the inhabitants of this world against him.' See de Maistre, *Works*, selected and trans. by Jack Lively (London, 1965), p. 254.

38 *War and Peace*, VI, xxv, 90.

39 Lawrence (D. H.), *Women in Love* (London, 1954), ch. 2, p. 27.

CHAPTER TEN

1 'Some Words About *War and Peace*' is printed at the end of the World's Classics edition.

2 Scholes (Robert) and Kellogg (Robert), *The Nature of Narrative* (New York, 1966), p. 15.

3 Strakhov (N.), *Kriticheskie Staty ob Turgeneve i Tolstom* (St. Peterburg, 1899), p. 236.

4 *op. cit.*, p. 151.

5 Shklovsky (Viktor), *Material i Stil v Romane Tolstogo 'Voina i Mir'* (Moskva, 1928), pp. 396–397.

6 *op. cit.*, p. 58.

7 Eikhenbaum (Boris), *Lev Tolstoi*, t. 2, p. 262.

8 Shklovsky (Viktor), *op. cit.*, p. 394.

9 Proust (Marcel), *By Way of Sainte-Beuve*, trans. Sylvia Townsend Warner (London, 1958), p. 126.
10 *Ibid.*, p. 284.
11 In what follows I take issue with Jerome Thale's article '*War and Peace:* The Art of Incoherence', *Essays in Criticism*, vol. XVI, no. 4 (Oct. 1966), pp. 398–415.
12 *What is Art?*, p. 38.
13 Hagan (John), 'On the Craftsmanship of *War and Peace*', *Essays in Criticism*, vol. 13, no. 1 (Jan. 1963), pp. 17–49.
14 Proust (Marcel), *op. cit.*, p. 284.
15 Christian (R. F.), *Tolstoy's 'War and Peace': A Study*, pp. 149–150.
16 Schopenhauer (Arthur), *The World as Will and Representation*, trans. E. F. J. Payne (New York, 1958), section 55, vol. I, p. 293.
17 Rivière (Jacques), 'Marcel Proust and the Positive Mind' in *The Ideal Reader*, ed. and trans. Blanche A. Price (London, 1962), p. 129.
18 Scholes (Robert), *The Fabulators* (New York, 1967), p. 100.
19 Rivière (Jacques), *op. cit.*, p. 127.
20 Kuzminskaya (Tatyana), *Tolstoy as I Knew Him*, trans. Nora Sigerist and others (New York, 1948), p. 188.
21 Mink (Louis O.), 'History and Fiction as Modes of Comprehension', *New Literary History*, vol. I, no. 3 (Spring 1970), pp. 549–554.
22 Scholes (Robert) and Kellogg (Robert), *The Nature of Narrative* (New York, 1966), p. 197.
23 *War and Peace*, I, xxv, 118. John Hagan (*op. cit.*, p. 26) rightly sees this letter as expressing what he calls Tolstoy's 'own brand of Gospel Christianity'.

CHAPTER ELEVEN

1 Arnold (Matthew), *The Letters to A. II. Clough*, ed. H. F. Lowry (New York, reissued 1968), p. 97.
2 Berlin (Sir Isaiah), *The Hedgehog and The Fox*, pp. 36–37.
3 *Ibid.*, p. 6.
4 Scholes (Robert) and Kellogg (Robert), *The Nature of Narrative*, pp. 272–273.
5 Berlin (Sir Isaiah), *op. cit.*, p. 67.
6 Hagan (John), 'On the Craftsmanship of *War and Peace*', *Essays in Criticism*, vol. 13, no. 1 (Jan. 1963).
7 *Ibid.*, p. 26.
8 Wittgenstein (Ludwig), *Tractatus Logico-Philosophicus*, trans D. F. Pears and B. F. McGuinness (London, 1961), proposition 6.4311, p. 147.

9 Leontiev (Konstantin), *The Novels of Count L. N. Tolstoy: Analysis, Style and Atmosphere*, 1890, in *Essays in Russian Literature: The Conservative View: Leontiev, Rozanov, Shestov*, ed. and trans. Spencer E. Roberts (Athens, Ohio, 1968), p. 284.

CHAPTER TWELVE

1 Leavis (F. R.), *The Great Tradition* (London, 1950), p. 124.
2 Arnold's essay is printed in *Essays in Criticism: 2nd Series*.
3 Maude (Aylmer), *Life*, vol. I, pp. 306–307.
4 *What is Art?*, pp. 199–200.
5 *Pedagogical Articles*, trans. Leo Wiener (London, 1904), p. 207.
6 See Robertson (J. M.), *Explorations* (London, n.d.), pp. 69–111.
7 See Redpath (Theodore), *Tolstoy* (London, 2nd edn 1969), p. 66.
8 See the *Memoir* of Lawrence by E. T. (Jessie Chambers), the prototype of Miriam in *Sons and Lovers*.
9 Hare (Richard), *Portraits of Russian Personalities Between Reform and Revolution* (London, 1959), p. 207.
10 *What is Art?*, p. 178.
11 Leavis (F. R.), *Anna Karenina and Other Essays* (London, 1967), p. 12.
12 Wittgenstein (Ludwig), *Tractatus Logico-Philosophicus*, trans. D. F. Pears and B. F. McGuinness (London 1969), proposition 6.422, p. 147.
13 The Socialist Revolutionaries who were to assassinate Tsar Alexander II in March 1881 adopted the name 'Narodnaya Volya', 'The People's Will'.
14 Leavis (F. R.), *Anna Karenina and Other Essays* (London, 1967), p. 21.
15 *Ibid.*, pp. 16–17.
16 See Lawrence's stories 'St Mawr' and 'Daughters of the Vicar' respectively.
17 See *New Light on Tolstoy*, ed. René Fülop-Miller, trans. Paul England (London, 1931), p. 301.
18 Leavis (F. R.), *Anna Karenina and Other Essays*, p. 23.
19 Weitz (Morris), *Philosophy in Literature* (Detroit, 1963), p. 29.
20 *Ibid.*, p. 35.
21 For 'the paradox of tolerance' see Sir Karl Popper, *The Open Society* (London, 1969), vol. I, p. 265. Just as we may claim 'the right not to tolerate the intolerant' so we may, perhaps, claim the right to judge those who judge.
22 Flaubert (Gustave), *Madame Bovary*, trans. Alan Russell (Harmondsworth, 1950), p. 335.

CHAPTER THIRTEEN

1   *A Confession*, pp. 18, 21 and 24.
2   Santayana (George), *Some Turns of Thought in Modern Philosophy: Five Essays* (Cambridge, 1933), pp. 88–89.
3   *Ivan Ilych . . . and Other Stories*, p. 45.
4   *A Confession*, p. 20.
5   I take issue here and in much of what follows with Professor A. G. N. Flew's stimulating article 'Tolstoi and the Meaning of Life', in *Ethics*, vol. LXXIII, no. 2 (Jan. 1963), pp. 110–118.
6   *A Confession*, pp. 50–51, 56.
7   For the above see *A Confession*, pp. 57, 58, 62 and 67.
8   On the absurdity of this quest by some existentialists see Edwards (Paul), 'Existentialism and Death; A Survey of Some Confusions and Absurdities', in Morgenbesser (Sidney), Suppes (Patrick) and White (Morton), *Philosophy, Science and Method: Essays in Honour of Ernest Nagel* (New York, 1969), p. 473–505.
9   Wittgenstein (Ludwig), *Tractatus Logico-Philosophicus*, trans. D. F. Pears and B. F. McGuinness (London, 1969), proposition 6.4311, p. 147.
10 *Ivan Ilych . . . and Other Stories*, pp. 44–45.
11 *Ibid*, p. 62.
12 For other comments see Phillips (D. Z.), 'Moral Presuppositions and Literary Criticism', *The Human World*, No. 6 (February 1962), pp. 24–34, and Speirs (Logan), *Tolstoy and Chekhov* (Cambridge, 1971), pp. 141–147.

CHAPTER FOURTEEN

1   *Diary*, 1853–1857, p. 114.
2   The first two are printed in the volume *A Confession, The Gospel in Brief and What I Believe*, the third in the volume entitled *The Kingdom of God and Peace Essays* and the fourth in *Essays and Letters*, trans. Aylmer Maude (London, 1903), pp. 288–337.
3   Quoted in Christian (R. F.), *Tolstoy's 'War and Peace': A Study*, pp. 178–179.
4   Hick (John), *Faith and Knowledge* (London and Melbourne, 1967), p. 3.
5   *Ibid*. pp. 3–4.
6   *A Confession*, p. 62.
7   Hick (John), *op. cit.*, p. 7.
8   *Ibid.*, p. 239.
9   In *Twenty-Three Tales*, pp. 1–10.

10 For an example see Florovsky (Georges), 'Three Masters: The Quest for Religion in Nineteenth Century Russian Literature', in Panichas (George A.), *Mansions of the Spirit* (New York, 1967), pp. 157–179.

11 *What I Believe* in *A Confession*, p. 362.

12 *Ibid.*, pp. 316–317.

13 Schopenhauer (Arthur), *The World as Will and Representation*, trans. E. F. J. Payne (New York, 1966), vol. I, pp. 523–524.

14 *Diary*, 1852–1857, p. 114.

15 Goldenveizer (A. B.), *Talks with Tolstoy* (Richmond, 1923), p. 146.

16 *The Many Faced Argument*, ed. John Hick and Arthur C. McGill (London, 1968), p. 356.

17 Gorky (Maksim), *Literary Portraits*, trans. Ivy Litvinov (Moscow, n.d.), p. 23.

18 'A Letter to M. A. Engelhardt', 1882, printed at the end of *What Then Must We Do?*, p. 391.

19 *What I Believe* in *A Confession . . .*, p. 346.

20 Perrin (Norman), *Rediscovering the Teaching of Jesus* (London, 1967), p. 109.

21 *Ibid.*, p. 48.

22 See Davies (W. D.), *The Setting of the Sermon on the Mount* (Cambridge, 1964).

23 Perrin (Norman), *op. cit.*, pp. 147–148.

24 *Ibid.*, p. 146.

25 See Moore (G. E.), 'The Nature of Moral Philosophy', in *Philosophical Studies* (London, reprinted 1958), p. 320.

26 Jeremias (Joachim), *New Testament Theology* (London, reprinted 1958), vol. I, pp. 63–68.

27 *What I Believe* in *A Confession . . .*, p. 344.

28 Matthew XVII: 24–27, *The Gospel in Brief* in *A Confession . . .*, p. 227.

29 In *Ivan Ilych and Other Stories*, pp. 227–384.

30 Malcolm (Norman), *Ludwig Wittgenstein: A Memoir* (London, 1958), p. 43.

31 *Ivan Ilych and Hadji Murad . . .*, p. 281.

CHAPTER FIFTEEN

1 See *What I Believe* in *A Confession . . .*, p. 379 footnote.

2 I use J. C. Fenton's translation in the Pelican Gospel Commentaries (Harmondsworth, 1963), p. 88.

3 *op. cit.*, p. 378.

4 See J. C. Fenton's Pelican translation and commentary, p. 309.

5 *Ibid.*, p. 310.

6   *The Gospel in Brief* in *A Confession* . . ., p. 227.
7   Printed in *Essays and Letters*, trans. Aylmcr Maude (London, 1903), pp. 36–52.
8   See *What I Believe* in *A Confession* . . ., p. 379 footnote.
9   Maude (Aylmer), *Life*, vol. II, p. 70.
10 *Ibid.*, pp. 108–109.
11 *Ibid.*, pp. 149–150.
12 *Essays and Letters*, trans. Aylmer Maude, p. 46.
13 *The Kreutzer Sonata* . . ., p. 156.
14 Quoted in Leon (Derrick), *Tolstoy: His Life and Work* (London, 1944), p. 247.
15 *The Countess Tolstoy's Later Diary, 1891–1897*, trans. Alexander Werth (London, 1929), p. 28.
16 Spence (G. W.), *Tolstoy the Ascetic* (Edinburgh and London, 1967), pp. 105–106.
17 *The Kreutzer Sonata* . . ., pp. 129, 133, and 147.
18 *Ibid.*, pp. 149 and 152.
19 Maude (Aylmer), *Life*, vol. II, p. 262.
20 *Essays and Letters*, p. 46. See also Maude, *Life*, vol. II, p. 271.
21 Printed in *The Kreutzer Sonata, The Devil and Other Tales*, pp. 299–357.
22 *Ibid.*, p. 307.
23 *Ibid.*, p. 326.
24 Avvakum, *Life* . . ., trans. Jane Harrison and Hope Mirrlees (London, 1924), p. 44.
25 Gorky (Maxim), *Literary Portraits*, trans. Ivy Litvinov (Moscow [n.d.]), pp. 29–30.
26 Printed in *Twenty-Three Tales*, pp. 102–130.
27 Gorky (Maksim), *op. cit.*, p. 27.
28 Printed in *The Kreutzer Sonata, The Devil and Other Tales*, pp. 235–296.
29 In what follows I draw on Maude, *Life*, vol. II, pp. 338–402.
30 In what follows I am indebted to Troyat (Henri), *Tolstoy*, trans. from the French by Nancy Amphoux (New York, 1965), pp. 62–63.
31 *Ibid.*, p. 541.
32 Quoted from Sonya's diaries by R. F. Christian in his *Tolstoy: A Critical Introduction* (Cambridge, 1969), p. 219.
33 Quoted in Troyat (Henri), *Tolstoy*, p. 544.
34 Maude, *Life*, vol. II, p. 401.

CHAPTER SIXTEEN

1   Redpath (Theodore), *Tolstoy* (London, 2nd edn 1969), p. 20.

2 Weber (Max), *The Sociology of Religion*, trans. Ephraim Fischoff (reprinted 1966), p. 238.

3 In *Recollections and Essays*, p. 411.

4 In *Essays and Letters*, pp. 43–44.

5 *The Countess Tolstoy's Later Diary, 1891– 1897*, trans. from the Russian by Alexander Werth (London, 1929), p. 13.

6 *Ibid.*, p. 90.

7 *Pedagogical Articles*, p. 214.

8 *Pedagogical Articles*, p. 130.

9 Leon (Derrick), *Tolstoy: His Life and Work* (London, 1944), p. 240.

10 *Ibid.*, pp. 240–241.

11 *New Light on Tolstoy*, ed. René Fülop-Miller, trans. Paul England (London, 1931), p. 329.

12 Maude, *Life*, vol. II, p. 354.

13 *Ibid.*, p. 355.

14 Bulgakov (V. F.), *The Last Year of Leo Tolstoy*, trans. Ann Dunnigan (London, 1971), p. 87.

15 Tolstoy (Sergey), *Tolstoy Remembered*, trans. Moura Budberg (London, 1961), p. 97.

16 Maude, *Life*, vol. II, p. 355.

17 Sonya quoted the proverb 'Let the child amuse itself as it likes, so long as it doesn't cry' in a letter to Tolstoy on 23 October 1884, quoted in Maude, *Life*, vol. II, p. 153.

18 Bulgakov (V. F.), *op. cit.*, p. 13.

19 Maude, *Life*, vol. I, pp. 59–60.

20 *Ibid.*, vol. II, p. 368.

21 *Ibid.*, vol. I, p. 432.

22 *Ibid.*, vol. I, pp. 422–424.

23 *Ibid.*, vol. II, pp. 290–317.

24 *Ibid.*, vol. II, p. 385.

25 *Ibid.*, vol. II, p. 322.

26 *Ibid.*, vol. II, pp. 391–392.

27 *Ibid.*, vol. I, pp. 59–60.

28 *Ibid.*, vol. II, p. 470.

29 *Ibid.*, vol. II, pp. 140–141.

30 *Ibid.*, vol. II, pp. 108–109.

31 *Ibid.*, vol. II, pp. 149–150 and p. 533.

32 Leon (Derrick), *Tolstoy: His Life and Work* (London, 1944) p. 227.

33 Maude, *Life*, vol. II, p. 473.

34 *Ibid.*, vol. II, p. 507.

35 *Last Diaries*, trans. Lydia Weston-Kesich (New York, 1960), p. 144.

36 *Ibid.*, p. 215.
37 *Family Views of Tolstoy*, ed. Aylmer Maude (London, 1926), p. 195.
38 Scheler (Max), *On the Eternal in Man*, trans. Bernard Noble (London, 1954), p. 399.
39 Bulgakov (V. F.), *op. cit.*, p. 91.

Bibliography

This is a selected bibliography listing only those works referred to in the text and notes. Tolstoy's own works are listed alphabetically by title as they appear in the Maude translations in the World's Classics series. Other works are listed alphabetically by author.

WORKS BY TOLSTOY IN WORLD'S CLASSICS

Anna Karenina

Childhood, Boyhood and Youth

A Confession, The Gospel in Brief and What I Believe

Essays and Letters (contains 'An Afterword to *The Kreutzer Sonata*', 1890, and 'What is Religion and Wherein Lies its Essence?', 1902)

Ivan Ilych and Hadji Murad and Other Stories (contains *Memoirs of a Madman*)

The Kingdom of God and Peace Essays

The Kreutzer Sonata, The Devil and Other Tales (contains *Family Happiness, Father Sergius* and *The Porcelain Doll*)

On Life, and Essays on Religion

Recollections and Essays

Resurrection

The Snow Storm and Other Stories (contains *A Billiard Marker's Notes, A Landlord's Morning, Lucerne, Three Deaths, Polikushka, Strider: The Story of a Horse*)

Tales of Army Life (contains *The Raid, The Wood-Felling*, the Sevastopol stories, *The Cossacks*)

Twenty Three Tales (contains *God Sees the Truth, but Waits* and *Two Old Men*)

War and Peace

What is Art? and Essays on Art

What Then Must We Do?

WORKS BY TOLSTOY IN OTHER EDITIONS

The Diaries of Leo Tolstoy, trans. from the Russian by C. J. Hogarth and A. Sirnis, 'Youth', 1847–1852 (London, 1917).

Last Diaries, trans. Lydia Weston Kesich (New York, 1960).

Letters, traduites et annotées par Benjamin Goriely, t. I, 1842–1860 (Paris, 1954).
'The Meaning of the Russian Revolution', 1906, in *Russian Intellectual History: An Anthology*, ed. Marc Raeff (New York, 1966).
Pedagogical Articles . . . trans. by Leo Wiener (London, 1904). (Contains 'Education and Culture', 'Progress and the Definition of Education'.)
The Private Diaries of Leo Tolstoy, 1853–1857, ed. Aylmer Maude and trans. Louise and Aylmer Maude (London, 1927).
Sobranie Sochinenii, t. 17–18 (*Pisma, Letters*) (Moskva, 1965).
Tolstoy's Love Letters with a Study . . . by Paul Biryukov, trans. from the Russian by S. S. Koteliansky and Virginia Woolf (Richmond, 1923). (Contains an account of Tolstoy's relationship with Valeria Arsenieva, the background to *Family Happiness*.)

MEMOIRS, ETC., MENTIONING TOLSTOY

Bulgakov, V. F., *The Last Year of Leo Tolstoy*, trans. Ann Dunnigan (London, 1971); Fülop-Miller, René (ed.), *New Light on Tolstoy*, trans. Paul England (London, 1931); Goldenveizer, A. B., *Talks with Tolstoy*, trans. S. S. Koteliansky and Virginia Woolf (Richmond, 1923); Gorky, Maxim, *Literary Portraits*, trans. Ivy Litvinov (Moscow, [n.d.]); Gusev, N. N., *Letopis Zhizni i Tvorchestva L. N. Tolstogo, 1828–1890* (Moskva, 1958); Kuzminskaya, Tatyana, *Tolstoy as I Knew Him*, trans. Nora Sigerist and others (New York, 1948); Maude, Aylmer, *Family View of Tolstoy* (London, 1926); Tolstoy, Sergey, *Tolstoy Remembered*, trans. Moura Budberg (London, 1961); Tolstoy, Sophia Andreevna, *The Countess Tolstoy's Later Diary, 1891–1897*, trans. Alexander Werth (London, 1929).

BIOGRAPHIES OF TOLSTOY

Leon, Derrick, *Tolstoy: His Life and Work* (London, 1944); Maude, Aylmer, *The Life of Tolstoy*, 2 vols in one (London, reprinted 1953); Troyat, Henri, *Tolstoy*, trans. from the French by Nancy Amphoux (New York, 1965).

CRITICAL STUDIES OF TOLSTOY

Bayley, John, *Tolstoy and the Novel* (London 1966); Berlin, Sir Isaiah, *The Hedgehog and the Fox* (London, reprinted 1954); Christian, R. F., *Tolstoy: A Critical Introduction* (Cambridge, 1969); Christian, R. F., *Tolstoy's 'War and Peace': A Study* (Oxford, 1962); Dragomirov, Mikhail Ivanovich, *Étude du Roman 'La Guerre et La Paix'* . . . *Au Point de Vue Militaire* (Paris, [1896]); Eikhenbaum, Boris, *Lev Tolstoi*, Nachdruck der Ausgabe Leningrad 1928/31, Wilhelm Fink

Verlag, München, (2 t. in one, 1968); Eikhenbaum, Boris, *Lev Tolstoi: Semidesiatye Gody* (Leningrad, 1960); Leontiev, Konstantin, *The Novels of Count L. N. Tolstoy: Analysis, Style and Atmosphere*, 1890. In *Essays in Russian Literature: The Conservative view: Leontiev, Rozanov, Shestov*, ed. and trans. Spencer E. Roberts (Athens, Ohio, 1968); Myshkovskaya, L. M., *Masterstvo L. N. Tolstogo* (Moskva, 1958); Redpath, Theodore, *Tolstoy* (London, 2nd edn 1969); Shestov, Leo, *Dostoevsky, Tolstoy and Nietzsche*, trans. Bernard Martin (Ohio University Press, 1969); Shlovsky, Victor, *Material i Stil v Romane Tolstogo 'Voina i Mir'* (Moskva, 1928); Speirs, Logan, *Tolstoy and Chekhov* (Cambridge, 1971); Spence, G. W., *Tolstoy the Ascetic* (Edinburgh and London, 1967); Strakhov, N. N., *Kriticheskie Staty ob Turgeneve i Tolstom* (S. Peterburg, 1899); Vitmer, A., *1812 God v Voine i Mir* (S. Peterburg, 1869).

PERIODICAL ARTICLES

Duffy, Christopher, 'Borodino', *The Listener*, vol. 88, no. 2269 (21 September 1972); Flew, A. G. N., 'Tolstoi and the Meaning of Life', *Ethics*, vol. LXXIII, no. 2 (Jan. 1963); Hagan, John, 'On the Craftsmanship of *War and Peace*', *Essays in Criticism*, vol. XIII, no. 1 (Jan. 1963); Laqueur, Walter, 'Literature and the Historian', *The Journal of Contemporary History*, vol. 2, no. 2 (April 1967); Mink, Louis O., 'History and Fiction as Modes of Comprehension', *New Literary History*, vol. I, no. 3 (Spring, 1970); Phillips, D. Z., 'Moral Presuppositions and Literary Criticism', *The Human World*, no. 6 (Feb. 1962); Sorel, Albert, 'Tolstoi Historien', *Revue Bleue* (Paris, 1888); Struve, Gleb, 'Monologue Intérieur: The Origins of the Formula', *P.M.L.A.*, vol. 69, no. 5 (Dec. 1954); Thale, Jerome, '*War and Peace*: The Art of Incoherence', *Essays in Criticism*, vol. XVI, no. 4 (Oct. 1966).

GENERAL WORKS

Arnold, Matthew, *Essays in Criticism: Second Series* (London, reprinted 1898); Arnold, Matthew, *The Letters to A. H. Clough*, ed. H. F. Lowry (New York, reissued 1968); Avvakum, Protopope, *The Life of the Archpriest Avvakum by Himself*, trans. Jane Harrison and Hope Mirrlees (London, 1924); Borger, Robert and Cioffi, Frank (eds), *Explanation in the Behavioural Sciences* (Cambridge, 1970; contains J. W. N. Watkins's 'Imperfect Rationality'); Chambers, Jessie, *D. H. Lawrence: A Personal Record*, by E. T. [Jessie Chambers] (London, 1935); Chandler, David, *A Reader's Guide to the Battlefields of Europe*, vol. 2 (London, 1965; contains an account of the battle of Borodino by Brigadier P. Young); Clausewitz, Karl Von, *The*

Campaign of 1812 in Russia, trans. from the German (London, 1843); Davies, W. D., *The Setting of the Sermon on the Mount* (Cambridge, 1964); Dostoevsky, Fyodor, *Notes from Underground . . .* trans. Andrew R. MacAndrew (New York and Toronto, 1961); Duffy, Christopher, *Borodino and The War of 1812* (London, 1972); Elton, G. R., *Political History: Principles and Practice* (London, 1970); Fenton, John Charles, *The Gospel of St Matthew* (The Pelican Gospel Commentaries, Harmondsworth, 1963); George, Hereford Brooke, *Napoleon's Invasion of Russia* (London, 1899); Gerstein, Linda, *Nikolai Strakhov: Philosopher, Man of Letters, Social Critic* (Cambridge, Mass., 1971); Geyl, Pieter, *Napoleon For and Against*, trans. from the Dutch by O. Renier (London, revised edn 1964); Hare, Richard, *Portraits of Russian Personalities Between Reform and Revolution* (London, 1959); Herzen, Alexander, *My Past and Thoughts*, trans. Constance Garnett, 6 vols (London, 1924–1927); Hick, John, *Faith and Knowledge* (London and Melbourne, 1967); Hick, John, and McGill, Arthur C. (eds), *The Many Faced Argument* (London, 1968); Hook, Sidney, *The Hero in History* (London, 1945); Ivanov-Razumnik, R. V., *Lev Tolstoi* (S. Peterburg, [n.d.]); Jeremias, Joachim, *New Testament Theology*, vol. I, trans. from the German by John Bowder (London, 1971); Lampert, E., *Sons Against Fathers* (Oxford, 1965); Leavis, F. R., *Anna Karenina and Other Essays* (London, 1967); Leavis, F. R., *The Great Tradition* (London, 1950); Lemon, Lee T. and Reis, Marion J. (trans.), *Russian Formalist Criticism: Four Essays* (Lincoln, Nebraska, 1965; contains Victor Shklovsky's 'Art as Technique'); Maistre, Joseph de, *Works*, selected and trans. Jack Lively (London, 1965); Malcolm, Norman, *Ludwig Wittgenstein: A Memoir* (London, 1958); Moore, G. E., *Philosophical Studies* (London, reprinted 1958); Morgenbesser, Sidney, Suppes, Patrick and White, Morton, *Philosophy, Science and Method: Essays in Honor of Ernest Nagel* (New York, 1969; contains Paul Edwards's 'Existentialism and Death; A Survey of Some Confusions and Absurdities'); Nettl, J. P., *Rosa Luxemburg*, 2 vols (London, 1966); Nietzsche, Friedrich, *The Twilight of the Idols . . .* trans. R. J. Hollingdale (Harmondsworth, reprinted 1969); Ortega y Gasset, José, *The Dehumanization of Art, And Other Essays . . .*, trans. Helen Weyl (Princeton, N. J., 1968; contains 'Notes on the Novel'); Panichas, George A. (ed.), *Mansions of the Spirit* (New York, 1967; contains Georges Florovsky's 'Three Masters: The Quest for Religion in Nineteenth Century Russian Literature'); Pascal, Blaise, *Pensées*, ed. Louis Lafuma, trans. John Warrington (Everyman's University Library, London, reprinted 1973); Perrin, Norman, *Rediscovering the Teaching of Jesus* (London, 1967); Poggioli, Renato, *The Phoenix and the Spider* (Cambridge, Mass., 1957); Popper, Sir Karl, *The Open*

Bibliography

Society and Its Enemies, 2 vols (London, reprinted 1969); Popper, Sir Karl, *The Poverty of Historicism* (London, reprinted 1969); Proust, Marcel, *By Way of Sainte-Beuve*, trans. Sylvia Townsend Warner (London, 1958); Revel, Jean-François, *On Proust*, trans. Martin Turnell (London, 1972); Rivière, Jacques, *The Ideal Reader*, ed. and trans. Blanche A. Price (London, 1962); Robertson, J. M., *Explorations* (London [n.d.]); Santayana, George, *Reason in Science* (New York, 1962); Santayana, George, *Scepticism and Animal Faith* (New York, 1955); Santayana, George, *Some Turns of Thought in Modern Philosophy: Five Essays* (Cambridge, 1933); Scheler, Max, *On the Eternal in Man*, trans. Bernard Noble (London, 1954); Scholes, Robert, *The Fabulators* (New York, 1967); Scholes, Robert and Kellogg, Robert, *The Nature of Narrative* (New York, 1966); Schopenhauer, Arthur, *The World as Will and Representation*, 2 vols, trans. E. F. J. Payne (New York, 1958); Stewart, J. A., *The Myths of Plato* (London, 1905); Venturi, Franco, *The Roots of Revolution*, trans. from the Italian by Francis Haskell (London, 2nd impression, 1964); Vygotsky, Lev, *Thought and Language*, ed. and trans. E. Hanfmann and G. Vakar (Cambridge, Mass., 1962); Weber, Max, *The Sociology of Religion*, trans. Ephraim Fischoff (London, reprinted 1966); Weitz, Morris, *Philosophy in Literature* (Detroit, 1963); Wernham, James, C. S., *Two Russian Thinkers: An Essay in Berdyaev and Shestov* (Toronto, 1968); Wilson, Sir Robert T., *General Wilson's Journal: 1812–1814*, ed. Antony Brett-James (London, 1964); Wittgenstein, Ludwig, *Notebooks, 1914–1916*, ed. G. H. Von Wright and G. E. M. Anscombe (Oxford, 1969); Wittgenstein, Ludwig, *Tractatus Logico-Philosophicus*, trans. D. F. Pears and B. F. McGuinness (London, 1961).

Index